STRATEGIC IMAGINATION

ESSAYS IN HONOUR OF BRENDAN SARGEANT

STRATEGIC IMAGINATION

ESSAYS IN HONOUR OF BRENDAN SARGEANT

EDITED BY ANDREW CARR

Australian
National
University

ANU PRESS

Australian
National
University

ANU PRESS

Published by ANU Press
The Australian National University
Canberra ACT 2600, Australia
Email: anupress@anu.edu.au

Available to download for free at press.anu.edu.au

ISBN (print): 9781760466954
ISBN (online): 9781760466961

WorldCat (print): 1514336760
WorldCat (online): 1514337932

DOI: 10.22459/SI.2025

Cover design and layout by ANU Press. Cover photograph source: Coral Bell School,
The Australian National University.

This book is published under the aegis of the Asia-Pacific Security Studies editorial board
of ANU Press.

Contents

Abbreviations   vii

List of illustrations   ix

Contributors   xi

Preface   xvii
Greg Moriarty

1. Introduction   1
    Andrew Carr and Sita Sargeant

2. The Australian strategic imagination: Origins and form   9
    Brendan Sargeant

Part 1. The concept of strategic imagination

3. Concepts: What is strategic imagination?   37

4. A reconciled republic? The Australian Constitution,
    the Indigenous Voice to Parliament, the republic and the
    future of the Commonwealth   39
    Mark McKenna

5. Imagination and scholarship: The role of creativity
    and complexity   65
    Anthea Roberts

6. Imagination and policy   77
    Dennis Richardson

7. Thinking about strategic imagination   89
    Ian Hall

8. The strategist as author   99
    Andrew Carr

Part 2. The practice of strategic imagination

9. Strategic imagination: Practice   115

10. Imagination and the Korean crisis   117
    Roland Bleiker

11. Australia in a new era: Why strategic imagination matters   145
Tom Barber and Melissa Conley Tyler

12. The Indo-Pacific as strategic imagination   159
Rory Medcalf

13. Approaching Australian defence and strategic policy through strategic imagination   169
Stephan Frühling

14. Strategic imagination: The case of reimagining Nordic defence   181
Robbin Laird

Part 3. Remembrances of Brendan Sargeant

15. Remembrance foreword   201

16. Vale Brendan Sargeant   203
Evelyn Goh

17. Reflections on Brendan Sargeant   209
Amy King

18. Reimagining strategy and statecraft for the future   213
Jochen Prantl

19. The imagination of a bureaucrat   217
Hugh White

20. Grappling with the past and present through imagination   221
Meighen McCrae

21. Bridging the gap: Remembering Brendan Sargeant   225
Brendan Taylor

22. 'To see what is worth seeing': Keynote speech to the Strategic and Defence Studies Centre fiftieth anniversary dinner, 21 July 2016   229
Brendan Sargeant

Index   237

Abbreviations

ADF	Australian Defence Force
ANU	The Australian National University
ANZUS	Australia, New Zealand and United States Security Treaty
AP4D	Asia-Pacific Development, Diplomacy & Defence Dialogue
ASEAN	Association of Southeast Asian Nations
DFAT	Department of Foreign Affairs and Trade
DMZ	Korean Demilitarized Zone
EU	European Union
JSA	Joint Security Area
MP	Member of Parliament
NNSC	Neutral Nations Supervisory Commission
SDSC	Strategic and Defence Studies Centre
UK	United Kingdom
UN	United Nations
US	United States

List of illustrations

Figures

Figure 5.1 Creativity: Thinking with both sides of our minds 67

Figure 5.2 Looking backward and forward in complexity 73

Map

Map 7.1 The Indo-Pacific region 95

Plates

Plate 10.1 The author with North Korean officers, Panmungak,
Joint Security Area, Panmunjom, 1986–88 123

Plate 10.2 The author with South Korean officers, Seoul, 1986–88 124

Plate 10.3 South Korean soldier facing the military demarcation line,
1986–88 126

Plate 10.4 Military demarcation line inside the DMZ, 1986–88 126

Plates 10.5 and 10.6 'Northern' and 'Southern' soldiers in the JSA,
Panmunjom, 1986–88 128

Plate 10.7 Meeting of the Military Armistice Commission, JSA,
Panmunjom, 1986–88 130

Plate 10.8 Flying in a US Army helicopter 131

Plate 10.9 From inside a US Army helicopter, south of the DMZ 132

Plate 10.10 Man next to Kim Il-sung statue, Kaesong, North Korea,
1986–88 135

Plate 10.11 Hotel in Pyongyang, 1986–88   136

Plate 10.12 Woman collecting herbs in Pyongyang, 1986–88   137

Plate 10.13 Urban scene in Pyongyang, 1986–88   137

Plate 10.14 'The Land of No Smiles I', Man'gyŏngdae, North Korea,
    1986–88   139

Plate 10.15 'The Land of No-Smiles II', 1986–88   139

Plate 10.16 'Forever in front of them all', Camp Bonifas,
    UN Command, DMZ, 1986–88   140

Plate 10.17 Pyongyang, 1986–88   143

Contributors

Tom Barber is Program Manager at the Asia-Pacific Development, Diplomacy & Defence Dialogue (AP4D). He has previously worked as a research assistant at La Trobe Asia and Deakin University.

Roland Bleiker is Professor of International Relations, Director of the Rotary Peace Centre and Coordinator of the Visual Politics Research Program at the University of Queensland. Roland has a passion for cross-cultural and interdisciplinary learning. He has taught more than 60 courses at the University of Queensland, from introductory classes on peace studies to advanced subjects on international relations theory and masters seminars on nonviolent resistance, visual politics, ethics and human rights. Roland's research explores how images and emotions shape political phenomena, including humanitarianism, security, peacebuilding, protest movements and the conflict on the Korean Peninsula.

Andrew Carr is Associate Professor in the Strategic and Defence Studies Centre at The Australian National University. His research focuses on strategy and Australian defence policy. He has published in outlets such as *Survival, Parameters*, the *Journal of Strategic Studies, Australian Foreign Affairs, International Theory, The Washington Quarterly* and *Comparative Strategy*. He is the author or editor of five books with Melbourne University Press, Oxford University Press and Georgetown University Press.

Melissa Conley Tyler is Executive Director of the Asia-Pacific Development, Diplomacy & Defence Dialogue (AP4D). For 13 years she served as national executive director of the Australian Institute of International Affairs (AIIA). Under her leadership, the AIIA was recognised for three years running as the top think tank in South-East Asia and the Pacific and one of the top 50 think tanks worldwide in the University of Pennsylvania's Global Go To

Think Tanks Index. She joined the University of Melbourne in 2019 as director of diplomacy at Asialink and then as a Research Fellow/Associate in the Asia Institute.

Stephan Frühling is Professor at the Strategic and Defence Studies Centre, The Australian National University. Stephan is a chief investigator on the Australian Research Council's Discovery Project on 'The Ties that Bind? Expectations and Institutions in the US–Australia Alliance'. From September 2017 to January 2018, he was the Fulbright Professional Scholar in Australia–America Alliance Studies at Georgetown University, Washington, DC. From August to December 2015, he was the 'Partner across the globe' research fellow in the Research Division of the NATO Defense College in Rome. In 2014–15, Stephan was a member of the Australian Government's external panel of experts for the 2016 Defence White Paper.

Evelyn Goh is the Shedden Professor of Strategic Policy Studies at The Australian National University, where she is also Research Director at the Strategic and Defence Studies Centre. She has published widely on US–China relations and diplomatic history, regional security order in East Asia, South-East Asian strategies towards great powers and environmental security. These include *The Struggle for Order: Hegemony, Hierarchy and Transition in Post-Cold War East Asia* (Oxford University Press, 2013); 'Great Powers and Hierarchical Order in Southeast Asia: Analyzing Regional Security Strategies' (*International Security* 32, no. 3 [Winter 2007–08]: 113–57); and *Constructing the US Rapprochement with China, 1961–1974* (Cambridge University Press, 2004). Her latest book (co-authored with Barry Buzan) is *Rethinking Sino-Japanese Alienation: History Problems and Historical Opportunities* (Oxford University Press, 2020).

Ian Hall is Professor of International Relations at Griffith University. He is also an Academic Fellow of the Australia India Institute at the University of Melbourne. Before his appointment to Griffith, he taught at the University of St Andrews, the University of Adelaide and The Australian National University. He served as a co-editor of the *Australian Journal of International Affairs* between 2018 and 2023. He is the author of three books, including *Modi and the Reinvention of Indian Foreign Policy* (Bristol University Press, 2019), the editor of five volumes and several special issues and has published many scholarly articles and chapters.

Amy King is Associate Professor in the Strategic and Defence Studies Centre at The Australian National University, with expertise in Chinese foreign and security policy, China–Japan relations and the economics–security nexus in the Asia-Pacific region. She is also a research fellow with the Australia–Japan Research Centre, a research associate with The Australian National University's Graduate Research and Development Network on Asian Security and serves on the Editorial Board of the *East Asia Forum*. She currently holds both a Westpac Research Fellowship and an Australian Research Council DECRA Fellowship to investigate China's role in shaping the international economic order.

Robbin Laird is a military and security analyst. He has taught at Columbia University, Queens College, Princeton University and Johns Hopkins University. He worked with the Center for Defense Analysis and the Institute for Defense Analysis. He is a member of the Board of Contributors of AOL Defense and writes for *The Diplomat*. He is the Director of the International Council of Securities Associations, since 2000, and co-founder and editor of two websites, *Second Line of Defense* and *Defense.info*. He became a fellow of The Williams Foundation, Canberra, in 2018.

Meighen McCrae is an Associate Professor at the Strategic and Defence Studies Centre, which she joined in June 2018, and a historian of international history and the history of war. She is interested in three main areas: the way coalitions fight, notions of victory and how individuals think about future war during periods of conflict or great international tension. She was previously a lecturer in military history, strategic studies and intelligence studies as well as the deputy director of the Centre for Intelligence and International Security Studies in the International Politics Department, Aberystwyth University, Wales. Her monograph *Coalition Strategy and the End of the First World War: The Supreme War Council and War Planning, 1917–1918* (Cambridge University Press, Military Histories Series, 2019) focuses on the efforts of Britain, France, Italy and the United States to forge a tightly coordinated coalition in the final year of World War I.

Mark McKenna is one of Australia's leading historians, based at the University of Sydney as Professor Emeritus. He is the author of several prize-winning books, including *From the Edge: Australia's Lost Histories, Looking for Blackfellas' Point: An Australian History of Place* and *An Eye for Eternity: The Life of Manning Clark*, which won the Prime Minister's Literary Award for nonfiction and the Victorian, New South Wales, Queensland and South Australian premiers' awards.

Rory Medcalf is Professor and Head of the National Security College at The Australian National University. He has led the expansion of the college into policy engagement and futures analysis, as well as education, executive development and research, repositioning the college as 'more than a think tank'. His professional background involves three decades of experience across diplomacy, intelligence analysis, think tanks, academia and journalism, including as founding director of the International Security Program at the Lowy Institute from 2007 to 2015.

Greg Moriarty is a senior Australian public servant and diplomat and, since 4 September 2017, the Secretary of the Department of Defence. He was previously chief of staff to prime minister Malcolm Turnbull.

Jochen Prantl is a Professor at The Australian National University. He served as director of the Asia-Pacific College of Diplomacy in 2015–16 and deputy director (international engagement) in 2017–18 for the Coral Bell School of Asia Pacific Affairs. His research focuses on global governance, international security and strategic diplomacy. Previously, he held positions in the Department of Politics and International Relations and Nuffield College at the University of Oxford and the Lee Kuan Yew School of Public Policy at the National University of Singapore. He also served as acting director of Oxford's Centre for International Studies. In 2007, Dr Prantl was the inaugural recipient of the Zvi Meitar/Vice-Chancellor Oxford University Research Prize in the Social Sciences and, in 2008, the university's nominee for the AXA Prize for Innovative Research.

Dennis Richardson is an Australian retired public servant and diplomat who served as the secretary of the Department of Defence from 2012 to 2017 and secretary of the Department of Foreign Affairs from 2010 to 2012.

Anthea Roberts is Professor at the School of Regulation and Global Governance (RegNet), an interdisciplinary researcher and a legal scholar who focuses on new ways of thinking about complex and evolving global fields. She is the Director of the ANU Centre for International Governance and Justice and Chair of the Geoeconomics Working Group. Anthea is founder and Director of Dragonfly Thinking, which is a startup company employing structured analytic techniques and artificial intelligence tools to enable policymakers and businesses to view complex problems through multiple lenses and to develop integrative decision-making approaches, such as through applying her Risk, Reward and Resilience Framework.

Brendan Sargeant was one of Australia's most respected defence strategists, professor of practice in defence and strategic studies and head of the Strategic and Defence Studies Centre at the Coral Bell School of Asia Pacific Affairs at The Australian National University. Brendan served as the associate secretary of defence and deputy secretary of strategy before retiring from the Department of Defence in 2017.

Sita Sargeant is the founder of She Shapes History, a social enterprise offering engaging walking tours in Canberra that share the stories of women and queer people who have shaped history. Her aim is for guests to leave with a better understanding of the past, thereby engaging more thoughtfully with the present. Sita is aiming to expand her tours to every Australian capital city and run educational programs, making history relevant, accessible and unforgettable for all Australians.

Brendan Taylor is Professor of Strategic Studies and Head of the Strategic and Defence Studies Centre. He is a specialist on great-power strategic relations in the Asia-Pacific, East Asian 'flashpoints' and Asian security architecture. His writings on these subjects have appeared in such leading journals as *Survival, The Washington Quarterly, Australian Foreign Affairs, The Pacific Review, International Affairs* and *Review of International Studies.* He is the author or editor of 14 books, including *The Four Flashpoints: How Asia Goes to War* (Black Inc., 2018) and *Dangerous Decade: Taiwan's Security and Crisis Management* (IISS, 2019).

Hugh White is Emeritus Professor of Strategic Studies at The Australian National University. His work focuses primarily on Australian strategic and defence policy, Asia-Pacific security issues and global strategic affairs especially as they influence Australia and the Asia-Pacific. He has served as an intelligence analyst with the Office of National Assessments, as a journalist with the *Sydney Morning Herald,* as a senior adviser on the staffs of defence minister Kim Beazley and prime minister Bob Hawke, as a senior official in the Department of Defence, where, from 1995 to 2000, he was deputy secretary for strategy and intelligence, and as the first director of the Australian Strategic Policy Institute. He was the principal author of Australia's 2000 Defence White Paper. His major publications include *Power Shift: Australia's Future between Washington and Beijing* (Quarterly Essay 39, 2010), *The China Choice: Why America Should Share Power* (Black Inc., 2012), *Without America: Australia's Future in the New Asia* (Quarterly Essay 68, 2017) and *How to Defend Australia* (Black Inc., 2019).

Preface

Greg Moriarty

For those who knew Brendan Sargeant, it was scarcely surprising that the inspiration for his concept of 'strategic imagination' came from Odysseus, the eponymous hero of Homer's *Odyssey*. After all, what distinguished Brendan from other 'scholar-practitioners' in Australia was his ability to draw on his immense knowledge of literature and poetry to inform his understanding of strategic policy.

Brendan saw strategic challenges fundamentally as challenges to the imagination. Beyond calculations about the relationship between ends, ways and means, Brendan argued strategy reflected—and could indeed shape—a nation's collective imagination. Certainly, it was Brendan's own capacity for imagination that allowed him to contribute so valuably to Australia's defence landscape.

For Brendan, strategic imagination meant the ability to envision alternative futures beyond today's challenges, combining 'experience, manifested in the world as it is, and imagination, manifested in the world as it might be'. Brendan believed the act of defining new strategy lay in reconciling these forces—a process that, for nations, is given expression through political leadership. In developing this concept, Brendan was motivated by a deep conviction that traditional approaches to strategy often fell short, especially in a rapidly changing world. And, in applying this concept, he challenged conventional wisdom. Brendan believed crises throughout Australian history had forced Australia to 'envisage a future different from the continuities mandated by the past'. As part of the Department of Defence's senior leadership group, he never ceased encouraging his colleagues to think differently about the problems they faced.

While Brendan's professional journey began in 1983 with a job as an assistant research officer at the Department of Defence, his professional foundation was in his major in English literature earnt as an undergraduate at the Footscray Institute of Technology, Melbourne. Beyond fostering a lifelong passion for telling, and ultimately also writing, stories, Brendan's grounding in English literature informed his lifelong conviction that strategic thinking was fundamentally a process of telling stories about 'who we are and, more importantly, who we think we are'. Small wonder then that Brendan's love of literature and poetry quickly made an impression on those with whom he worked at Defence, including former first assistant secretary, Strategic and International Policy Division, Myra Rowling, who recalls a young Brendan joining her small team responsible for Australia, New Zealand and US policy and seamlessly weaving references to English poet William Blake into incisive policy work.

Throughout his career in the Australian Public Service, and with a solid foundation at Defence, Brendan's adaptability allowed him to thrive in roles at the Attorney-General's Department, Centrelink and the Department of Finance and Deregulation. Perhaps the turning point in his career was his return to Defence in March 2010 as deputy secretary of strategy (operations)—a lynchpin in the department's strategic centre. It was at Defence that Brendan began his deep association with The Australian National University's Strategic and Defence Studies Centre (SDSC), bridging the worlds of policy and academia. A frequent guest speaker at SDSC courses for graduates new to Defence, Brendan proved the value of combining the conceptual frameworks of scholarship and the experiences of a policy practitioner.

Brendan held the position of deputy secretary of reform and governance for almost two years, from 2010 to 2012, before becoming deputy secretary of strategy in 2012, which saw him author the *2013 Defence White Paper*— a document that officially birthed the concept of the Indo-Pacific, which shifted Australian strategic thinking. He served as associate secretary of Defence from 2013 to 2018, where he oversaw the First Principles Review— a reform effort that revitalised defence governance and planning. Though Brendan was characteristically humble, it is no stretch of the imagination to argue that both documents were, in his own words, 'strategic artefacts' that formed the contours of Australian strategic policy.

Brendan's fusion of fiction with the rigours of defence policy was exposed in a keynote speech he made in 2016 as associate secretary marking 50 years of SDSC at The Australian National University. Rather than citing Thucydides or Machiavelli—both mainstays of strategic thought—Brendan spoke about the Australian novel *The Plains* by Gerald Murnane, which talks about a fictional 'Outer Australia', which is a place of abundance, and 'Inner Australia', where people are devoted to the search for meaning. Brendan saw the work of strategy as a journey to 'Inner Australia'—and one that Defence should pursue alongside its daily operations. The challenge for any organisation, Brendan argued, was to 'reflect on the larger story that we are telling through what we do'.

These thoughts are especially prescient in light of the 2023 *Defence Strategic Review*, which reimagines Australia's strategic priorities and urges Australia to face up to the realities of the Indo-Pacific. Central to Brendan's philosophy was recognising the power of imagination in helping us avoid the pitfalls of history, and it is through documents such as these that the Department of Defence, as part of Australia's policymaking community, has shaped, and will shape, the country's strategic imagination.

After concluding his 35-year career in the Australian Public Service in July 2018, Brendan transitioned to The Australian National University. There, he became a professor of practice in defence and strategic policy and head of SDSC within the Coral Bell School of Asia Pacific Studies. At The Australian National University, he fervently shared his wealth of knowledge and experience, nurturing future leaders in Australian strategic and defence policy. Despite Brendan's generosity in giving advice and mentorship, he was always clear-eyed about the need to be 'ruthless in our self-analysis, about our strengths and weaknesses, and who we are'. This openness to contestation and debate was central to him becoming an accomplished scholar, strategist and mentor.

In 2021, Brendan approached Defence with a proposal for the SDSC to produce a series of volumes on the department's strategic guidance documents since 1976, with supporting essays providing commentary on the context in which these documents were produced. Brendan believed this would crucially bolster Defence's corporate memory of strategic policy, as well as position the SDSC to better support strategic policy development. Unfortunately, the contract for the project—now referred to as the 'History of Australian Strategic Policy Project'—was not signed until after Brendan's passing. Still, the project will make it easier for policymakers, academics and, indeed, the public to trace the evolution of Australia's strategic imagination over time and is a testament to Brendan's efforts to bridge the gap between academia and policymaking.

In some ways it is unsurprising that Brendan married the concepts of strategy and imagination; he had long meshed his experiences as a writer, policy practitioner and professor. Former first assistant secretary of strategic policy at Defence Peter Sawczak thought of him as a 'poet-scholar' for whom inspiration, no less than discipline, dictated the practice of the art of imagination. Indeed, Brendan published a book, *In the Path of the Elephant*, in 2014 and his short story, 'Lizard Boy', was shortlisted for the *Australian Book Review*'s Elizabeth Jolley Short Story Prize in 2019. Moreover, his legacy comprises many more stories of his humility, energy and mentorship by those with whom he worked.

The public testimonials that poured in after Brendan's passing speak to his remarkable character, intellectual prowess and lasting impact on those who had the privilege of knowing him. In the words of Brendan himself, 'the future belongs to those who can imagine it'. We would be wise to heed his advice as Australia's strategic environment becomes increasingly competitive, unstable and uncertain.

1

Introduction

Andrew Carr and Sita Sargeant

You can't depend on your judgment when your imagination is out
of focus.

—Mark Twain

The purpose of this book is to explore the concept of strategic imagination and, through it, to honour the person who developed it, Brendan Sargeant. Strategic imagination is an unusual intellectual conjunction. It unites the world of strategy, which prides itself on pragmatism and hard-headedness, with the world of imagination, which is often associated with an aesthetic, enlightened sensitivity.

To Brendan, a defence intellectual in the richest sense of that term, the union made perfect sense. Where strategy is the world of experience and action, imagination offers frameworks in which experience is reconciled with identity and history. These ideas create the contours for action to be developed and applied to the world. Each relies on the other and, given humanity's inherent desire to gather and tell stories about who we are and how we want to engage with the world, our societies cannot help but develop a strategic imagination. As Brendan observed in a 2021 paper outlining the concept:

> [A] country does not exist without the people who have created it out of their actions, stories, desires, and their sense of who they are and where they belong. A country will possess a strategic imagination which will have evolved over time in response to the influence of geography, history, culture, and the many other tangible

and intangible forces that go to create a community and its vision of itself. A country's strategic imagination is a living thing, dynamic and evolving in contact with the world, and full of contradictions.[1]

At the time of his unexpected passing in February 2022, Brendan was working on a manuscript-length study of strategic imagination. The introduction to that study is published here for the first time, as Chapter 2 of this volume. He saw this as urgent work if the world was to grapple with the historic shifts under way, in both the political order and the biophysical environment. In this book, *Strategic Imagination: Essays in Honour of Brendan Sargeant*, the authors have come together to tell their own stories about Brendan and to complete his project.

Together, we seek to provide an academic foundation for the idea of strategic imagination. While many of us see great merit in the idea, our intention is to propose rather than assert, to open it to the debate and disagreement that all academic concepts must rightly face if they are to enter common use. Many chapters are written by those who worked with Brendan, wanting to offer reflections on how he thought about and engaged with the world. Other authors contributed despite never meeting him, recognising in his concept of strategic imagination the gem of a new idea for interpreting the world.

The imagination of a strategist

Brendan, the administrator, engaged with the world before him, while Brendan, the reader and writer, engaged with the world that could be. His concept of strategic imagination emerged from a life at the borders of practical experience and creative pursuit. Brendan often said he was drawn to borders because they were where the new was born. You only had to look at regions like South-East Asia and north-east India to witness the conversation that occurs when two distinct cultures and histories meet. Borders are places of creativity, imagination and growth. They were places where Brendan could not help but find himself.

---

1   Brendan Sargeant, *Challenges to the Australian Strategic Imagination*, Centre of Gravity Series Papers 58 (Canberra: Strategic and Defence Studies Centre, The Australian National University, 2021), 5, hdl.handle.net/1885/233085, sdsc.bellschool.anu.edu.au/experts-publications/publications/8022/centre-gravity-series-challenges-australian-strategic.

For much of his life, Brendan worked as a bureaucrat in the Australian Public Service, authoring many significant strategy and policy documents, some publicly available but most still classified. After long days in the office and dinner with his family, he would sit at his desk, exploring and creating new worlds late into the night. Driven by a genuine interest in everything, he hardly discriminated in what he read or wrote. At the time of his death, his personal library contained more than 18,000 books. Brendan claimed to have read about one-third of them, saying he would read the rest in his retirement, though he knew he would never read them all.

Working with near-graphomaniacal intensity, Brendan produced thousands of poems, short stories, essays and novels. He completed two master's degrees: one in literature, with a thesis on the poetry of William Blake and William Wordsworth, and another in creative writing, during which he wrote a children's novel set in India. He also maintained a daily journal—a practice he began in his early thirties. All this he achieved while raising a family and working full-time in increasingly senior roles. Brendan's contributions to both worlds would have filled many lifetimes.

When Brendan was 18, he moved from Melbourne to Sydney to live in a derelict share house in Kings Cross with artists and screenwriters. He was determined to pursue a creative life, but, like many young people before and after him, he soon realised that life in Sydney was not cheap. Broke and finding the dole insufficient, he began working part-time as a bank teller. This income covered rent, cigarettes and, most importantly, books. He spent all his spare time exploring the city on foot, working on his first novel and reading everything he could get his hands on. During these years, he read many classics and fell in love with literary theory and criticism. While Brendan was never a quick reader, he was a close one, reading and rereading sentences until he fully understood their meaning. The beginnings of the canon from which he would draw for the rest of his life, particularly when it came to informing and inspiring his approach to policy and strategy, were being formed.

After a few years of working in various jobs and trying to make it as a writer, Brendan decided to go to university. He studied part-time while working full-time to support his family, having learned at the age of 22 that he was going to be a parent. After finishing his degree, Brendan applied for several graduate programs in the Australian Public Service and was hired by the Department of Defence. Joining the public service was, in many ways, a strategic choice for Brendan. He wanted a career that engaged only part of his creative capacity, wanting to preserve most of it for personal endeavours. This steered him away from academia and teaching.

From his first days at the Department of Defence, Brendan spent his spare time reading the department's historical documents: white papers, policy documents, ministerial correspondence—anything he could get his hands on. His years as a creative and his time at university had taught him the importance of understanding the broader context of his work. Despite not having previously studied defence policy or international relations, he intuitively recognised that understanding an organisation's history was key to making effective policy today. Brendan could not help but merge his new role as a public servant with his lifelong role as a creative thinker. Just as he had when he began his career as a writer, he formed a canon for the Department of Defence through close readings of its official and unofficial documents. This meant he understood on a very deep level how the department had evolved and how it articulated what it was, enabling him to write policy that built on this foundation in innovative ways. Looking through Brendan's library, you can see the different areas in which he worked reflected in the books in his collection. Whenever he entered a new area, he sought to learn as much as possible about its context and, in so doing, he added to his canon not only of Australian policy but also of literature.

With each passing year, the worlds of the writer and the bureaucrat became increasingly intertwined. Events in one world shaped his experiences in the other. Always on the hunt for a good story, Brendan took inspiration from the world around him, carrying a pocket-sized notebook and fountain pen wherever he went. He stained more than a few shirt pockets with fountain pen ink. Everyone had at least one great story to tell, and he wanted to hear it. He would reshare his favourites—perhaps, as his family would say, a few too many times—over the dinner table and with friends. Those who knew him best had probably heard these stories so often that they felt they had experienced them themselves. Brendan loved nothing more than reading or hearing and then subsequently sharing a great story.

In many of Brendan's poems and short stories, he referenced the life of the administrator. In one of his unpublished novels, 'The Great Library', the librarian is responsible for maintaining and organising the library but not questioning its existence or interpreting its contents. At one point in the novel, the librarian shares a story about another librarian who left the library searching for a book that held the inner consciousness of the universe. However, he quickly dismisses this as something he would not do and says, 'Of course, I do not engage in such speculation. As a practical administrator, I have my hands full with the world before me, including this Library.' The librarian spends his time overseeing the library, not imagining what could be; that is a task left to others. The role of an administrator was to focus on the practical aspects of managing the everyday rather than getting caught up in the more philosophical or interpretative aspects. Sometimes, Brendan's writing was pure imagination, but often you could find the world he experienced reflected in his work. Neither world existed in isolation. His writing, both for the public service and in his creative life, reflected a life straddling the borders of two worlds.

While the chapters in this book speak to Brendan's concept of strategic imagination, two great works were growing in his mind: the idea of strategic imagination and an Australian epic that would reflect all he had learned over the years. This epic novel had been building in his mind for at least a decade, but he had only begun seriously working on it in the months after he retired from the public service. It would engage with the Australian landscape and national identity and dive into the broader history of our region and a connected Australia. This was going to be the novel that truly delved into and explored many of the ideas he had spent decades thinking of while in the public service. The novel would explore his ideas in a way that only a creative piece can. Brendan would speak about his idea of strategic imagination and this unwritten novel with the same passion.

For Brendan, it was never enough to read or see something; it had to become something—whether a piece of writing or a conversation. As a result, he had more ideas than he knew what to do with. Regardless of when he died, his life would always be unfinished. His love of sharing, whether through poems, stories or book recommendations, is what many remember him for. It is what made him an excellent teacher. Brendan left the public service in 2018 and a few months later joined The Australian National University. For someone like Brendan, academia made a lot of sense and, if he had not valued his creative life as much as he did, it is a path he might have taken at a younger age. At The Australian National University, Brendan once again found himself at the intersection of two worlds. However, this time, he had shifted his focus from primarily living in the world of practical experience to living in the world of the in-between. He spent more time than ever actively working in the borderlands, using his experiences of both worlds to create something new that others could access. Brendan was working to become a more official bridge between these two worlds. His unique perspective allowed him to step outside each world and see it as both an outsider and an insider. Brendan had this exceptional ability to make his way of seeing accessible to everyone. He had a gift for clarifying complex concepts, making even the most esoteric topics clear and easy to understand. When Brendan explained them, they just made sense.

Through his concept of strategic imagination, Brendan takes us to the borderlands of two worlds. He shows us the power that comes from such a life. He challenges us to see beyond our expectations and perceptions and to envision new possibilities. With his concept of strategic imagination, Brendan has provided us with a way of viewing the world as he did naturally, distilling his innate approach into a framework accessible to all.

Structure of the book

While most books reflect their author, we are hopeful this book will reflect its subject. There is a deliberate eclecticism to the content and approach of this book. In disciplinary terms, our authors have backgrounds in history, strategic studies, policymaking, aesthetics, law and complexity science. Many of the contributors have worked as academics, some have been policy officials and a few have crossed between these lines, as did Brendan.

To properly think through the concept of strategic imagination, the book is divided into three sections. In section one, authors were asked to think about the *concept* of strategic imagination. Why is it necessary and how should it be understood? In section two, authors apply the *practice* of strategic imagination. How can different ways of viewing strategy and imagination improve analysis and clarity for policy choices? Finally, in section three, SDSC staff offer a series of remembrances of Brendan. What was he like as a colleague and friend, and how did he seek to view the world? The last word, then, fittingly, goes to Brendan, in a speech he gave at the fiftieth anniversary dinner for SDSC in 2016. Brendan took as his theme the novel *The Plains* by Australian author Gerald Murnane. In this text, a young filmmaker tries to move to 'interior Australia', seeking endlessly to 'see what was worth seeing'.

That struggle to see clearly, to go beyond impressions to the truer core, is a fitting way to understand the concept of strategic imagination and the mindset needed to utilise it. Across the concept, practice and remembrance sections, a common theme is that strategic imagination encourages us to seek fresh ways of viewing situations, looking out for what is new or unusual to see more clearly what is meaningful in a situation. We hope this book will inspire current and subsequent generations of scholars and practitioners to engage with the concept of strategic imagination. There are many topics that are ripe for consideration under the strategic imagination framework that we did not have space to address. Climate change, for instance, may require fundamentally new forms of relations between humanity and its habitat, along with bold efforts to think through the various scenarios and prepare our societies adequately. Artificial intelligence is another subject that challenges our wish for a comfortable world that slowly evolves, rather than occasionally revolts and shakes as new eras are born. Strategic imagination is a tool for thinking through such challenges and the way in which our societies may better approach them. This book offers a starting point for others to explore its merits, grapple with its challenges and hopefully use it as a bridge to reach a better world.

2

The Australian strategic imagination: Origins and form

Brendan Sargeant

'A Little Fable'

'Alas,' said the mouse, 'the world is growing smaller every day. At the beginning it was so big that I was afraid, I kept running and running, and I was glad when at last I saw walls far away to the right and left, but these long walls have narrowed so quickly that I am in the last chamber already, and there in the corner stands the trap that I must run into.' 'You only need to change your direction,' said the cat, and ate it up.

—Franz Kafka

Introduction

The Australian strategic imagination is structured by the claims and imperatives of empire in its various manifestations over time in tension with the claims and imperatives of the nation as a continually evolving imagined community. Australian grand strategy has been the ongoing work of reconciling these potentially conflicting imperatives in ways that maintain strategic stability. When there is a strategic crisis, the management of this tension is often at the core of crisis management and resolution.

In this essay, I want to explore in a preliminary way the idea of the Australian strategic imagination. Questions that arise include: How is the Australian strategic imagination created? What form does it take and how does it work? How does it evolve? Can the idea of strategic imagination be applied to other countries?

I have personal and professional reasons for my interest. I worked in strategic policy in the Department of Defence for many years and was the principal author of major strategy and policy documents—some publicly available, many still classified. Reflecting on my experience, I am struck by the degree of continuity in Australian strategic policy over many decades. I have also been struck by the operational focus of strategy as developed within Australian policy communities. We argue in policy and academic communities about how it has changed and what those changes mean, but the larger story is how it has not changed in its essentials over the past century. This begs the question: why not?

Imagination and strategy

One of the reasons it has been hard to talk about strategic imagination and why it does not appear much in the lexicon of the discourse on strategy is that strategy tends to focus on method. It is less concerned with the why and more concerned with the how. Lawrence Freedman defines strategy as 'the central political art, the capacity to get more from any given situation than the starting conditions would suggest are possible'. When I first met him in the early 2000s (before his *Strategy: A History* had been published), I asked him what his definition was.[1] He said it was 'the path to power'. There are many other definitions, but when you delve into them, they do not say much more than Freedman; they tend to be definitions that arise out of the context of the time or circumstances that are being discussed. In this sense, strategy comes alive in specific case studies and that is often the best way to study it.

The discourse on strategy has not developed a vocabulary to describe imagination and its workings. Another way of saying this is that it does not have a theory of imagination. This is not surprising. Imagination is a complicated idea that dissolves into many different meanings depending on

---

1   Lawrence Freedman, *Strategy: A History* (New York: Oxford University Press, 2013).

the context in which it is discussed. Divorced of context, it is a very abstract idea. It comes alive in context where it is visible through its manifestations and can be analysed in terms of its reality and consequences.

Strategy, because it is method and process, exists in many different contexts that govern the nature of the problem to which it is responding and hence the specific forms it assumes. When we discuss Australian strategic policy and strategy, the context is Australia's participation in the international system. How we describe that system—the theory we use—contextualises how we might understand strategy. Different models of the international system, built on different theories, will mandate different forms of strategy. In this context, to explore the idea of a strategic imagination necessarily requires an exploration of the idea of imagination in international relations. From my reading (admittedly very cursory: Tim Aistrope, Roland Bleiker), international relations theory is not comfortable with the concept of imagination and has not found a way of incorporating it into the mainstream of its discourse. I have not yet found a well-developed theory of imagination in international relations theory, though Bleiker's work in *Aesthetics and World Politics* opens suggestive pathways towards this.[2] This, I suppose, is a way of suggesting that the idea of a theory of strategic imagination implies the need for a theory of imagination in international relations.

The *Oxford Dictionary* definition of imagination is that it is a 'faculty that enables one to envisage objects not present to the senses'. Imagination is central to our humanity, our ability to live, desire and create. It is the energy that drives change in the world through the action of humans as they try to envisage and create a world different to the one in which they live. It is also critical to the life of academic disciplines because it enables people to step beyond the boundaries of the discipline, even if the discipline will have its own method to adapt to these new boundaries. My own belief is that we create the intellectual structures within which we live and work and which we sometimes call disciplines, and these intellectual structures are works of imagination that connect to the world in a multitude of ways. For example, in my view, the major theories that structure the discipline of international relations are works of imagination and can be understood and analysed as such. Bleiker, in a striking paragraph in the conclusion of chapter one of *Aesthetics and World Politics*, uses the striking metaphor of an art gallery

---

2   Roland Bleiker, *Aesthetics and World Politics* (London: Palgrave Macmillan, 2009), doi.org/10.1057/9780230244375.

where the major and minor theories of international relations are assembled as paintings, some large, classical and popular, others to the side and smaller, and so on.

The importance of thinking about imagination and its relationship with policy and academic discourses in strategy, security and international relations is that it can illuminate the meaning and limitations of the structures that we have built in these fields in ways that can open richer ways of thinking about them and, in some circumstances, new pathways for action. It opens the gap between the object of contemplation and our descriptions of it, and it is in this gap that meanings reside.

Towards a theory of the Australian strategic imagination

In developing this essay, I am working towards a theory of the Australian strategic imagination. I draw from eclectic sources, particularly some aspects of literary theory. I do this because literary theory offers the richest and deepest analysis and exploration of the idea of imagination. It does this because it tends to focus on those artefacts of the imagination that we call works of literature, and it tries to understand and explain them and, in many ways, connect them with larger movements in social, cultural and political life. This has produced a rich body of knowledge. While recognising the problems of transposing from one context to another, I believe some aspects of literary theory offer a rich conceptual and interpretative toolkit for exploring and developing the idea of the Australian strategic imagination. I also believe that no theory can account for the world or all the rich variety of beings and objects it comprises, but different theoretical frameworks offer insight, much as the light at different times of the day will allow us to see different aspects of the same landscape. My own experience is that no single theory will exhaust all the possible meanings in a text.

In the first part of this essay, I discuss the idea of the imagination, particularly the English Romantic imagination. I will then suggest how this conception of imagination provides a framework for understanding the origins of the Australian strategic imagination in the context of Australian settlement. I conclude this part of the essay with a discussion of the shape and structure of the Australian strategic imagination.

The second part of the essay explores how the Australian strategic imagination develops and evolves. It will put forward the proposition that the strategic imagination exists as a set of dynamic relationships that evolve over time. In other words, the relationship between artefacts of imagination is of more significance in understanding the strategic imagination than the artefacts themselves. In this discussion, I will draw on Harold Bloom's theoretical work in relation to poetic influence and misreading.[3] I will also draw on formalist theory, particularly the work of Caroline Levine, to discuss how we can consider the Australian strategic imagination as a structure with temporal and spatial dimensions.[4] This means that it can be conceptualised as an object that can be described and analysed from a range of theoretical perspectives that can yield fresh insight. We can understand how form structures the strategic discourse, governs the type of language that can be used and establishes frameworks within which decisions and institution-building occur. Bloom's and Levine's works are in many ways antithetical; Bloom was not a formalist, nor were the critics with whom he was associated. If one wanted to integrate these quite antithetical approaches to literary and cultural artefacts, Bloom's work, and the work of theorists like him, focuses on the inner dynamics of an evolving discourse. Levine's work, on the other hand, sets out the idea that establishes the structure and boundary within which the discourse develops.

Expanding on the above, Australian strategy can be conceptualised as a series of interventions over time in response to a changing external environment. The development and construction of these interventions occur within the context of previous interventions and ideas about Australia's relationship with the world. We can often trace continuities and discontinuities over time using certain ideas and language. We can understand the way in which ideas evolve and struggle against each other. We can understand the inner dynamics of the strategy discourse, its convergences, tensions and lacunae. The Australian strategic imagination conceptualised as an enabling and constraining form establishes the limits within which the discourse occurs. The dilemma for those who work in strategy, particularly in the face of the need to undertake major change, is how to construct a discourse that can step outside or challenge the form that has been created and that

---

3   Harold Bloom, *The Anxiety of Influence: A Theory of Poetry* (New York: Oxford University Press, 1973).
4   Caroline Levine, *Forms: Whole, Rhythm, Hierarchy, Network* (Princeton: Princeton University Press, 2015), doi.org/10.23943/princeton/9780691160627.001.0001.

mandates certain approaches and limits. This is where imagination becomes important. Levine's work also illuminates how different forms can reinforce, disrupt, contend and constrain.

The idea of strength is a central term that I take from Bloom. In Bloom, a strong imagination is one that can establish primacy over precursor imaginations. The strength of Wordsworth or Blake, for example, is their ability to create in the shadow of Milton. A strong imagination represents a discontinuity and may manifest in the emergence of new modes of expression and new forms. In this respect, a strong imagination asserts primacy over the continuities represented by tradition. An example of this in international relations, I suggest, is explored in Evelyn Goh and Barry Buzan's book *Rethinking Sino-Japanese Alienation: History Problems and Historical Opportunities*.[5] The discussion in relation to the coexistence of China and Japan over centuries is in part about how each seeks to create both priority and space. Each of them seeks primacy. Each wants to create a consciousness that is so large it absorbs or embraces all other consciousnesses within its orbit; the struggle is to assert imaginative strength. China has the advantage of scale and a vast civilisation; Japan is perhaps a more derivative culture, and its strategy is to create identity through separation and distancing. Within the strategic system in which they exist, the conflict is a struggle of imaginations in which each seeks priority and control of the past, which in turn establishes the future. It is a struggle for primacy, to be first and for the power that comes from primacy.

The Romantic imagination in Blake and its lessons for strategy

The imagination is an abstract idea. It becomes visible in the reality of its creations and its artefacts. The writers whom I have found the most useful in helping me think about what the imagination is and how it works in the world are those who have tried to describe its workings directly—mostly Romantic poets and their critics. These writers offer a vision of the human world as an act of ongoing creation. They call the force that drives human creation the imagination. They describe this force, this faculty, in many ways. Yet, behind the theory and practice, it might be considered as a mode

---

5   Evelyn Goh and Barry Buzan, *Rethinking Sino-Japanese Alienation: History Problems and Historical Opportunities* (Oxford: Oxford University Press, 2020).

of apprehension distinct to humans that gives the world—the human world—the capacity to develop a deeper sense of the nature of reality, an understanding that reality is contingent on its status as an act of creation.

Some writers, such as Coleridge, saw the imagination as a creative force like the creative power of God. For Coleridge, imagination is a kind of divinely mandated creative force; it acts as a force of enlivening change on the world that, in its natural state as dead and fixed objects, resists it. The imagination is life; reality untouched by imagination represents death. Critics such as Bloom argue that the Romantic project was in part an attempt to overcome through the creative agency of imagination the reality of death in all its manifestations.

Other later poets, such as the American Wallace Stevens, saw the imagination as a mysterious yet potent first cause that enabled the poet to begin to make his or her world. To be human is first to imagine:

> Yet the absence of the imagination had
> Itself to be imagined.[6]

To my mind, William Blake is the poet who provides the most useful description of the imagination and how it might be used as a mode of perception that enables creation. His conception of imagination enables him to see and understand the world from many different perspectives simultaneously:

> The world of imagination is the world of eternity. It is the divine bosom into which we shall all go after the death of the vegetated [that is, mortal] body. This world of imagination is infinite and eternal, whereas the world of generation is finite and temporal.[7]

Blake contrasts the world of imagination and the world of generation, this material world. What imagination provides is the capacity to apprehend this world from a larger or more complete perspective: outside the limits of nature and time or other demarcations used to limit perception and understanding of reality. In this passage, we can see the Christian myth of the fall and redemption and hovering also the ghost of Plato. If we accept that these are metaphors for a mode of apprehension, Blake is arguing that the imagination—this capacity to create—provides access to a mode of

---

6   Wallace Stevens, 'The Plain Sense of Things', in *The Collected Poems of Wallace Stevens* (New York: Alfred A. Knopf, 1954).
7   William Blake, *A Vision of the Last Judgement* (painting, 1808).

apprehension that enables us to step outside the world apprehended through our limited perception to see both more of and more in the world. In his major works, he takes the reader through the transformation; the act of reading, as Blake teaches, potentially offers access to a larger consciousness. The relevance to strategy is that such a mode of apprehension provides the ability to understand and shape strategy with a greater sense of what it might mean and be able to achieve.

An important aspect of Blake's work is an exploration of the psychological process by which individuals might apprehend the world through their imagination. For Blake, our social and political categories are created by our modes of perception. Our normal modes of understanding are limited, and this is manifest in the difficulty we have accessing through our normal processes of perception anything more than a partial understanding of the world. The work of the imagination is that of showing how we might see beyond these categories to a larger intelligibility.

A deep reading of Blake teaches us to see outside the categories that our minds create. A good illustration of this is his *Songs of Innocence and Experience*, in which he explored what he called the two contrary states of the human soul.[8] The term 'soul' is Blake's and out of fashion these days, so perhaps consciousness is a more useful term for our purposes.

Blake used the idea of the imagination as a means of seeing how those states of the consciousness constructed partial representations of reality. In *Songs of Experience*, in poems such as 'London' or 'The Tyger', he shows consciousness trapped within the world of experience, unable to see beyond that world and therefore unable to understand the nature of that world and its place in it. Similarly, in his *Songs of Innocence*, in poems such as 'The Chimney Sweep', he shows a consciousness that embodies innocence and is unable to understand how its perception of reality is partial and makes it a victim. The inability of this consciousness to see beyond the world constructed within this partial reality, and therefore to either escape from or overthrow it, is the source of its oppression. As an aside, when I read Blake, I am struck by how the implied consciousness embodied in realist theories of international relations resembles the trapped consciousness we find in his poems of experience.

---

8   William Blake, *Songs of Innocence and Experience* (London: Penguin Classics, 2017).

To understand these poems, the reader must step outside the consciousness created by the poems to see that neither state nor the combination of the states gives full access to meaning. Blake is asking us to read them with a larger consciousness than that embodied in the world of the poems. To read them, we must have a strong imagination—one that can break through the limiting categories (forms) that structure our perception. One way of describing this larger consciousness with its greater cognitive capacity is the term Blake used: imagination. In so doing, we see that the consciousness embodied in the poem's speaker conveys only a partial representation of reality and limits access to truth.

The insight that Blake provides is that any representation of reality is partial. The work of imagination is to see beyond the limitations of that representation, to understand it and to assert human primacy over the construction of representations of the world. He also, in the detailed anatomy of the creative imagination that emerges in his work, provides a description of those obstacles to imagination, the 'mind forged manacles'. These include self-doubt, fear, jealousy, hate and the other negative emotions. These colour perception, narrow the world and create social and political structures that dehumanise in both explicit and subtle ways. We see these pathologies at work in our public space in policies and institutions conceived by fear.

I have spent some time on Blake because he is the writer who brings the most conceptual clarity to discussion of the imagination. Another major theorist of the imagination, as noted above, was Coleridge, with his ideas of the primary and secondary imagination:

> The primary Imagination I hold to be the living Power and prime Agent of all human Perception, and as a repetition in the finite mind of the eternal act of creation in the infinite I Am …

> The secondary Imagination I consider as an echo of the former, co-existing with the conscious will, yet still as identical with the primary in the kind of its agency, and differing only in degree and in the mode of its operation. It dissolves, diffuses, dissipates in order to recreate; or where this process is rendered impossible yet still at all events it struggles to idealize and to unify. It is essentially vital, even as all objects (as objects) are essentially fixed and dead.[9]

---

9   James Engell and W. Jackson Bate, eds, *The Collected Works of Samuel Taylor Coleridge. Volume 7: Biographia Literaria* (Princeton: Princeton University Press, 1985).

But every major Romantic writer built their own theory in the context of the project that they were pursuing. If we stand back and consider the Romantic imagination from a broader perspective, what binds all the writers is the idea that the role of the imagination is fundamentally redemptive, and that it is in dialogue with the external world to prevent the intrusion of that world into the poet's consciousness in ways that would threaten or destroy its integrity. The imagination struggles against the material world to prevent that world from destroying it.

In the context of literature, we see this dialogue play out in many ways. I have discussed Blake. In Wordsworth, it was an attempt to protect the integrity of the self from the depredations of the city, of politics, of the mechanisation of society. Ultimately, as we find in Wordsworth, there is an attempt to overcome the reality of death and its avatars, whether they be industrialisation, the mechanisation of daily life, poverty, the depredations of ageing and death and so on. In Blake, it included the positivist science that led to the world view of Sir Isaac Newton, the injustices of empire and the modes of thinking that resulted in what he described as the dark satanic mills: the Industrial Revolution built on a reductive and mechanistic view of reality. In the Romantic imagination, the external world is the world of death, the extinction of the living imaginative self. The great Romantic writers had imaginations of enormous strength because they challenged comprehensively the way in which society was constructed and ordered, not only at the level of its processes and artefacts, but also in the major thinking that led to such a society. They searched for a language, a mode of apprehension, that challenged the state of being and the world view that underpinned the society in which they lived, and in which we still live.

Imagination as power

One implication of Romantic theories of imagination is that imagination is a source of power. The Romantic writer seeks power over the 'universe of death' through the exercise of imagination.[10] Each writer seeks through the exercise of imagination some power over material reality. Poems are the record of this struggle and embody the poet's strategy to achieve their imaginative vision. The Romantic imagination in this context takes many different forms. Each writer failed when measured against their

---

10 Harold Bloom, *Take Arms Against a Sea of Troubles: The Power of the Reader's Mind Over a Universe of Death* (New Haven: Yale University Press, 2020), doi.org/10.12987/9780300255812.

ambition because all came up against the inability of external reality to accommodate unlimited human desire. In my own study of Wordsworth, I concluded that it is ultimately a desire to overcome the reality of death and, for Wordsworth, death established the boundary of his imagination and its capability. The larger conclusion of this struggle of imagination and reality is that imagination will push up against limits and become visible in terms of effect and structure. The imagination is the exercise of power— over death, over nature, over language, over the brute reality of the material world, over the forces of industrialisation, of mechanistic science and so on. It is the exercise of a desire for more life and all the things that 'life' might symbolise and embody: love, choice, self-creation, agency. The stronger the imagination, the more successful it is. In this context, I note that in his book *On Grand Strategy*, John Lewis Gaddis defines grand strategy as 'the alignment of potentially unlimited aspiration with necessarily limited capabilities'.[11] In the terms of this essay, he is describing strategy as the pathway between imagination as desire and reality as constraint.

I have spent some time on this because an examination of the Romantic imagination gives us a way of thinking about the structure of the Australian strategic imagination. I would argue that the Australian strategic imagination can be understood as the outcome of the dialogue between imagination and the constraints of what we might describe as the material world in all its manifestations.

The birth of the Australian strategic imagination

There continues to be a debate on why Australia was settled. When I was in primary school, we were taught that it was established as a prison in which to put people who committed crimes in England. We were also taught that the early governors were kind and visionary men and that the convicts eventually became settlers and undertook the task of settling and farming the land. The Indigenous peoples were presented as a backdrop, not central to the drama of settlement beyond being an element of a hostile country. Several generations of historians have challenged this narrative, but it still has some hold in popular thinking and is certainly the preferred story of conservative politicians and their cultural gatekeepers.

---

11   John Lewis Gaddis, *On Grand Strategy* (New York: Penguin Press, 2018), 21.

The story less often told is that Australia was settled as part of an imperial project; it was a strategic location to strengthen the British Empire's position against the French and other competitors. There may have been many other convenient reasons for settlement, but the imperial imperative was central and the most important. It is in this moment that the Australian strategic imagination was born. In this moment two conceptions of Australia came into being. One is of Australia as an integral part of the British Empire. On strategic matters, it could exercise no independent agency. Its security and defence were guaranteed and undertaken by the empire in accordance with imperial imperatives. The other, much more fragile conception was of Australia as a community, an emerging nation that had to exercise agency independent of empire to build its identity. We see the beginnings of the idea of an Australian nation, though it took more than a century for the idea to mature. It was an idea built on the experience of the development of the colonies and the emergence (and imagining) of an Australian identity that was related to the experience of Australia as a place and as a unique community.

The Australian strategic imagination is structured by the conflict between the imperatives of empire and the location of strategic identity within an imperial framework, and the emergence of the idea of an Australian nation that is independent of empire to the extent that it has a separate strategic identity. Over the past century, we have seen the end of the British Empire and the rise of the United States as a global power, but this does not challenge the foundations of the Australian strategic imagination because we have seen the substitution of one empire for another: American hegemony rather than British hegemony. The British Empire also still has a life as a particularly hungry ghost in current Australian strategic policy and its effect plays out in various nostalgias and ideas of strategic identity. If we want to frame this in terms of grand strategy, Australia's grand strategy has been the work of managing the tension between the imperatives of the hegemon (the United Kingdom, then the United States) and those of the nation in ways that maximise Australian security and agency. My argument would be that the history of Australian strategic policy both as a series of documents and as actions can be understood through this lens.

Earlier in this essay I discussed the concept of imagination with reference to the work of William Blake. I did this for two reasons. First, Blake, to my mind, is the most profound theorist of the imagination in our culture and offers the most comprehensive discussion and anatomy of its expression in both art and the world.

My second reason is that Blake wrote at the height of English Romanticism, which was during the period in which Australia was settled by Europeans. Blake was a critic of empire and Australia was a product of empire. As Blake describes the world of experience in his poems and prophetic books, which included his analysis of the pathologies of oppression, we were seeing in Australia the establishment of a prison colony that in its structure and functioning both embodied and gave expression to the world of experience as Blake describes it.

If we consider this world in terms of the categories that we see in the Romantic imagination, the early Australian settlers were living in Blake's world of experience. His poem 'London', an extraordinary critique of empire, creates a world that in its political and social hierarchies and structures of oppression is one that the early colonists would have recognised. Empire establishes and sustains its forms of oppression in all places simultaneously. Blake's *Songs of Experience* illuminate the psychology of oppression. The speakers of these songs are trapped in that world and do not have the imaginative strength to break out. The First Fleet sailed into Botany Bay in 1788. 'London' was published in 1794.

Another way of thinking about this would be to argue that the circumstances and the environment in which these settlers found themselves were a cognitive and imaginative crisis because much of what they were seeing and experiencing in this new environment was outside any frame of reference they had brought with them. It was an enormous imaginative challenge and these settlers had limited cognitive resources to meet this challenge. Their imagination was not strong. Trapped in a world of experience, empire becomes a trope for stability, order and continuity. Empire confers both material and psychic security. It becomes a major source of identity, but also incarnates the world of experience and its inhabitants in Australia, as in Blake's poem, cannot see any reality beyond it.

The early years of settlement were characterised by violence and resource shortages and many difficulties understanding the rhythms of the seasonal cycle and how the land might be understood and farmed. The landscape was challenging and perhaps, more importantly, did not fit with any conceptions that the early inhabitants brought with them. There was a vast and unknown interior and the Indigenous inhabitants were often hostile. There has been much scholarship on this, in terms of both how early settlers saw the country and, more recently, the resistance of the Indigenous inhabitants. Noting this, I believe it is reasonable to argue that Australia was born in warfare, half-starved, a fragment of empire and frightened that it may not survive. Survival depended on collective action in the government and administrative culture that favoured intervention. This, too, has shaped the Australian strategic imagination in ways that are still with us today.

But empire is challenged by local community—the life of individuals in place—which also works to create identity. We also see the stirrings of an idea of nation that in time would create an emergent strategic identity.

The imagination in Australia has always struggled to find its full expression. The forces arrayed against it have been formidable. Everyone will have their own list, but mine includes the continuing domination of Australian culture by empire and, later, by the memory of empire; the challenge of nature in Australia—so often a source of disappointment; the legacy of conflict and violence in the country's origins and subsequent history, shrouded in silence until recently; the challenge of absorbing into consciousness a completely different landscape that did not fit into familiar categories derived from the other side of the world; and the incomprehension of and inability to engage with what was available to the settler culture through a relationship with the Indigenous inhabitants.

Australian culture has always privileged the practical over the visionary, the doing over the thinking. It seeks to live in this world, rather than contemplate some other. The mainstream story of our art is its struggle to come to terms with the landscape. In literature, one of the major tropes has been the confrontation of the isolated and diminished self with natural and social forces beyond their control. Eccentricity, silence, escape, exile, madness, death and transcendence are some of the coping strategies of the Australian imagination under challenge (Patrick White and Henry Handel Richardson are exemplars of this). The Australian strategic imagination is a subset of the Australian imagination and the demarcation is not a simple one. However, we can see its expression in a strategic culture of pragmatism, predominantly realist traditions of statecraft, a pessimism about the world, a reflex to fortress Australia in times of crisis and a willingness to surrender strategic policy to the current hegemon.

These are, of course, generalisations, and there are many exceptions to what I have described. However, a reading of Australian literature and art reveals an attempt to come to terms with, comprehend and represent the Australian reality in ways that do full justice to both the present moment and what the future that might be. As Mark McKenna, in his essay *The Moment of*

Truth, argues, our culture's imagination of Australia is incomplete and, in some areas, characterised by avoidance and silence.[12] For McKenna, our failure to achieve a republic that incorporates the reality of the Indigenous experience of this country since settlement is a failure of imagination and, I would suggest, our biggest contemporary crisis. In Blake's terms, modern Australia was created in the world of experience and has not yet had the strength to imagine its way beyond this reality. In this sense, and drawing on Bloom's concept of strength, the Australian strategic imagination has struggled to achieve strength, and we still see that struggle in contemporary policy debates.

The contours of the Australian strategic imagination

If we consider the history of Australia, there are several crises that give insight into the development of Australia's strategic imagination. These include, but are not limited to, settlement and the wars of Indigenous dispossession, exploration, Federation, World War I, World War II, the wars in Korea and Vietnam, the post–Vietnam War strategic reorientation and, notably, the current China crisis. Each of these moments represents a crisis. Each is a moment of discontinuity, a moment that requires an act of imagination strong enough to envisage a future different from the continuities mandated by the past and powerful enough to generate a strategy sufficient to chart a path towards this future. When they occur, moments in history such as those mentioned above represent an enormous challenge because it means overcoming the forces of continuity and all that they represent in tradition, culture, practice and established relationships. Just as some of these moments of transition are navigated successfully, there are also failures. These failures are failures of imagination, which in turn give birth to weak or ineffective strategies.

We can also see some enduring themes that give us a sense of the shape and contours of the Australian strategic imagination and the tensions that it has tried to resolve as it has sought to respond to the future. Exploring these tensions helps us understand and identify the boundaries of the Australian strategic imagination. Debates about strategy, no matter how arcane, are

---

12 Mark McKenna, *The Moment of Truth: History and Australia's Future*, Quarterly Essay 69 (Melbourne: Black Inc., 2018).

not just technical, but also go to the question of our national identity and its construction and expression through the choices that we make. I identify some of these below. It is by no means a complete list, but notable is that each is a manifestation of what I have termed the tension between empire and nation.

There is a tension between fear of abandonment (from empire) and the desire for strategic autonomy (nation). This is discussed extensively in Alan Gyngell's history of Australian foreign policy in the twentieth century, *Fear of Abandonment*.[13] Gyngell explores how the fear of abandonment was embedded in the Australian imagination from the earliest moments of settlement and has shaped our attempts to influence and manage the larger strategic systems in which we participate. The tension to which strategic policy has since sought to respond is that of being a nation in command of its own destiny, while at the same time needing and wanting the support and protection of larger powers (empire).

Are we part of the world or a fortress kingdom unto ourselves? Australia has a history of sending expeditionary forces to other parts of the world as part of a larger imperial alliance or coalition engagement. This derives from a perception that Australian security is often best served by participation in and maintenance of larger global systems from which Australia benefits. Yet, Australia is also an island continent, which brings with it a concomitant obligation to provide for its own security and defence.

Australia is a trading nation that depends for its prosperity on the free flow of goods in our surrounding maritime environment. This creates a tension between maritime and land-based strategies for the construction and disposition of the armed forces. The challenge for Australian strategy is to resolve this tension to provide the most flexibility and embody the best recognition of the reality of our strategic environment. As one unpacks this dilemma, it becomes clear very quickly that the debate about the most appropriate strategy is one about what sort of country Australia is and should be: part of empire with the obligations of empire or an entity separate and autonomous. This tension flows through all debates about the development of strategic policy. It is why we have two different policies in relation to the US alliance in the *2020 Defence Strategic Update*. This debate was salient in our Covid-19 moment.

---

13   Allan Gyngell, *Fear of Abandonment: Australia in the World since 1942* (Melbourne: La Trobe University Press, 2021).

Geography haunts Australian strategy. Australian strategic policy has always grappled with the profound influence of geography as both a constraint and a strategic opportunity. To come to terms with Australian geography from a strategic perspective is to recognise that history is not necessarily a guide to the future. At the technical level, Australian geography provides many challenges in communications, logistics and force disposition. It gives us both the luxury and the challenge of time and distance. One of the enduring debates in Australian strategic policy is whether our geography or our history (empire) is more important in shaping strategy.

In current debates about the role (and presence in Australia) of US forces in relation to Australian strategic policy, we are also seeing the tension between nation conterminous with geography and nation as participant with reduced agency in a hegemonic project. Australian strategic policy has always sought to increase capability through alliances that bring intellectual resources and technology. This is one of the major ways in which the constraints imposed by geography are mitigated. Strategic policy has in recent years sought to chart the path between leveraging the power of an alliance and at the same time establishing a separate and independent operational and strategic identity. Decisions such as the AUKUS have a defensible strategic logic, but also embody a desire for protection by a hegemon and include a surprisingly nostalgic vision of the United Kingdom's strategic role that is probably beyond its capacity.

Anxiety about the Anzac myth and attempts to anchor it as a foundation for national identity have their counterpoint in anxieties about the legitimacy of possession in relation to First Nations peoples. The Australian community validates through commemoration participation in foreign wars but is silent about the Australian frontier wars. The Australian Defence Force is increasingly aware of the contribution of First Nations peoples to the defence of Australia and has made important steps in recent years to incorporate it into its community and work. However, one of the great silences in Australian history and in our thinking as a community about strategic policy, defence and the role of armed forces in society has been the absence of public acknowledgement of and incorporation into the national conversation the reality of the frontier wars.

Australia was an imperial project and the First Nations peoples were conquered. It is arguable whether the Australian strategic imagination has yet incorporated the reality and meaning of the frontier wars. In this sense, strategic policy does not yet speak to the full reality of the development of Australian nationhood and its history. There are often strange or confused attempts to reconcile history and geography. This debate is also partly a surrogate for debates about the nature of settler possession and its legitimacy. There is a theme in Australian mythologies of nation that Australia's possession was legitimised by sacrifice in war. Prime minister John Howard argued that our history and geography could be reconciled. Another way of framing this is to argue that our historical experience is imperial, but we live on an island continent remote from the concerns of empire. The current solution is an insecure nostalgia.

The enduring challenge of defending Australia and its interests remains a relatively small population seeking to exercise sovereignty over a very large land and maritime area. This shapes perceptions about the nature of the strategic challenge and imposes limits on what strategies might be viable. It also increases anxiety about strategic challenges in the neighbourhood. Related to this is fear of the 'other'—a persistent theme in Australia's strategic history. Australia has been a very welcoming country to migrants, but it also practices policies of exclusion and vilification, often in the service of an idea based on racial and political stereotypes. The 'other' has been a complex figure in Australian strategic history and has taken many forms, ranging from fear of Asian contamination of Australia's Anglo (and imperial) heritage to more recent vilification of refugees. The role of the other in Australian strategic history would make a major study in its own terms, but for the purpose of this essay, it is one of the structuring elements of the Australian strategic imagination and embodies over time many of the contradictions that the Australian strategic imagination seeks to resolve.

How can we conceptualise the Australian strategic imagination?

I have given a very cursory list that would come alive in more detailed case studies. What I am trying to demonstrate is that these contours add up to a structure and they relate to and come within a larger enabling form: empire and nation.

I have suggested that the Australian strategic imagination becomes visible in a crisis when decisions are made, but also in the documents and speeches that chart the evolution of policy and strategy. At the beginning of this essay, I suggested that one question in which I was interested was how that imagination evolves and changes, but also what has been the source of its remarkable stability over a very long period. The standard answer to this question is that Australia has enduring features of geography, its location in the international system is relatively secure and it has responded to crises pragmatically with an understanding of national capacity and limits, drawing on strategic and local resources as required. Over time, this experience shapes institutions that codify its routines of response into practice. For example, as a young policy officer, I was taught how to think about problems and the routines and rituals of response. I was being taught to operate with forms that shaped what responses are acceptable. It was not so different to an apprentice learning a craft.

This work generally takes place within a 'realist' understanding of the international system. This is certainly the theoretical framing that underpins most official strategic policy documents. This explanation makes sense within a positivist and realist understanding of Australia's strategic environment. In this context, strategy is about problem-solving in the context of resource constraints, however they are manifest. There is not much room for imagination as I have discussed it earlier in this essay because imagination is superfluous to the task of problem-solving. My criticism of this framework—which I believe is the dominant approach to strategic policymaking in Australia and the one that has most salience in contemporary strategic studies—is that it lacks an awareness of the way in which a strategy discourse can frame and shape artefacts and decisions. It is insufficiently self-conscious of the way the discourse shapes perceptions of the world and sets the parameters for policy development and decisions. It reduces human agency in relation to the world by assuming that the world in which we live is somehow independent of the minds that create it. In Blake's terms, it cannot find its way out of the world of experience.

I propose two different ways of thinking about Australian strategic policy over time, including how we might understand and analyse it as a manifestation of a strategic imagination that has its own imperatives inherent in its structure.

Strategic imagination as dialogue over time

As I have suggested, Australia's strategic imagination can be understood as a continuing dialogue over time between the imperatives of nation and empire, which may manifest as competing imaginings of Australia's future. It is also the result of the dialogue between possible futures and a past undergoing continuing reinterpretation. Within this frame, it may be considered as an evolving set of relations over time. It exists both within and outside time but is constrained by the path the world sets for it. It is movement, insight, response—visible in its moments of crisis; it is how humans live in the world by creating it as they move in the world through time. In this respect, it embodies potential and works against structure. It is many voices talking to one another across time.

The inner struggle of Australian strategic policy is between various forms of realism, rooted in geographical reality and imperial legacy, and various forms of constructivism, perhaps manifested in an internationalism that would step away from empire. This larger structure shapes the discourse over time. This reading of the Australian strategic imagination suggests that the path to understanding it lies along an analysis of the relationship between its different manifestations. This approach would consider, for example, how documents and decisions over time embody and reconcile the tension between empire, on one hand, and nation in the context of the circumstances at play. For example, an enduring feature of Australian strategic policy has been the need or the desire to reconcile the imperatives of continental defence with the need for a maritime strategy that recognises our participation in larger regional and global systems and relationships. One question that would be salient is the extent to which documents and decisions reference past documents and decisions or speak to the future. What is the relationship between these artefacts and how does that relationship work to shape Australian strategic policy? Another example are the three recent defence white papers, from 2009, 2013 and 2016, and the *2020 Defence Strategic Update*. Each white paper presents a specific argument about Australia's strategic environment. They argue with each other, misread each other, shift the meanings of key words. They can be read as discrete objects—'well-wrought urns'—and analysed as such. Or they can be read as a dialogue, the workings of a single imagination trying to grapple over time with an evolving challenge. They can be read against and with earlier documents[14] for continuities and lacunae. Out of this approach we could construct a conceptualisation of Australia's strategic imagination that comprehends it as a set of dynamic and evolving relationships in time. From this perspective, it is not a set of discrete events or artefacts, but a single continuum—an object that has both spatial and temporal dimensions.

On a more personal note, having worked to write, critique and implement strategic policy since the early 1980s, it is a curious experience. On one hand, you are conscious of history and the external world, and your work must respond to that. On the other, you are engaged in debates that lie outside time. The *1987 Defence White Paper* and the *2020 Defence Strategic Update*, for example, can merge in an uncanny ahistorical space to become one text with variation. Each new document reorders and reinterprets the past and seeks to change the future. The creation of a new document at a textual level engages with precursor documents. You enter a world of misreading, 'anxiety of influence', hauntings and ghosts. In this reality, the relationship between documents over time will give us greater insight than any single document.

Strategic imagination as form

We can understand the Australian strategic imagination as a form and this approach to analysis can yield useful insights about how it operates to shape artefacts and decisions over time and how it works to maintain stability and respond to change in the external environment. In undertaking this approach, I am borrowing heavily from literary theory and, behind my thinking, debates in recent decades about the relative utility of different theoretical approaches to texts. My own approach to literary works is to consider them as silent objects. As the Canadian critic and theorist Northrop Frye said, a work of literature is silent. This sounds counterintuitive, but what it means is that it is an object we interpret to determine its meaning. We can use a variety of interpretative approaches to do this. Different theoretical approaches or readings are likely to yield different meanings. Without interpretation, it remains a silent object.

---

14   For example, Paul Dibb, *Review of Australia's Defence Capabilities* (Canberra: Department of Defence, 1986) [*Dibb Review*]; and *The Defence of Australia 1987*, Department of Defence White Paper (Canberra: AGPS, 1987), www.defence.gov.au/sites/default/files/2021-08/wpaper1987.pdf.

In this section of the essay, I am responding to the work of the formalist critic and theorist Caroline Levine. Her ideas and methodological approach are set out in her 2015 book, *Forms: Whole, Rhythm, Hierarchy, Network,*[15] in which she proposes that formalist approaches can be used to analyse the relationship and interaction between works of art and broader cultural, social and political formations. Her book sets out an understanding of forms and how they work to constrain, establish difference, overlap, intersect, migrate and situate what we might describe as content. She extends her analysis and thinking to how the study of forms in literary texts can illuminate and help us understand political and social forces. She distinguishes between form and content, recognising that one form can organise many different types of content. She takes the idea of affordances from design theory to talk about how forms enable the emergence of—or 'afford'—a range of manifestations.

Affordance is a term used to describe the potential uses or actions latent in materials and designs. Glass affords transparency and brittleness. Steel affords strength, smoothness, hardness and durability. Designed things may have unexpected affordances generated by imaginative users—for example: we may hang signs or clothes on a doorknob or use a fork to pry open the lid, so expanding the affordances of an object.[16]

The power of Levine's idea is that it allows us:

> to grasp both the specificity and the generality of forms—both the particular constraints and possibilities that different forms afford, and the fact that those patterns and arrangements carry their affordances with them as they move across time and space.[17]

Levine discusses four major organising forms that can operate in many different contexts: whole, rhythm, hierarchy and network. In each discussion, she analyses how these forms can organise and structure our understanding of and participation in our environment and shape cultural, social and political organisation, and how they can compete and disrupt. From my perspective, she offers a way of thinking about the Australian strategic imagination's incarnation as an object with spatial and temporal dimensions, and how that object has a form that in turn enables the organisation of content that has implications for our understanding of the formation and the implementation of strategic policy within a very

---

15   Levine, *Forms.*
16   ibid., 6.
17   ibid., 6.

wide range of contexts. In this respect, it provides a container or, to use Levine's terminology, establishes it as a 'whole' within which many other forms emerge and interact. In this respect, it allows us to understand more deeply what I have described as a conversation over time generated by the Australian strategic imagination.

Towards some case studies

The Australian strategic imagination from the perspective of form has as its core organising structure an unstable hierarchy comprising the claims of empire against the claims of nation. This hierarchy is unstable to the extent that over time the relative claims of each element can shift and vary because of circumstances. This hierarchical structure embodies a whole to the extent that it establishes boundaries within which strategic policy is developed and expresses itself. In contemporary policy, empire is a trope for the Australia–US alliance, and this is a form that establishes what can be considered or incorporated into policy and what may not. It competes with, or is in relation to, the claims of nation and notions of national interest built on the foundations of an understanding of an independent Australian community.

The Australian strategic imagination creates a form that operates within a larger system of forms constructed by the interaction of ideas and states. One way of thinking about the contemporary moment is that we are seeing the emergence of competing hierarchies in the Indo-Pacific, each of which would establish a different order. This competition, which is unstable, represents disruption across the larger strategic system that has the potential to disrupt the stability of the form that expresses the Australian strategic imagination. The result is that we are in a period of crisis.

Within the overall form of the Australian strategic imagination—what I have described as an unstable hierarchy, but which also establishes a bounded whole that functions to exclude as well as include—we can see the emergence and interaction of other subordinate forms. For example, we can see how strategic policy documents can act as a 'whole', both including and excluding ideas. For example, the 1985 *Dibb Review* established the idea of Australia as a bounded space conterminous with geography.[18] Policy is concerned with managing the relationship between what is included and

---

18   Dibb, *Review of Australia's Defence Capabilities.*

what is excluded, from both geographical and force-structure perspectives, and establishing a hierarchy of force-structure and operational priorities. This in turn determines the shape and function of the institutions that are tasked with implementation.

As a form, the Dibb document provides an organising framework for many subsidiary decisions, including the development and shaping of institutions. It also establishes the framework for positioning the near region as an 'Arc of Instability'. We can see how Dibb's framework functions as a form to shape content over time. When Joanne Wallis argued against Dibb by reframing the 'Arc of Instability' as the 'Arc of Opportunity', she not only was challenging a policy idea but also had conceptualised Australia and the region within a different 'whole' that implied different hierarchies and presented a form that disrupted the one developed by Dibb.[19] The policy significance is that the form shapes ideas about what is legitimate in terms of operational policy. To be crude, the Arc of Instability deriving from Australia as a bounded whole means that outside those boundaries comes threat and the response tends to be exclusion. The Arc of Opportunity means Australia is part of a larger whole within which engagement and opportunity become a viable, perhaps necessary, policy response.

The 1985 *Dibb Review* document was challenged by the United States for its exclusions and, in this context, its disregard of the centrality of the alliance in Australian strategy (and its importance to US defence). It challenged in a small way the balance of the hierarchy that is the major form of Australia's strategic imagination. The resulting compromise was contained in the 1987 White Paper, which expressed policy as self-reliance within a framework of alliances and agreements. We can see here how the larger hierarchical structure of the Australian strategic imagination (empire/nation) flows through and shapes policy documents, but how ideas that embody a form can challenge or disrupt existing forms.

In those elements that I described as forming the contours of the Australian strategic imagination, we can see how they respond to and are structured by this larger form. However, even though forms are forces for stabilising strategic policy at the macrolevel, at the microlevel, forms interact, compete, destabilise and organise, as discussed in relation to Dibb and Wallis.

---

19   Joanne Wallis, 'The Pacific: From "Arc of Instability" to "Arc of Responsibility" and then to "Arc of Opportunity"?', *Security Challenges* 8, no. 4 (2012): 1–12.

Another example is that, if we consider strategic policy over decades, there are certain rhythms. There is a crisis, followed by some form of policy change and usually some consequential capability adjustment and administrative reorganisation. This rhythm establishes the cycle of organisational development and change within the defence institutions and, from my own research, takes place over about a decade. It operates within the larger hierarchical form but establishes how we might understand time and threat and capability cycles, which in turn flows through to the cycle of institutional change. The recent debate about warning time is an attempt to disrupt this well-established rhythm. Whether it is a sufficiently powerful disruption remains to be seen.

One question that arises out of this is: if the strategic imagination generates relatively enduring forms, how might change occur? This is a central question for the current moment. My view is that the forms within which we live, notwithstanding that they are created human artefacts, are extraordinarily powerful forces for continuity. Change occurs because of our adaptation to the world as it changes. But if we consider forms as forces that shape and organise the world, change is problematic because forms work to stabilise. The moment in which we are living is potentially very dangerous, because we are seeing the emergence of competing forms within the Indo-Pacific that are potentially powerful enough to disrupt those forms within which we currently function. This, for me, is why we need to understand our strategic imagination, its limitations and how it works. Formalist approaches to analysis can yield insight.

Some thoughts on implications

My intuition is that out of all this one could develop a broader theory of imagination and form that would enable comparative discussion. For example, realist theory in international relations, which sits behind Australian strategic policy and is the theoretical foundation for much thinking in defence and intelligence communities, is a form that guides and shapes, and one that I think the Australian strategic imagination finds too congenial. Is it a useful or adequate form to shape our engagement with the wider world? Should we disrupt it? Is the challenge to Australian strategic policy from the Pacific Islands (the Blue Pacific Continent) a disruption or the presentation of an alternative organising set of forms: the whole and a network rather than a hierarchy? We have also seen attempts to build new forms in Australian strategic policy, drawing on constructivist approaches, though we are not presently in a constructivist moment. A text, a decision, can be a site where multiple and contending forms intersect.

The discussion above is very abstract. I am not an advocate of an unthinking formalism, in literature, life or the development of strategic policy. Content matters. However, content is contextualised by form, which works to shape it. Even as we can undertake the type of interpretative analysis that I described earlier in this essay, it is also important to understand how that analysis operates within a larger framework of forms that guide us in so many ways.

As I noted earlier, one of the interesting features of Australian strategic policy is that it changes very little when looked at from the perspective of a century. We must ask whether we have allowed ourselves to limit our capacity to imagine alternative pathways into the future. Is our imagination strong enough to disrupt and break the forms that shape and bound it? For example, if we were to abandon the idea that we need the protection of a hegemon, what would that do to strategic policy? It would have profound implications at every level and in every manifestation, including institutional. In that respect, I believe that if we are to challenge and change our strategic imagination, we need to understand its form in time and space and how that in turn shapes our thinking and decisions.

Part 1.
The concept
of strategic
imagination

3

Concepts: What is strategic imagination?

The most striking part of the concept of 'strategic imagination' is its second word, 'imagination'. Today the word 'strategic' is overused, often signifying nothing more than significance. 'Imagination', however, is increasingly rare in common language. It is not a word often seen in public or academic conversations about nation-states, bureaucracies and the craft of scholars. In Carl von Clausewitz's famous 'paradoxical trinity', he assigned to the government the provision of 'reason', providing the logic and rationality that underpin strategy, in contrast to the 'chance' of military outcomes and the 'passions' of the body politic.[1] So, too, many who study or work on strategic issues describe themselves as 'realists'—a term that implicitly denies any sense of imagination and creativity in their approach to the world. If we are to properly assess this conjunction of 'strategic imagination', we must first examine some of these long-held assumptions.

In this section on 'concepts', we begin with three chapters that take on this question, examining imagination and the nation, imagination and scholarship, and imagination and policy. Each shows that in the day-to-day practice of political leaders, officials and academics, creativity and imagination are essential to success, and their absence or denial can be harmful. In Chapter 4, Emeritus Professor Mark McKenna considers the role of imagination in Australian life. He does so by considering two moments in which a significant question was put before the Australian people: the 1999 republic referendum and the 2023 Voice to Parliament referendum. Both

---

1   Carl von Clausewitz, *On War*, translated by Colonel J.J. Graham (New York: Barnes & Noble, 2004).

votes asked the public to imagine a different kind of Australia. The rejection of these proposals, along with the absence of compelling alternative visions by those who opposed them, suggests a nation stuck in an unimaginative rut. This is a concern that Brendan Sargeant identified in the previous chapter as a troubling position for a nation facing turbulent seas beyond its shores.

We then hear from Professor Anthea Roberts, in Chapter 5, who urges the use of imagination as a spur to scholarship that is appropriate for the challenges of our era. Roberts starts with the distinction between 'day science' and 'night science', illustrating how the rigour we associate with the term 'scholarship' makes its mark only when combined with creativity and boundary-pushing to test, check and rethink our assumptions. Then, in Chapter 6, Dennis Richardson, the former secretary of the Department of Defence, offers his thoughts on imagination in policymaking. He explains how Brendan drew on his literary background to inform and support his policy work and discusses some of the challenges of their period leading the department.

In Chapter 7, Professor Ian Hall highlights the ways philosophers and scholars have considered imagination and culture in their study of politics. Hall distinguishes between 'creative' and 're-creative' imagination and looks at the mindsets needed for scientists and public servants to learn from each other in creation of 'imaginative strategy'. To round out this section, Andrew Carr in Chapter 8 focuses on the mechanism through which so much of imagination occurs: the written word. Strategists do not build the machines of war, give the order to fight or fire the gun. Instead, it is through their words, helping others to see, to experience and ultimately to imagine the outcome of actions, that they can shape their environment.

Clausewitz's essential point in his 'paradoxical trinity' was not to put reason on the highest peak above passion and chance. There was, this Prussian Romantic philosopher realised, a necessary interdependence between these themes. His masterpiece, *On War*, can and should be read as a decrial of the search for purely rational approaches to war that were championed by rival military theorists such as Antoine-Henri Jomini and the 'Military Enlightenment' school.[2] What strategic imagination does most powerfully is not suggest there is a place for imagination in how nations, governments and intellectual life is shaped, but remind us that these fields cannot exist without its presence. We must directly engage and nurture it if we are to understand and thrive in the world as it really is.

---

2   Armstrong Starkey, *War in the Age of the Enlightenment, 1700–1789* (London: Bloomsbury, 2003), doi.org/10.5040/9798216033653.

4

A reconciled republic?
The Australian Constitution,
the Indigenous Voice to
Parliament, the republic
and the future of the
Commonwealth

Mark McKenna

Westminster Abbey, 11 am, Friday, 7 July 2000. It was billed as 'A Service for Australia'—the highlight of a week's commemorative events to mark the centenary of the passage of the *Commonwealth of Australia Constitution Act 1900* through the British Parliament. It was this legislation, largely forgotten today, that approved the Australian Constitution—already sanctioned by the Australian people through a referendum—and enabled the Federation of the Australian colonies on 1 January 1901.

Looking around the abbey (I had a pew because I was teaching at the Menzies Centre for Australian Studies, London), it seemed that Australia's entire political class was present: prime minister John Howard, opposition leader Kim Beazley, state premiers, judges, senior public servants, corporate executives and various characters who could be loosely defined as 'professional Australians'.

Queen Elizabeth II and Prince Philip were certainly in attendance, along with a sprinkling of 'lesser-known royals', as they are politely described in the trade. Australian High Court judges Ian Callinan and Kenneth Hayne sat directly in front of me. As the congregation rose to its feet to sing *God Save the Queen*, I peered through the gap between the judges' wives' hats to see NSW premier Bob Carr and his Victorian counterpart, Steve Bracks, standing together in silence.

Archbishop Peter Hollingworth delivered a worthy homily, John Howard recited a few verses from Philippians 4 in his typical nasal tone and the choir delivered a stirring performance of Bruce Woodley's *I Am Australian*— familiar from a well-worn trail of television commercials, including the 'Yes' referendum campaign in 1999. We did not need the libretto. Then, almost as an afterthought, the sound of a lonely didgeridoo drifted around the abbey.

The entire week seemed to be an endless procession of 'official' openings and drawn-out closings. But one event in particular, a gathering to celebrate the impending centenary of Federation and the recent opening of a major Arthur Boyd exhibition, was unforgettable for its sheer abandonment. Hundreds of Australians were crammed into Australia House on The Strand. I had heard people say that coming to London allowed you to see Australia more clearly, but that was untrue. London was where you came to be more Australian than you were at home.

On the ground floor of Australia House, champagne flowed like water. One famous Australian talked to another famous Australian as they looked over their shoulder to spot the next famous Australian: actors, musicians, journalists, artists and writers were just an hors d'oeuvre away. Past and present prime ministers—John Gorton, Malcolm Fraser, Bob Hawke, Gough Whitlam and Howard—were there, too. Bob Menzies's ghost hovered over the proceedings. Paul Keating, the prime mover of the recently failed movement for an Australian republic, was conspicuously absent.

Howard, his face beaming with pride, worked the room effortlessly. Like everyone else, he was well oiled. At one point, he stopped briefly to talk to me. I introduced myself as a disappointed republican, which elicited a wry chuckle. Just as he remarked implausibly that 'the whole event this week was republic neutral', the artist Margaret Olley, who was stalking celebrities mischievously with her camera, snapped his photo.

Later, as I stumbled along Kingsway towards Holborn tube station, I imagined Olley's photographs gracing the walls of some future exhibition of bacchanalia at Australia House. Hundreds of Australians had flown from the opposite end of the world for an almighty bash in London. For many, it did not seem to matter that the week's events were a stark reminder that Australia had yet to outgrow its colonial mentality, and that we had failed to grasp the true indicator of this mindset. We'd had a good time.

I have often looked back to that morning in Westminster Abbey. Over time, its significance has changed. At first, it seemed only to reinforce the failure of the republic referendum in November 1999. After a decade of campaigning, the republican movement ended defeated and divided. Eight months later, we were in London, commemorating the fact that the Australian Constitution was born within a statute of the British Parliament, when we could have been celebrating Australia's first year as an independent commonwealth with its own head of state.

Gough Whitlam could not have been more correct when he remarked that the road of the constitutional reformer in Australia is long and hard. Twenty-two years on, the Australian Constitution remains frozen, while the republic—a national political project struggling for relevance in an era of global political crises—kneeled dutifully in the abbey, waiting for the Queen's casket to be carried down the aisle. Despite the Queen's death in September 2022, we have come no further and, if recent polls are any indication, the passion for change seems lukewarm at best.[1]

Where to from here?

From the moment the modern republican movement began in the early 1960s, with the writings of Geoffrey Dutton and Donald Horne, the vision of an Australian republic was grounded in a set of familiar arguments that have shifted surprisingly little since. Dutton, in 1963, with his characteristic patrician flair, claimed that our failure to become a republic was 'the most monumental tribute to our national intellectual indolence'. We had not reached 'an adult relationship' with Britain. Instead, he argued, we had traded our independence for a 'stucco portal of ancient pomposities' and the 'syrup of a Royal visit'.[2]

---

1   The details of the service at Westminster Abbey come from my own notes at the time.
2   Geoffrey Dutton in Donald Horne, *The Coming Republic* (Melbourne: Sun Books, 1992), 6–8.

In *The Lucky Country* (1964), Horne insisted that the time had come to end the cultural cringe and break free from Australia's 'provincial' image as the home of 'backwater colonialism'. Only a republic could put an end to Australia's psychological dependence on Britain and create a less 'derivative', more confident and mature society. Or, in the words of countless newspaper opinion pieces over the years, it would represent Australia's 'coming of age'—one of the tiredest cliches in the lexicon of Australian nationalism.[3]

The masculine pride of republican intellectuals was affronted; they were embarrassed by Australians' willingness to cling to the 'apron strings' of the mother country and worried about what overseas visitors would think of us. As Dutton lamented, 'Australians are anonymous, featureless, nothing-men.'[4] Similar feelings of humiliation underwrote the foundation of the Australian Republican Movement in 1991.

On Australia Day 1988, Malcolm Turnbull watched 'from the top of a big building' in Sydney's CBD as a large crowd of dignitaries gathered at the Opera House. 'The most important [speech],' he recalled, 'the longest one, the one accorded the place of honour, was not uttered by an Australian. It was given by an Englishman, Prince Charles … [O]ur own national leaders were just warm-up acts for the Prince of Wales.' It was this rooftop epiphany that sparked Turnbull's resolution to campaign for an Australian republic. The whole bicentennial year, he thundered, 'was a year of shame. Every major event was presided over by a member of the British royal family.'[5]

When author Thomas Keneally launched the Australian Republican Movement at The Rocks, Sydney, in July 1991, with Turnbull and Horne sitting beside him, he spoke of the movement's determination to overturn the 'inherent inferiority' complex that had convinced Australians that they were not worthy to manage their own affairs or 'speak with an independent voice'. Until we became a republic, Keneally told the assembled media, Australia would remain a 'stunted nation' with a divided 'soul'.[6]

It was hardly surprising that the Australian Republican Movement's raison d'être was grounded in the cultural nationalism of the 1960s, when the first stirrings of modern republicanism emerged. All this talk of undersized

---

3   Donald Horne, *The Lucky Country* (Melbourne: Penguin 1986), 105, 107.

4   ibid., 107.

5   Malcolm Turnbull, *The Reluctant Republic* (Melbourne: Mandarin, 1994), 1, 3.

6   Thomas Keneally, Speech at launch of Australian Republican Movement, The Rocks, Sydney, 7 July 1991.

blokes who needed to stand on their own two feet harked back to Henry Lawson's *A Song of the Republic* (1887), which dramatically called on the 'Sons of the South'—'aroused at last'—to make a choice between the 'Old Dead Tree and the Young Tree Green'.[7]

While the Australian Republican Movement rejected the racist bedrock of Lawson's republicanism and fervently embraced British parliamentary and legal institutions, its platform echoed the poet's juxtaposition of a youthful, democratic, patriotic Australian republic with the hierarchical, class-ridden society of the Old World, which the British monarchy spectacularly embodied. At its core, an Australian republic has always been about severing the remaining constitutional ties to the United Kingdom. It is the continued existence of these *external* ties—this lingering British connection, this foreign head of state—that, for republicans, has long represented the persistence of Australia's colonial mentality.

Since the failure of the republic referendum in November 1999, and indeed well before, there have been two main problems with this way of thinking. As Australia's economic, cultural and political ties gradually shifted away from Britain and towards the United States and Asia in the latter part of the twentieth century, the British connection withered in spite of the fact that Australia remained a constitutional monarchy. This, combined with the increasingly multicultural fabric of Australian society, undermined the purchase of the old arguments for republican independence, which had continually been framed purely in terms of Australia's relationship with Britain and its increasingly dysfunctional if somewhat amusing royal family. Hovering above a succession of tabloid scandals, the Queen reigned in lonely dignity, seemingly untouchable, attracting more public affection as she aged. But the greater problem—the real blind spot and failure of imagination, the true marker of Australia's colonial mentality—had still not been placed in the same field of vision.

The program for the 'Service for Australia' at Westminster Abbey in July 2000 proudly proclaimed that 'the Australian people [had] created one of the world's most democratic constitutions'. 'The Commonwealth,' it declared, 'had been forged with the consent of the people. The people of Australia entered the 20th century as a nation with a united destiny.'[8] Yet, how could

---

7   Henry Lawson, *A Song of the Republic* (1887), available from: www.ironbarkresources.com/henry lawson/SongOfTheRepublic.html.
8   'A Service for Australia', Westminster Abbey, July 2000.

this be true when the dispossession and disenfranchisement of Australia's First Peoples were the starting point of the new federation? The very basis of the Constitution and the Commonwealth's creation rested on the exclusion of Indigenous Australians.

When we consider the frontier wars that were ongoing in the early twentieth century, particularly in the centre and north of the continent, we can no longer see Federation as 'peaceful' but, rather, as deeply implicated in legitimising the taking of Indigenous lands without treaty, consent or compensation. One hundred years later, in the heart of the former British Empire, it seemed impossible to acknowledge these basic historical facts.

Even today, our concept of the Australian polity fails to be genuinely inclusive. We sleepwalk in the footsteps of our colonial forebears, who introduced both responsible government and Federation without negotiating with Indigenous Australians. We have imagined our full constitutional independence, our republican future, as simply being a question of deleting the monarchical references from the Constitution. At the same time, despite the referendum on 14 October 2023 to recognise First Nations peoples and enshrine an Indigenous Voice to Parliament in the Constitution, the discriminatory race power (Section 51, xxvi) still stands. With the referendum's failure, Indigenous Australians remain invisible in our founding document. Two nation-defining issues—one shelved indefinitely, the other inching forward at glacial pace, both tightly controlled by those in power—have played out in parallel universes.

In the wake of the *Uluru Statement from the Heart* and its call for a constitutionally enshrined Voice to Parliament, the time has come to place our constitution on what Noel Pearson has called 'just foundations', rethink the rationale for an Australian republic and finally come to grips with what it means to end our colonial mentality once and for all. To do so, Australians must once more ask themselves: Does their conception of Australia include Indigenous people or not? Without a proper, constitutional response to this fundamental question, how can Australia hope to become a fully reconciled republic?

The true source of Australia's shame is not the delivery of a speech by the British monarch, but the continued exclusion of Australia's First Nations peoples from the Constitution. The persistence of Australia's colonial mentality—our failure to become a genuinely postcolonial nation—has little to do with the British royal family and everything to do with our reluctance to genuinely break away from our colonial past.

As the late Galarrwuy Yunupingu, former leader of the Gumatj clan of the Yolngu people, wrote in *The Monthly* in July 2016, if a 'settlement' between the Commonwealth and First Nations people is to be achieved, 'a prime minister must lead and complete it'. 'Let us have an honest answer from the Australian people to an honest question,' he implored. As the *Uluru Statement from the Heart* makes clear, the completion of any future settlement obviously entails a treaty and truth-telling.[9]

While Opposition Leader Peter Dutton and his fellow naysayers might be willing to support a legally non-binding recognition of Indigenous Australians in the preamble to the Constitution, similar to John Howard's proposal in 1999—precisely the weak symbolic change that the *Uluru Statement* rejected in favour of a constitutionally enshrined voice—they remain steadfast in their opposition to any revision of the Constitution proper.

Given the constrictive mechanism for change that is hardwired into the Constitution—Section 128, which requires a double majority of states and voters if any referendum is to pass—Dutton and likeminded conservatives frequently argued that the October referendum should have been abandoned to avoid damaging the cause of reconciliation.

For conservatives such as Dutton, the Constitution, like Australia Day, is stitched up. It requires no rethinking and no significant change. Their constitution and their country are already complete. This complacent view, of course, is one conceived of from inside the structures of power and consistently fails to see the perspective of those on the outside, who have long been excluded. Such is the fortune of those who can see their faces in the Constitution, whether they are constitutional monarchists or republicans. Even Turnbull, who led the charge to make minimal changes to the Constitution so that Australia could become a republic, was not willing, as prime minister, to support the substantive change that would enshrine an Indigenous Voice to Parliament.

In the leadup to the referendum, I spoke with Yuin elder Ossie Cruse and Djiringanj-Yuin spokesperson Warren Foster. Both men argued that Indigenous sovereignty had never 'been extinguished' and that the Constitution was foisted on their people without their consent, like so many other aspects of whitefella law and culture. When I asked Cruse about the

---

9   Galarrwuy Yunupingu, 'Rom Watangu', *The Monthly*, July 2016, www.themonthly.com.au/issue/2016/july/1467295200/galarrwuy-yunupingu/rom-watangu.

dismissal of the *Uluru Statement*'s call for a constitutionally enshrined voice by prime ministers Turnbull and Scott Morrison, he shrugged his shoulders. 'They can only respond like that,' he said, 'because they can't understand the *left-outness* of Aboriginal people; they can't see history from our perspective.'

Foster was even more pointed:

> We are one of the poorest people. We've suffered a lot from the taking of our land and yet we're still willing to walk forward with other Australians, but only on an equal basis. Back then, we didn't have a voice. We're not part of that constitution. We weren't party to it. We couldn't have a say. We're not there. We're not written in it. So how come they think they have jurisdiction over us?[10]

The legacies of suffering and exclusion of which Foster speaks have been evident in the long and complex relationship between Indigenous Australians and the Crown. Aboriginal people have petitioned the Crown for land rights, recognition and justice since the mid-nineteenth century. In the twentieth century, petitions gradually came to speak not only for the Aboriginal people of one locality or region, but also for those across the entire nation.

In 1933, Burraga (Joe Anderson), a Dharawal elder from Thirroul, south of Sydney, pleaded for all Aboriginal peoples in New South Wales to petition King George V for guaranteed Aboriginal 'representation in federal parliament' (as existed in New Zealand). He wrote:

> Before the white man set foot in Australia, my ancestors were as Kings in their own right. And I, Aboriginal chief Burraga, am a direct descendant of the royal line … One hundred and fifty years ago the Aboriginals owned Australia, and today he demands more than the white man's charity. He wants the right to live.[11]

One year later, Yorta Yorta activist William Cooper drafted a similar petition to the king, although he did not deliver it to prime minister Joseph Lyons until September 1937. Lyons refused to support Cooper's petition, which was signed by 1,800 Aboriginal people from across the country, or forward it to the king—by that time, George VI. In 2014, Cooper's grandson Uncle

---

10   The comments of Foster and Cruse are drawn from interviews conducted by the author.
11   Heather Goodall, '1933—Joe Anderson's Speech', in *The Quest for Indigenous Recognition, Australian Dictionary of Biography* (Canberra: National Centre of Biography, The Australian National University, 2006–24), adb.anu.edu.au/the-quest-for-indigenous-recognition/joe-anderson.

Boydie Turner finally submitted the petition via governor-general Sir Peter Cosgrove to Queen Elizabeth II. Almost 90 years since Cooper wrote the petition, there has still been no official response from the British monarch.[12]

The venerable, majestic crown—at once object, person and synonym for state authority—is the cloak that legitimised the taking of Indigenous land by force. Despite the many appeals made by Indigenous Australians to the person of the monarch throughout the nineteenth and twentieth centuries, and the handful of more recent meetings between the monarch and Indigenous representatives in London, there is little evidence that these interactions have made a substantial difference to the social, legal and political status of Indigenous Australians. At best, they have offered the possibility of highlighting government inaction on Indigenous issues. At worst, they are a reminder of the monarch's aloof distance and powerlessness to effect real change in the lives of Aboriginal people. In any event, a polite 'audience' with the king cannot atone for more than two centuries of profound neglect. As William Cooper wrote to the Lyons government in 1935, even though they are the 'original owners of the country', Indigenous Australians have 'no voice' in the government of the Commonwealth.[13]

This history points to the urgency of an Indigenous Voice to Parliament and why, in essence, the Voice is a fundamentally republican proposal: not only because it disperses power and protects Aboriginal peoples from arbitrary and potentially harmful policies, but also because it circumvents any need to petition a distant royal intermediary, by bringing the representatives of Indigenous peoples to the heart of power in Canberra, which is where so many of the decisions that affect their lives are made.

If Australians are to learn from their history, as politicians are constantly asking them to do, recognition of Indigenous Australians surely must be more than ornamental—more than a paragraph of beautiful words that soothe the soul and change nothing. It requires something much harder. It requires the Commonwealth to cede ground—not only to share history but also to share decision-making power. This is another reason the referendum in October 2023 was so important for Australia's future.

---

12   Bain Attwood, '1937—William Cooper's Petition', in *The Quest for Indigenous Recognition*, *Australian Dictionary of Biography* (Canberra: National Centre of Biography, The Australian National University, 2006–24), adb.anu.edu.au/the-quest-for-indigenous-recognition/william-cooper.
13   ibid.; Mark McKenna, *Moment of Truth*, Quarterly Essay 69 (Melbourne: Black Inc., 2018), 2–4.

The missing story

In her recent book, *The Gun, the Ship and the Pen: Warfare, Constitutions and the Making of the Modern World*, British historian Linda Colley argues that 'a constitution … like a novel, invents and tells the story of a place and a people'. But what story of 'place and people' is told by Australia's Constitution?[14]

'Humbly relying on the blessing of Almighty God', the Constitution's preamble proclaims that the Australian people 'have agreed to unite in one indissoluble Federal Commonwealth under the Crown'. The Constitution is 'enacted by the Queen's most Excellent Majesty, by and with the advice and consent of the Lords Spiritual and Temporal, and Commons'. In other words, the implicit sovereignty of the Australian people is underwritten by the archbishops of Canterbury and York, the bishops of London, Durham and Winchester, other bishops of the Church of England, life peers, the Earl Marshal, Lord Great Chamberlain, hereditary peers elected under the Standing Orders and the House of Commons. So the 'spiritual' sovereignty inscribed in the Australian Constitution emanates from the Church of England and the queen or king who stands as its titular head.

But today, who aside from a deluded monarchist rump, would seriously argue that our constitution should continue to be grounded in the spiritual leadership of the Anglican Church? Or the monarch's ailing majesty for that matter? The story laid down in the preamble to the Australian Constitution—written half a century before the legal category of Australian citizenship existed—is broken. It no longer reflects who we are. It speaks only to constitutional lawyers and of times past, when we were British subjects enmeshed in empire rather than citizens of a democratic nation.

As for the Constitution itself, while it lives as a legal document, it has little meaning in the body politic. Ignorance is pervasive. From the first sample surveys conducted in the 1960s to the extensive *Civics Expert Report* conducted in 1994, and more recent Australian Electoral Commission surveys and parliamentary committees, there is widespread consensus that the lack of understanding of the Constitution in the general community

---

14   Linda Colley, *The Gun, the Ship and the Pen: Warfare, Constitutions and the Making of the Modern World* (London: Profile Books, 2021), 12.

remains the most substantial obstacle to future constitutional reform. Contrary to conventional wisdom, the Australian people are not attached to the Constitution; they are attached to the idea of not changing it.

While most Australians believe Australia to be an independent nation, few would be able to identify the point at which it became independent. Nor would they try to demonstrate their independence by quoting passages from the Constitution. They have rarely if ever looked to the Constitution to express their identity. As the historian John Hirst pointed out in 2002, Australian society is characterised by 'that strange gap, that lack of attachment between a democratic society and its democratic institutions of government'.[15] If we do have an attachment to constitutional principles, it exists in ideas like a 'fair go' and other ill-defined democratic freedoms— ideas that are given force and meaning through an understood contract of civil society. Ours is a constitution more imagined than material, more the stuff of abstract faith and belief, however misplaced, than ink, text and parchment.

For all the Constitution's silence on citizenship and the democratic principles Australians supposedly share, there is a glaring dissonance at its heart. It is entirely disconnected from the place and country in which we live, severed from the spiritual sovereignty of Indigenous Australians that has reigned in Australia for more than 60,000 years.

This is the missing story in the Constitution, the absence of which constitutes the colonial mentality that must still be shattered. It is their spiritual sovereignty—'the ancestral tie between the land or mother nature and the Aboriginal and Torres Strait Islander peoples', as the *Uluru Statement* makes clear—that 'has never been ceded or extinguished, and co-exists with the sovereignty of the Crown'.[16]

New historical knowledge has the capacity to change the way Australians think and act on Country. The growing awareness of the inseparable connection between Country and culture—such a defining feature of Indigenous Australia—is slowly permeating Australia's entire society, shifting the way Australians see the nation's past, present and future. With the release of the *Uluru Statement* in 2017, Uluru became a sacred text as well as a sacred place. Together with the statement—more poetic, inspiring

---

15   John Hirst, *Australia's Democracy: A Short History* (Sydney: Allen & Unwin, 2002), 328.
16   *Uluru Statement from the Heart* (2017), ulurustatement.org/the-statement/view-the-statement/.

and reflective of the country in which we live than the Constitution itself—this new historical knowledge has the potential to transform our attitude to constitutional change.

For anyone who has read even a handful of the histories published since the 1980s that completely overturned the myth of Australia being settled peacefully, it is possible to comprehend why and how the Constitution embodies the big lie that the land was there for the taking, as though Indigenous Australians were rightly dispossessed and merely destined for extinction. The laws of federal and state governments that attempted to govern every aspect of Indigenous peoples' lives since the invasion began in the late eighteenth century were conceived, written and legislated without consultation with those affected by them. This is why the framers of the *Uluru Statement* have demanded that any future reform goes well beyond symbolism.

Story alone is not enough. Nor is an 'acknowledgement of Country'. The glaring inequalities of power embedded in the Constitution must be addressed. Throughout the referendum, it was argued that constitutional enshrinement of a Voice to Parliament was fundamental to *makarrata* ('a coming together after a struggle') and truth-telling. Professor Megan Davis, one of the architects of the *Uluru Statement*, sought to remind us of the underestimated power of a 'constitutional moment':

> A First Nations voice in the Constitution, established by referendum, would shift Indigenous affairs out of the realm of ideological party politics, where our issues are ruthlessly measured against utilitarian rule. Such a voice would be imbued with the legitimacy of the First Nations peoples and the Australian people voting in unity at a referendum and conducting a dialogue with each other through the parliament for the century ahead. Symbolic and substantive.[17]

In recent years, Australia's political leaders have lost the ability to enlarge the vision of the nation—to give it life imaginatively and positively through political speech and to lay down a path of renewal and change. A complacent, self-satisfied thumbs-up seems to be the best we can do. When Keating addressed Federal Parliament in June 1995 and outlined his government's rationale for a republic, he loaded his vision with a multitude of possibilities:

---

17   Megan Davis, 'Voice at a Crossroads', *The Monthly*, March 2021, www.themonthly.com.au/issue/2021/march/megan-davis/voice-crossroads.

> The creation of an Australian republic is not an act of rejection. It is one of recognition: in making the change we will recognise that our deepest respect is for our Australian heritage, our deepest affection is for Australia, and our deepest responsibility is to Australia's future … An Australian head of state can embody our modern aspirations— our cultural diversity, our evolving partnerships with Asia and the Pacific, our quest for reconciliation with Aboriginal Australians, our ambition to create a society in which women have equal opportunity, equal representation and equal rights.[18]

Almost 30 years later, we can see how Keating asked the impossible: believing that a minimalist republic that prided itself on little change would completely transform the nation's identity. What Keating believed was implicit in the declaration of an Australian republic must now be made explicit. The act of recognition that he placed first, an Australian head of state, must now come second to the more fundamental act of recognising Indigenous Australians in our constitution.

The republican vision of Australia's independence—for so long conceived narrowly as the mere severing of an external connection with a withered, anomalous crown—must finally be grounded on our own soil and on thousands of generations of Indigenous occupation.

In essence, this is an entirely different conception of Australian independence—one that grows out of the country itself, begins with a central act of recognition, enshrines a new relationship with First Nations peoples on an equal basis and lays the just foundations of Australia's Constitution and the future of the Commonwealth.

Only a fully reconciled Australian republic can genuinely address the dispossession and persecution of Indigenous Australians that the Crown propelled and sanctioned. This is yet another reason a resounding 'Yes' vote in the referendum was essential not only for Indigenous Australians, but also for the nation as a whole—a point powerfully made by Noel Pearson when he appeared before the joint select committee hearings on constitutional recognition in May 2023:

---

18   Paul Keating, 'An Australian Republic: The Way Forward', Speech, House of Representatives, Canberra, 7 June 1995, www.paulkeating.net.au/shop/item/an-australian-republic-the-way-forward---7-june-1995.

> The country is going to change the minute we vote on this, and change for the better. We'll put a lot of bad things behind us when we do it. It's a simple change, but it's very profound. The impact of it is going to be absolutely tectonic. It's going to change the country in a good way.[19]

The true challenge of the 2023 Voice referendum was to consider nothing less than the beginning of the creation of a new foundational language for the Commonwealth—one in which the Constitution and the people's willingness to reform it will become central to the stories we tell about Australia's independence, history and identity.

The politics of the 2023 referendum

Two months out from the referendum, there were many in the political class who believed that it had already been lost. In November 2022, The Nationals announced they would oppose the proposal for a constitutionally enshrined Voice to Parliament. In April 2023, Opposition Leader Peter Dutton followed suit, confirming that the Liberal Party would advocate for a 'No' vote. In the interim, MPs on the progressive left such as Victorian Greens Senator Lidia Thorpe and those on the far right such as Queensland Senator Pauline Hanson also announced their opposition to the proposal. Consequently, the Yes campaign faced opposition across the entire political spectrum. Any dreams of bipartisan support in the Federal Parliament were dashed. In addition, major opinion polls showed a steady decline in support for the Yes case, from more than 60 per cent support in 2022 to less than 50 per cent in mid-2023.[20]

This decline demonstrated the effectiveness of Dutton's scare campaign. Together with other key leaders of the No campaign such as Nationals Senator Jacinta Price and Warren Mundine, Dutton continued to accuse

19   Josh Butler, 'Noel Pearson Says Tony Abbott's Call to Scrap Voice Referendum "Absurd"', *Guardian*, 1 May 2023, www.theguardian.com/australia-news/live/2023/may/01/australia-news-live-indigenous-voice-cost-of-living-budget-economy-jobseeker-interest-rates?filterKeyEvents=false; Josh Butler, 'Noel Pearson Warns of "Almost Endless Protest" if Indigenous Voice Referendum Fails', *Guardian*, 1 May 2023, www.theguardian.com/australia-news/2023/may/01/noel-pearson-warns-of-almost-endless-protest-if-indigenous-voice-referendum-fails.
20   Nick Evershed and Josh Nicholas, 'Voice Referendum 2023 Poll Tracker: Latest Results of Opinion Polling on Support for Yes and No Campaign', *Guardian*, 13 October 2023, www.theguardian.com/news/datablog/ng-interactive/2023/oct/13/indigenous-voice-to-parliament-referendum-2023-poll-results-polling-latest-opinion-polls-yes-no-campaign-newspoll-essential-yougov-news-by-state-australia.

the Labor government of failing to provide sufficient detail about how the Voice would work after the referendum. The Yes campaign often appeared trapped.

Fail to provide the detail and your opponents will argue you are asking for a blank cheque. Provide the detail and they will find the devil in it. Say the Voice is a modest proposal and they will say it is radical, or not radical enough. Put the Voice forward as the first necessary reform and so-called progressive No-voters will argue that other reforms such as treaty or truth-telling should happen first; while in parliament, Dutton fearfully portrayed the Voice as inevitably leading to a treaty. See a blue sky and the No campaign will see a raging storm.

The most convincing argument against providing too much detail on the Voice was made by Megan Davis, who repeatedly stressed that the Voice did not threaten the supremacy of parliament and that parliament would frame and adapt the legislation that determined how the Voice operated. All the more reason, then, that voters should not be asked to vote on the specifics of legislation that would inevitably change over time.

Social media allowed the Voice campaign to mobilise wide sections of the electorate that increasingly fall outside the grip of the major political parties. Yet, this same media landscape also distorted, exaggerated and manipulated Indigenous opposition to constitutional enshrinement of the Voice, whether it was from the left or the right, particularly through the many actors on social media who magnified or distorted their views. Due to the No campaign's deliberate strategy of sowing confusion and fear wherever possible, and the rampant spread of misinformation and lies on social media, it proved difficult for the Yes campaign to keep the debate focused on the specific proposal put forward in the referendum, and to stop the debate from fracturing. The No campaign advanced its case under three key slogans:

- Vote 'No' to the 'Canberra Voice' (a product of 'academics' and 'elites')
- Don't know? Vote 'No'
- Don't change the Constitution. Vote 'No' to the Voice of Division.

Variations on the above themes were numerous. It was argued that the Voice would entrench racial division and give one group of Australians special privileges that no others possessed. Australians were told to vote 'No' to the Voice because enshrinement would hand more power to Canberra and 'academics'. Decision-making would be removed from local Indigenous communities and given instead to a handful of bureaucrats and unelected judges on the High Court.[21]

Nor would enshrinement improve social and economic outcomes or help to 'close the gap'. The referendum was 'a complete waste' of money, according to Lidia Thorpe.[22] 'Parliamentary democracy' as Australians knew it would be 'dead' (according to unnamed 'silks' confiding their darkest secrets to Janet Albrechtsen in the *Australian*).[23]

Then there was the exploitation of voters' ignorance and fear. Enter former prime minister Tony Abbott. Speaking on ABC *Radio National* with Patricia Karvelas, Abbott intoned gravely:

> I am very uncomfortable with this voice … I'm uncomfortable with what Malcolm Turnbull called a third chamber of parliament. I'm uncomfortable with electing a body determined by race … You really can't ask the people for a blank cheque on something as significant as this … [I]f the people are asked to vote in favour of an entirely unspecified voice the natural response will be to say well, 'If you don't know, vote no'.[24]

Closely aligned with Abbott's scare tactics were the tried and tested arguments that appealed to stasis: 'if it ain't broke, don't fix it'. Variations on this mantra were numerous: we could recognise Indigenous peoples without damaging a constitution that has 'served Australia well'. The existing framework for an Indigenous voice and improved consultation and deliberation with Indigenous communities were already under way. There was no need to change the Constitution to achieve these objectives. Once the Voice was in the Constitution, it would be there to stay. Far better to retain flexibility and allow parliament to abolish the Voice if it saw fit. In any case, Indigenous peoples can stand for parliament. There were at the time 11 Indigenous parliamentarians in the Federal Parliament; this remained a far better solution than a constitutionally enshrined Voice.

21   Nyunggai Warren Mundine, *X* [*Twitter*] post, 28 May 2022, 8.54 am, twitter.com/nyunggai/status/1530321573504163841.
22   Sarah Collard, 'Referendum on Indigenous Voice to Parliament a "Complete Waste" of Money, Lidia Thorpe Says', *Guardian*, 1 September 2023, www.theguardian.com/australia-news/2022/sep/01/referendum-on-indigenous-voice-to-parliament-a-complete-waste-of-money-lidia-thorpe-says.
23   Janet Albrechtsen, 'The Albanese Amendment', *Weekend Australian*, 13–14 August 2022: 18.
24   In Patricia Karvelas, 'Tony Abbott on Shinzo Abe', [Interview], *Radio National Breakfast*, ABC Radio, 12 July 2022, www.abc.net.au/radionational/programs/breakfast/tony-abbott-on-shinzo-abe/13969192.

All the arguments above, many of them echoing the 'No' case arguments in the republic referendum of 1999, damaged the Voice campaign. It proved easier to refute concrete arguments against enshrinement (that it represented a 'third chamber' of parliament) than it did to counter more general myths that tapped into deeply entrenched views in the electorate ('the Constitution has served us well') or arguments that played to widely held perceptions about equality (the Voice would divide Australians and make them less equal as citizens). The positive connection between a constitutionally enshrined Voice and the enhancement of democracy, fairness and equality was not widely accepted or understood.

Given the Australian electorate's longstanding preference for practical change, the Voice was also vulnerable to any suggestion that constitutional change would not improve the lives of Indigenous peoples. The benefit argument was made but it failed to cut through. In addition, the Yes campaign found it difficult to counter the fact that two of the No campaign's most prominent leaders, Mundine and Price, were Indigenous. Voters who paid little attention to politics and had little knowledge of the mechanics of constitutional change concluded crudely that if Aboriginal people could not agree on the referendum proposal, why should they as non-Indigenous Australians vote yes?

Crossing this political minefield was a tall order. As ever, the task of the naysayers was easier than it was for the advocates of change. Even pointing out the lies in the No campaign's arguments did not dent their political effectiveness. By comparison, the politics of the 1967 referendum (when there was bipartisan support for the proposal and there was no formal 'No' case), appeared less complex, less polarised and less precarious.

The most substantial arguments against the Voice were refuted. The Voice would not enshrine 'race' in the Constitution; that word is already present courtesy of the racist mentality that prevailed in Australia when the document was written in the 1890s. Section 51 (xxvi) originally gave the parliament the power to make laws with respect to '[t]he people of any race, other than the Aboriginal race in any State, for whom it is deemed necessary to make special laws'. As a result of the 1967 referendum, the highlighted words were deleted, but the so-called race power remained.[25] Offensive as

---

25   Russell Taylor, 'Indigenous Constitutional Recognition: The 1967 Referendum and Today', Lecture, Senate Occasional Lecture Series, Parliament House, Canberra, 26 May 2017, www.aph.gov. au/-/media/087AC476528E42C7A97738235B1B17BA.ashx.

this provision is, proponents of the Voice decided to focus their attention on constitutional enshrinement, not because they wanted to insert 'race' into the Constitution—after all, the entire constitution is a racist construct because it denies their very existence—but because they wished to ask the Australian people to recognise their unique cultural status as Australia's First Nations peoples.

The Voice was an attempt to directly addresses historical *inequality*. It was a simple, forceful and elegant response to a longstanding injustice that has seen successive state and federal governments pass legislation that impacts the lives of Indigenous Australians without any requirement to negotiate with them.

Nor is the Voice separate from truth-telling. It remains a possible instrument of truth-telling—the first and most important step, because it directly addresses the lie with which Australia has been content to live for far too long: the exclusion of Indigenous Australians from the nation's founding document. And because it tackles the fundamental issue of power, ensuring a permanent First Nations' seat at the decision-making table and a voice in the framing of Commonwealth legislation that they have long been denied. The Voice could also help lay the basis for *makarrata* because its existence signals that First Nations peoples are within rather than outside the halls of power.

The referendum was also an opportunity for truth-telling. It implicitly asked the majority of Australians to recognise and understand a historical experience different to their own; to recognise that, for Indigenous Australians, the history of the past 235 years has been far removed from the stories of peaceful progress that have comforted white Australians for so long. In other words, the referendum asked Australians to do what prime minister Paul Keating suggested in his Redfern Park speech in 1992: to imagine that 'we' had suffered the 'murders', 'discrimination and exclusion'. 'With some noble exceptions,' said Keating, 'we failed to make the most basic human response ... to ask how would I feel if this were done to me? As a consequence, we failed to see that what we were doing degraded all of us.'[26]

---

26   Tom Griffiths, '1992—The Redfern Park Speech', in *The Quest for Indigenous Recognition, Australian Dictionary of Biography* (Canberra: National Centre of Biography, The Australian National University, 2006–24), adb.anu.edu.au/the-quest-for-indigenous-recognition/the-redfern-park-speech.

When Peter Dutton stoked fear and anxiety by claiming that a constitutionally enshrined Voice would see the greatest change to our system of government since Federation, he both wildly exaggerated the risks and failed spectacularly to demonstrate empathy.[27] What of the changes forced on First Nations peoples by invasion and dispossession? What of the changes wrought by more than two centuries of government policies designed to eradicate Aboriginal and Torres Strait Islander cultures and dictate every aspect of their peoples' lives? What of their long struggle for their rights? And what of their exclusion from the Constitution?

In grave tone, Dutton warned Australians about a constitutional amendment that would genuinely and positively include Indigenous peoples in our constitution for the first time since 1901. He stressed the virtues of the Constitution's stability and continuity. As he and others have so often reminded us, the Constitution has 'served Australia well'. But whom has it served well? And for whom has it provided 'stability and continuity'?

Because of their exclusion from the nation's founding document, Indigenous Australians understand the Australian Constitution far better than other Australians. They do not have the luxury of ignorance.

Over the past 50 years, the presence of Indigenous culture and history has become more visible in Australia's public culture: from Welcome to Country ceremonies, to Indigenous placenames, art, dance, music and literature, and the opening ceremonies of football finals, school assemblies and, since 2008, of Federal Parliament after each federal election. For many Australians and certainly for visitors from overseas, this is *the* most distinctive aspect of Australian culture.

How long can Australians remain content to draw on this rich Indigenous knowledge and heritage as mere symbolism? Surely, we must give more. Surely, we must demonstrate that we have listened to and *heard* Indigenous Australians by agreeing to establish a First Nations Voice, which, as Davis argued, would constitute a 'dialogue for time immemorial between the First Nations and the Australian people'.[28] This was the 'constitutional moment' of reckoning that the referendum placed before us.

---

27 'Labor's Voice to Change Our System of Government in Ways We Haven't Contemplated', *Sky News*, 5 April 2023, resourcessl.newscdn.com.au/cs/video/vjs/stable/build/index.html?id=5348771529001-6324007711112.
28 Megan Davis, *Voice of Reason*, Quarterly Essay 90 (Melbourne: Black Inc., 2023).

In its measured tone and gracious request, the *Uluru Statement from the Heart* calls to mind previous invitations from Aboriginal and Torres Strait Islander peoples to their fellow citizens.

Among the thousands who walked across Sydney Harbour Bridge in May 2000, there were undoubtedly many reasons for attending. But the overwhelming expression of support for reconciliation would lodge permanently in the nation's memory. So, too, would the simple act of walking, which became one of the most powerful metaphors employed by Indigenous leaders when seeking support from their fellow Australians.[29]

In October 1992, the Council for Aboriginal Reconciliation explained that the process of reconciliation 'involves all of us walking together to find a better path to the future of this nation'. In May 2017, the final words of the *Uluru Statement from the Heart* invited Australians 'to walk with us in a movement of the Australian people for a better future'.[30]

I can only admire the optimism and determination of Indigenous leaders who continued to hold out their invitation to Australians to 'walk' with them.[31]

The referendum was a once-in-a-lifetime opportunity to make the Voice work to the betterment of Indigenous Australians and the entire nation.

The post-referendum environment and the need for 'strategic imagination'

Confronting the cold, hard fact that 61 per cent of the Australian electorate rejected the constitutional recognition of Indigenous Australians and a constitutionally enshrined Indigenous Voice to Parliament, Australian reformers now look for a rescue narrative of some kind that will enable us to find a fragile patch of common ground.[32]

---

29   Mark McKenna, '2000—Walk across the Bridge', in *The Quest for Indigenous Recognition, Australian Dictionary of Biography* (Canberra: National Centre of Biography, The Australian National University, 2006–24), adb.anu.edu.au/the-quest-for-indigenous-recognition/walk-across-the-bridge.

30   ibid.

31   Davis, 'Voice of Reason'.

32   Australian Electoral Commission, 'National Results', *Tallyroom* (Canberra: AEC, Last updated 2 November 2023), results.aec.gov.au/29581/Website/ReferendumNationalResults-29581.htm.

If you believe the platitudes ('the Australian people always get it right') or the spin (the emphatic result was explained by the 'robust common sense' of the Australian people), you might imagine that Australians, having carefully studied the proposal to alter the Constitution and the arguments for and against change, delivered their judiciously reasoned response: 'No.'[33]

But the truth is both more bitter and more complicated. Although much has been made of the similarities between the recent referendum and the 1999 referendum on the republic—including education as a key determinant of voting behaviour and the respective No campaigns' reliance on the same mind-numbing slogans ('If you don't know, vote no')—the tenor of the republic debate appears tame by comparison.

While misinformation and scare-mongering certainly abounded in 1999, there was nothing like the outpouring of resentment and prejudice towards one group of Australians that First Nations' peoples endured in 2023, much of it effectively licensed by Nyunggai Warren Mundine and Senator Jacinta Nampijinpa Price, who appeared on some No campaign leaflets that showed a fist full of dollars accompanied by a dire warning: 'How much will compensation cost?' The implicit message—featuring two Indigenous leaders but cynically targeting the lowest base of a non-Indigenous audience—was not difficult to decipher: 'They've got too much already. Now they'll want even more and we'll have to pay.'[34]

By the time Price stood before the media to bask in the triumph of the result on referendum night, echoes of the Howard-era culture wars were omnipresent. Australia was 'not a racist country', she declared: 'We are one of, if not *the* greatest nation on the face of the earth. And it is time for Australians to believe that once again, to be proud to call ourselves Australian.'[35] The most significant thing about this seductive cocktail of denial and self-congratulation was not that it was new—Price's comments were strikingly reminiscent of Howard in 1996 telling Australians they did

---

33   Samantha Maiden, 'Richard Marles Says "Australian People Always Get It Right" as He Reveals Voice Disappointment', *News.com.au*, 15 October 2023, www.news.com.au/national/politics/richard-marles-says-australian-people-always-get-it-right-as-he-reveals-voice-disappointment/news-story/9cade79258347f9c648aab3a73bf1ee2#:~:text=Richard%20Marles%20says%20%27Australian%20people,"always%20get%20it%20right"; Tony Abbott, 'Voice Defeat Delivers Opening Salvo against Identity Politics', *Australian*, 20 October 2023, www.theaustralian.com.au/commentary/voice-defeat-delivers-opening-salvo-against-identity-politics/news-story/e8bbab6b2d88e5bf8745dbf4232c773b.

34   This No campaign leaflet appeared in my own mailbox.

35   Jacinta Price, 'Australia Votes "No" to the Prime Minister's Divisive Voice, Treaty, Truth Proposal', Press conference, [Transcript] (Canberra: Liberal Party of Australia, 16 October), peterdutton.com.au/leader-of-the-opposition-transcript-joint-press-conference-brisbane/.

not have 'a racist, bigoted past'—but that it was uttered in the context of this particular referendum and intended to resonate with non-Indigenous voters who did not want to hear about the history of violent dispossession that marked modern Australia's foundation. The pitch proved to be remarkably successful.[36]

Of all the reasons given by the pollsters for voting no, one of the most disheartening and widely registered was the low priority accorded to Indigenous issues by many voters. This was not ignorance so much as a failure of empathy and understanding—a failure to care about anyone's concerns or disadvantage other than their own. In the dying days of the campaign, Noel Pearson appealed to Australians' sense of morality, arguing there was only one 'morally correct' choice and that the alternative would only bring 'shame and dishonour', which we would have to wear 'for a long time to come'.[37] Offering his support, former High Court chief justice Robert French put the case eloquently. The referendum, he explained, was a 'once-in-a-lifetime opportunity for Australia to fill a moral and historic shortcoming in the constitution—to recognise our first history and the First Peoples who bear it and the painful legacy of its collision with the second history of colonisation'.[38] The result on 14 October 2023 pointed to the failure of this moral argument. An obvious question surfaces: how is it possible for Australians to understand the moral case for change if they do not understand Australia's history?

In the wake of the referendum, and at a time when the future of history and the humanities is under threat in our universities, the need for truth-telling, history and civics education is more urgent than ever before. If truth-telling of any kind is to change minds and hearts, it must begin at a local level, where it cannot be so easily kept at a distance or imagined as an abstraction. And while telling the truth is one thing, hearing the truth and taking it in are something else entirely. Nor will truth-telling necessarily lead

---

36 John Howard, 'John Laws Programme Radio 2UE', [Transcript] (Canberra: Department of the Prime Minister and Cabinet, 24 October 1996), pmtranscripts.pmc.gov.au/release/transcript-10149.

37 Natasha May and Emily Wind, 'Noel Pearson Warns Australia May "Never Live It Down" if Voice Referendum Fails', [Live blog], *Guardian*, 9 October 2023, www.theguardian.com/australia-news/live/2023/oct/09/australia-news-live-penny-wong-israel-commonwealth-games-inquiry-referendum-indigenous-voice-to-parliament-labor-victoria-nsw-sa-plane-crash-queensland.

38 Ellie Dudley; 'Indigenous Voice: Former High Court Justices Say "Vague" Wording Is the Right Choice', *Australian*, 23 March 2023, www.theaustralian.com.au/nation/indigenous/indigenous-voice-former-high-court-justices-say-vague-wording-is-the-right-choice/news-story/d620e391869cc46770cce45d994d7e38.

to different political outcomes. At the very least, a broader understanding and acceptance of Australia's history might help to create a more informed political culture and more informed votes in future referendums.

Despite the understandable uncertainty and pessimism about the way forward after 14 October, questions surrounding truth-telling and the need for a lasting settlement between Indigenous and non-Indigenous Australians remain. At the age of 90, esteemed Yuin elder Ossie Cruse was one of the signatories of the *Uluru Statement* and has lived through decades of racist policies and failed government attempts to address Indigenous disadvantage.

He told me:

> This referendum was really about one thing: it was an opportunity to say that Australia is not a racist country and that failed. The true message of the *Uluru Statement* was drowned out. The reason for saying No is not there … [W]e can't really see all the reasons people voted No. There was no [alternative] proposal from them.

In the face of a referendum that saw Cruse's community in Eden on the NSW Far South Coast vote 'No', he was adamant that the spirit of the *Uluru Statement* should not be forgotten:

> The promise held out by the *Uluru Statement* is that our children—white and black—would walk together into the future. We wanted to build something that would bring our future generations together. And it's for them that we have to keep setting an example whatever the cost and press on.[39]

It is now, in the post-referendum environment, that Brendan Sargeant's work on Australia's 'strategic imagination', which he argued was still structured by the 'claims and imperatives of empire', offers both solace and guidance. 'In those rare moments in a country's history where a genuine choice must be made and action taken,' he wrote, 'a country's strategic imagination becomes most visible.'[40]

---

39 Ossie Cruse to author, 17 October 2023.
40 Brendan Sargeant, *Challenges to the Australian Strategic Imagination*, Centre of Gravity Series Papers 58 (Canberra: Strategic and Defence Studies Centre, The Australian National University, 2021), hdl. handle.net/1885/233085.

With these words in mind, and given the decisive result in the 2023 referendum, it is tempting to conclude pessimistically that a project that began in the early 1990s—reconciliation and the republic or, to put it more precisely, a reconciled republic—has come to an end. Meaningful constitutional reform will probably never achieve bipartisan support, while the constitutional reform that will achieve bipartisan support is likely to be so uncontroversial that it will hardly seem worthwhile. But Sargeant's argument for a constantly re-examined and renewed strategic imagination holds true for Australia after the referendum even more than it did before. In this instance, it is the *strategy* of the referendum mechanism as a vehicle for reform that has failed, not our capacity for an imaginative response to the situation in which we find ourselves.

Given the parlous state of so many social indicators of the lives of Indigenous Australians—including life expectancy, health, imprisonment rates and education—retreat and negativity are not an option. As Sargeant maintains, Australia needs 'a larger conception of strategy, a richer discourse, and a more searching questioning of the assumptions that underpin' its strategic imagination, which includes the questions surrounding constitutional reform.[41]

The result of the 2023 referendum was largely due to three factors: the adversarial structure of federal politics; a cynical, dishonest and manipulative No campaign; and the simplistic Yes–No binaries that were given false equivalence by the referendum process and the media. Yet, there is no reason to assume that the current political alignment—both between and within the major political parties (and outside them for that matter)—will remain unchanged. Just as the generation of politicians at the time of Federation could not foresee the political configuration of today's parliament, we cannot foresee the political alignments of the future. But we can work to shift them in ways that encourage the emergence of a political and electoral environment that is more receptive to change. And it is for this reason that Indigenous leaders such as Megan Davis, Thomas Mayo and Rachel Perkins have recently stressed that the *Uluru Statement* still stands and they will continue their work to fulfil its aspirations.[42]

---

41   ibid.

42   Josh Butler, '"The Uluru Statement Stands": Key Yes Campaigners to Keep Working towards Indigenous Voice', *Guardian*, 6 November 2023, www.theguardian.com/australia-news/2023/nov/06/voice-to-parliament-referendum-yes-campaign-where-now-next-steps-raise-awareness.

Although the term reconciliation is still bandied out—alive or dead?—it no longer seems the right word for Australia's predicament. After all, what do Aboriginal people have to reconcile? And why should they accept the only hand that non-Indigenous Australians are willing to offer them? 'Conciliation' seems a more appropriate term for the post-referendum environment. In the short term, Australia will be forced to live with the ignominy of a constitution that excludes Indigenous Australians. Yet, there is no reason the reforms sought by Indigenous leaders (voice, treaty and truth) cannot be achieved through legislative and other means. If these reforms can be achieved to the satisfaction of a majority of Indigenous and non-Indigenous Australians, the possibility of finding an appropriate form of constitutional recognition that will secure bipartisan support becomes more likely. As for the prospect of a republic, one fundamental truth remains: there is no just foundation for an Australian republic until the exclusion of Indigenous Australians from the nation's founding document is addressed.

Finally, it is important to see the 2023 referendum as part of the seismic shift that has taken place in Australia's thinking about Indigenous Australians since the late twentieth century. Between 1967 and 2023, as the White Australia policy slowly came to an end, Australian governments rejected the oppressive policies of assimilation, ceased the removal of Indigenous children from their families, introduced land rights legislation and established departments of Aboriginal affairs and Indigenous advisory bodies. In addition, the High Court overturned the doctrine of *terra nullius* and recognised the continuing existence of native title in the common law (including its right to coexist on pastoral leases). Meanwhile, across the nation's public and ceremonial culture, Indigenous cultures, histories, protocols, countries and languages were recognised and embraced as the bedrock of Australian identity in the twenty-first century. These are just some of the changes that have taken place and, while they are by no means satisfactory or complete, they point to the spirit of change, which, however slowly and falteringly, is clearly moving towards greater respect and recognition for First Nations peoples.

The broad sweep of this historical movement for change continues to unfold and, despite its sometimes glacial rate of progress, its overall direction is undeniable and transcends the 2023 referendum. The result on 14 October was particularly devastating for Indigenous Australians, but it cannot and will not be the final word. In 50 or 100 years from now, it is entirely possible that the *Uluru Statement from the Heart* will be seen as even more significant than it is today.

5

Imagination and scholarship: The role of creativity and complexity

Anthea Roberts

It is no secret that Brendan Sargeant was one of my favourite people at The Australian National University.

On a superficial level, he and I were an unlikely pair. He had grown up in the world of public sector administration and defence strategy. I had little interest in management and struggled to distinguish one end of a submarine from another. He had spent most of his career in Australia, contemplating our nation's place in the region and the world. I had spent most of my career outside Australia and tended to adopt an international perspective more readily than a national one.

On a deeper level, however, Brendan and I shared striking commonalities in our approach to the world. We struck up a friendship after he began attending meetings of the Geoeconomics Working Group that I chaired. Our conversations were wideranging, from ideas about complexity and strategy to our shared interest in fostering creativity. Our proclivities were often similar, including our tendency to zoom up to consider issues in broader ways and over longer time frames than was often encouraged in our environments.

Brendan and I had a meeting of minds that turned into a friendship, as often happens between academics.

We talked about the macro-changes facing the world, such as the problem of climate change and how China's rise was producing tensions with the West—in particular, the United States. We spoke about the importance of stepping away from the hustle and bustle of short-term demands to pursue innovative longer-term projects with uncertain payoffs. We considered the strategic capabilities our nation should develop to navigate the next few decades, marked by increasing and colliding geopolitical threats and natural hazards. And, of course, because it was Brendan, we talked about William Blake.

In this short essay, I want to introduce two themes about imagination and scholarship that animate my thinking as an academic and typify the types of discussions I had with Brendan. The first is the importance of preserving or reclaiming imaginative, artistic and creative ways of thinking in the academy. The second is how to understand and act in a complex and unpredictable world. As you will see, long time horizons play a crucial role in both themes. And, because I am inclined to think with images, I employ two images that capture the essence of my points.

I am often struck by how our ideas of what it means to be a scientist or a social scientist tend to focus on the lefthand side of the image in Figure 5.1. We are taught to be rigorous and empirical. We create and test hypotheses. We separate and analyse. We compare and contrast. We count and calculate. We scrutinise and rationalise. We distinguish causation from correlation. We evaluate explanations and identify causal mechanisms. We present things as orderly and linear: a problem, a hypothesis, a test, findings, a discussion and a conclusion. We play by the established rules.

This is what it means to be rigorous in our thoughts.

But it can also lead to rigor mortis in our thinking.

Figure 5.1 Creativity: Thinking with both sides of our minds

Source: John Hain, pixabay.com/illustrations/mindsets-approaches-knowledge-3988226/.

I frequently feel like a conceptual artist caught in the confines of academia. In looking at Figure 5.1, I identify more readily with the righthand side. My work is often intuitive, attempting to sketch complex, emerging and contested phenomena by embodying multiple mindsets. I like to transcend particular debates by zooming up to the macroscopic level to see what is revealed and obscured by the different perspectives. I enjoy playing with metaphors and analogies for both theory generation and conceptual communication. Having too much accumulated expertise in an area makes me feel weighed down; breaking free in search of new grounds makes me feel animated and alive.

To develop good scholarship, we must use both sides of our brains—individually and collectively. We must recognise the importance of 'night science', not just 'day science'. We need to engage in exploration as well as exploitation. So, what do I mean by these two juxtapositions?

François Jacob used the phrase 'day science' to capture the hypothesis-testing mode of science that operates within the confines of a scientific field or intellectual paradigm. Highly specialised experts design experiments and follow protocols to move step by step from a hypothesis to a conclusion, incrementally advancing the state of knowledge in a field. The moves are relatively predictable and the returns are reasonably probable. Day science tends to be compartmentalised and disciplined. It is a classic case of the exploitation of existing knowledge and capabilities.

By contrast, Jacob invokes 'night science' to describe the much less structured process through which new ideas arise and questions and hypotheses are generated. Less linear, night science is more creative and associational. It is interdisciplinary, often involving the connection of disparate insights or fields. It is where intuition takes hold and large leaps of logic occur. Nothing is certain or predetermined in night science; with no map, a prescribed and predictable route cannot be followed. Instead:

> Night science wanders blind. It hesitates, stumbles, recoils, sweats, wakes with a start. Doubting everything, it is forever trying to find itself, question itself, pull itself back together. Night science is a sort of workshop of the possible where what will become the building material of science is worked out.[1]

Night science is to exploration what day science is to exploitation. The explore–exploit dilemma is a classic problem that we face in our lives and work—within and beyond the academy. It revolves around the question of how to balance exploiting existing opportunities and capabilities with exploring new ones. As the organisation scholar James March explained, exploration includes the various behaviours captured by terms such as search, variation, risk-taking, experimentation, play, flexibility, discovery and innovation. Exploitation is captured by terms such as refinement, choice, production, efficiency, selection, implementation and execution.[2]

---

1   François Jacob, *The Statue within: An Autobiography* (New York: Cold Spring Harbor Laboratory Press, 1988).

2   James G. March, 'Exploration and Exploitation in Organizational Learning', *Organization Science* 71, no. 2 (1991): 71–87, at 71, doi.org/10.1287/orsc.2.1.71.

Exploitation involves obtaining short-term rewards from existing opportunities and capabilities. Exploration involves searching for new opportunities or building new capabilities that could bring future rewards. Given that individuals and organisations have finite time and means, they often must decide how to allocate limited resources between these two sometimes conflicting goals. But over-focusing on pole one at the expense of the other can be problematic. '[M]aintaining an appropriate balance between exploration and exploitation is a primary factor in system survival and prosperity,' March concluded.[3]

The same holds true for academics and academic fields. We must balance exploration of new knowledge and fields, which often spurs innovation and creativity, with exploitation of existing knowledge and fields, which often allows for rigorous testing and refining of ideas. Some of us will incline more towards exploration or exploitation, based either on our proclivities or on external incentives and constraints present or absent at different stages of our careers. But for our academic ecosystems to be sustainable and resilient as a whole and over time, we must maintain a healthy balance between these two approaches.

We need both night and day science.[4] Night science fuels our imagination, encouraging us to think up new directions and ideas; day science restrains us to laboriously test, apply, extend and qualify them. Both types of science matter, but our method courses and the method sections in our academic papers often focus only on the day science aspect of our experiences and fields. Day science is treated as scientific and something that can be taught, whereas night science is viewed as something spontaneous that either happens or does not. Further, night science tends to be hard to discuss in academic company because it is not seen as fully 'academic'.

Even though paradigm shifts in science often arise from moments of inspiration in night science, somehow, we neglect these moments in our understanding of the scientific method. Einstein's insights about the theory of relativity came to him while he was engaging in thought experiments

---

3   ibid., 71.
4   Itai Yanai and Martin Lercher, 'Night Science', *Genome Biology* 20, no. 179 (2019), doi.org/10.1186/s13059-019-1800-6; Itai Yanai and Martin Lercher, 'What Is the Question?', *Genome Biology* 20, no. 289 (2019), doi.org/10.1186/s13059-019-1902-1; Itai Yanai and Martin Lercher, 'Renaissance Minds in 21st Century Science', *Genome Biology* 21, no. 67 (2020), doi.org/10.1186/s13059-020-01985-6.

about jumping in an elevator.[5] Darwin developed his theory of evolution by sketching multiple metaphors to help capture his thinking, including the tree of life (which took off as the governing metaphor) and the coral of life (which did not gain traction then but may be re-emerging as a more accurate understanding of evolution).[6] Innovation often results from making wild associational leaps, connecting one field or set of ideas to another.

Too much focus on filling one's day with the production of demonstrable outputs risks crowding out the space and time necessary to think big thoughts, search for new ideas, stray far from the beaten track and play with concepts unrestrained. In the short term, this focus on efficiency might produce a promising yield. In the long term, however, it seems destined to sap one's creativity and stifle innovation. It does not surprise me, for instance, that levels of productivity in science have gone up in recent decades while measures of disruptive innovation have gone down.[7] What looks efficient in the short term often looks inefficient in the long term and vice versa.

I often think about this dilemma through analogies to farming and ecosystem management. Quantifiable metrics in academia often encourage young academics to focus on planting and yielding a certain number of readily harvestable carrots each year. But this insistence on short-term and efficient deliverables crowds out the space to plant and nurture slower-growing plants like oak trees. And 100 yearly crops of carrots do not an oak tree make. Instead, monocropping and overfarming can lead to desolate and depleted lands. As Jenny Odell observes in her book *How to Do Nothing*:

> Just as practices like logging and large-scale farming decimate the land, an overemphasis on performance turns what was once a dense and thriving landscape of individual and communal thought into a Monsanto farm whose 'production' slowly destroys the soil until nothing more can grow. As it extinguishes one species of thought after another, it hastens the erosion of attention.[8]

---

5   Sabine Hossenfelder, 'Lost in Thought—How Important to Physics Were Einstein's Imaginings?', *Scientific American*, 1 September 2015, www.scientificamerican.com/article/lost-in-thought-how-important-to-physics-were-einstein-s-imaginings/.

6   Olivia Judson, 'Our Earth, Shaped by Life', *Aeon*, 18 November 2022, aeon.co/essays/the-insight-of-darwins-work-on-corals-worms-and-co-evolution.

7   Michael Park, Erin Leahey, and Russell J. Funk, 'Papers and Patents Are Becoming Less Disruptive over Time', *Nature* 613 (4 January 2023): 138–44, doi.org/10.1038/s41586-022-05543-x; 'Is Scientific Progress Slowing? With James Evans', *Big Brains Podcast*, Episode 89 (31 March 2022), news.uchicago.edu/scientific-progress-slowing-james-evans.

8   Jenny Odell, *How to Do Nothing: Resisting the Attention Economy* (New York: Melville House Publishing, 2019), xix.

Given the current state of our academy, we must do more to highlight and encourage the night science part of academia and to bridge the gap between and incentives to pursue exploration and exploitation. If we do not, we may find ourselves in a world of diminishing scientific returns. While a focus on short-term exploitation often leads to incremental improvements, this can displace the sort of exploration that increases the chances of both failure, from which we can learn, and true breakthroughs. Being too risk averse in the short term increases risk in the long term. For our innovation ecosystems to be healthy in time, we need both exploration and exploitation. It is not a question of either/or. It is a question of both/and.

Complexity

'Both/and' thinking is the basis of complexity theory.

Brendan told me that when he was young he worked in a laundromat. During long hours working alone, he found himself engrossed in reading one book again and again. It was *Steps to an Ecology of Mind* by Gregory Bateson.[9] Before Brendan died, he loaned me his copy of this treasured book.

Much of what Bateson says resonates with my thinking on creativity: '[A]dvances in scientific thought come from *a combination of loose and strict thinking*, and this combination is the most precious tool of science.'[10] Bateson liked to draw on wild analogies and metaphors: is a system radially symmetrical like a jellyfish or symmetrical in a transverse way like a lobster? He also aimed to build a 'double habit of mind' that involved developing wild hunches (loose thinking) and then subjecting those to rigorous examination (strict thinking).[11] What he describes is an internal embodiment of the cyclical movement between phases of night and day science.

Scientific advances often begin with loose thinking, followed by building structures on unsound foundations, then making corrections through stricter thinking and finally substituting new underpinnings beneath the already constructed mass, Bateson argued. We must first sketch something big before we can nail down the details, I would say. If we impose tests of rigour too early and too broadly, we will undermine the confidence of

---

9   Gregory Bateson, *Steps to an Ecology of Mind: Collected Essays in Anthropology, Psychiatry, Evolution, and Epistemology* (Northvale: Jason Aronson Inc., 1987).
10   ibid., 85 (emphasis in original).
11   ibid., 85.

and incentives for our academics to think in more creative and imaginative ways. We must value people who sketch the big picture as much as those who nail the smaller details because each approach is suited to different problems or aspects of problems at different stages in the evolution of thinking and fields.

Part of what fascinated Brendan about Bateson's book was its ecological way of thinking about the world. All systems were viewed as their own ecologies—whether an individual, a government, a university department or a country—and they nested within broader ecologies: individuals nested within families and communities, faculties nested within universities, departments nested within governments and countries nested within regions and the world. How those ecologies evolved was complex, depending on a myriad unpredictable interactions between a multitude of actors and factors. The question was not just one about parts, it was about how those parts related to create a whole.

In these ecologies, coevolution is common: actors shape and are shaped by their environments and their interactions. 'I pictured the relations between ethos and cultural structure,' Bateson mused, 'as being like the relation between a river and its banks—The river molds the banks and the banks guide the river.'[12] This coevolutionary dynamic pervaded Brendan's thinking about strategy. China was its own complex ecology, he would say, and not only were other countries having to respond to China's rise, but also China was having to evolve its approaches given its external environment was becoming more hostile. China affected other countries and other countries affected China.

Our world's complexity led both of us to have some doubts about the way in which many quantitative methods were being employed in the academy. Attempts to focus on one narrow element of the whole without understanding how it operated within a broader context seemed strange to us. How could you study the economy and treat political events as external shocks to the system when some of those political dynamics arose from the economic system itself? Efforts to hold everything else equal to investigate whether X caused Y often seemed problematic to us. We were instinctively drawn towards thinking in wholes rather than parts and towards focusing on complex, unpredictable and coevolutionary interactions rather than linear 'if X then Y' causal logic.

---

12   ibid., 93.

It struck me that many methods lauded in the academy as scientific involved looking at the past to say with some degree of certainty how we got to where we are now. Economics suffered from 'physics envy' and sought to align itself more with the rigour of a traditional natural science. Political science started doing likewise. But both seemed to be orienting themselves to the wrong type of physics, focusing on Newtonian stability and equilibrium rather than quantum-like probabilities and entanglement. Meanwhile, academia's focus on efficiency and optimisation brought forth the implicit mental model of a well-oiled machine rather than the unpredictable and ecological methods required for innovative thinking that are better reflected by metaphors of gardening.

Understanding our past does not always prepare us for the complexity and uncertainty we face when we look to the future. In thinking about this difference, I use Figure 5.2 to depict our relatively linear-seeming past and compare it with our complex and unpredictable future. The past often looks almost obvious or determined when viewed in retrospect; a lot of the contingency and complexity of what might have been seems to be forgotten or fades into the background. It can be hard to imagine how small changes at critical points could have led to a completely different present. With 20/20 hindsight, it is almost impossible to put yourself back into the fog of uncertainty that existed as events unfolded.

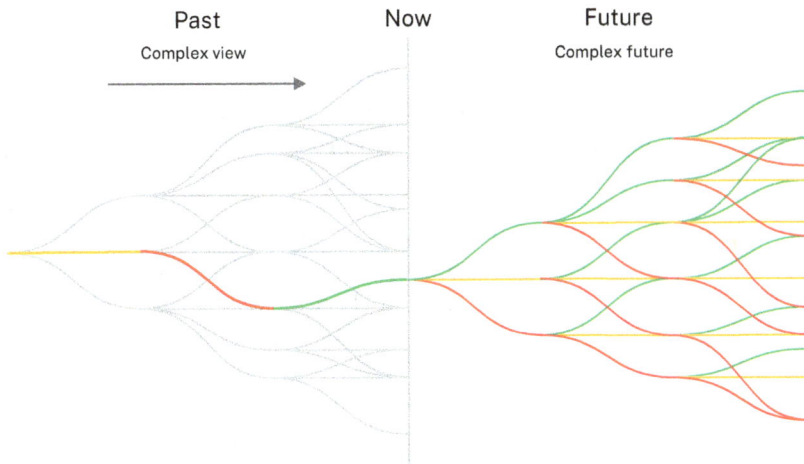

Figure 5.2 Looking backward and forward in complexity
Source: Anthea Roberts.

If often seems to me that academia is geared more towards methods for looking backwards so that we know with greater certainty how we got here, while policymaking, business and defence are geared towards developing tools and techniques for moving forwards in complex and uncertain environments. 'There is no data about the future,' the business professor Roger Martin likes to say.[13] The emphasis on rigour and modelling that I observed in economics and political science departments at many universities seemed a world away from the strategies I saw for coping with complexity and uncertainty on the battlefield or in business. It did not surprise me that Brendan, with a background in defence, chose to study at Wharton Business School rather than in an economics or political science department.

A cross-cultural element suffuses these differences as well. Linear ways of thinking are common in the West but less common in many other parts of the world. Many East Asian religions such as Buddhism or indigenous approaches have a stronger complexity basis, with a focus on the whole instead of the parts, on complex interdependencies and longer-term horizons. And some of the best books I have read that help to explain the evolution of the Chinese economy, for instance, have an explicit or implicit complexity basis with a focus on policy experimentation and adaptation rather than efficiency and optimisation. *How China Escaped the Poverty Trap* by Yuen Yuen Ang is one example, while *How China Escaped Shock Therapy* by Isabella Weber is another.

Some of the scholars who embrace complexity in their analysis also apply it to their scholarly approach. Take Ang as an example. In a discussion of one of her books on *Freakonomics Radio*, she and host Stephen Dubner had the following exchange:

> DUBNER: You write in the book that, 'data sets that are easily downloaded and plugged into regressions have shaped concepts, theories, and policies more profoundly than we'd like to admit'. So that sounds like a somewhat polite way of saying that academics and then perhaps policymakers talk about the things that are based on data that's easy to find. And if it's not so easy to find, we either

---

13   Roger Martin, 'Overcoming the Pervasive Analytical Blunder of Strategists: There Can Be No Data about the Future', *Medium*, 17 May 2021, rogermartin.medium.com/overcoming-the-pervasive-analytical-blunder-of-strategists-a5a4c52289b4; Roger Martin, 'Letter to the CEO', in *Strategy@work: From Design to Delivery*, edited by Brightline Initiative and Thinkers50 (London: Thinkers50, 2017), 43–44, thinkers50.com/wp-content/uploads/Thinkers50_Stratgey@Work_ONLINE-new.pdf?x30203&x72597.

forget about it or pretend it doesn't exist. And to me, that would describe a lot of the corruption that you're talking about. It's very hard to measure anything illicit, but especially illicit in the hands of the powerful because they have the means to prevent scrutiny. So to me, that's where you are unorthodox.

ANG: It's true that it's much easier to condemn corruption among the poor. Very difficult to talk about influence politics among the rich, it's a topic that people do not generally like to touch upon. I see this practical reality, that people will pick agendas that are easy. The analogy I would use is, have you heard of the term 'machine-friendly crops'?

DUBNER: I have not.

ANG: So, there are certain crops that are easily harvested by machines. And so, farmers would choose these crops simply because they can be easily mechanized. And I think that in the knowledge industry, we sometimes or maybe often see a similar dynamic, and I would call it a publication-friendly agenda. The incentives of the profession will lead people to overwhelmingly and disproportionately study certain kinds of topics in certain ways at the expense of truly important questions that frankly, very few people want to touch. I hope that doesn't get me into too much trouble.

DUBNER: I hope it does. I hope it does. The right kind of trouble.[14]

Brendan was not focused on machine-friendly crops. You can see this interest in complexity developing in Brendan's journal entries from his time at Wharton. Of a lecture by David Wessels, a professor of finance, Brendan recounts:

David made a very interesting comment. He said we live in the age of accountability. That is the story of his career—the era of ever increasing requirements for accountability in all spheres of life, including business. He said if you want people to be accountable, you then want to measure performance. So the culture drives a culture of measurement. The problem is you can measure really stupid things—measurement tends to take a very short-term focus. He said he is still thinking about this, but is wondering whether long-term performance would improve if they removed the requirement

14 Stephen J. Dubner, 'Is the U.S. Really Less Corrupt than China—and How about Russia? (Update)', *Freakonomics Radio Podcast*, Episode 481, 13 April 2022, freakonomics.com/podcast/is-the-u-s-really-less-corrupt-than-china-and-how-about-russia-update/.

on companies or teams within companies to actually measure their performance. The comment was probably the most interesting thing I have heard so far, particularly from a Professor of Finance, and one that raises the most profound questions for me about the nature of work, the nature of accountability and performance, and the role of performance measurement.[15]

Brendan led like a gardener, implicitly understanding the value of nurturing a diverse ecosystem and allowing different plants to grow or flower over different time scales. Do not overburden that promising mid-career academic with too many meetings with government officials, he would say; instead, let them write their second book as that will allow them to make a bigger contribution in the long term. Do not require a grantee to tell you exactly what they are going to do and how they are going to do it; instead, pick good people and important problems and give those people the space, time and funding to see what they produce. That ecosystem way of thinking, and that long-range temporal horizon, will always stay with me when I reflect on Brendan's way of looking at the world.

Conclusion

As with many people within and beyond The Australian National University and the Australian Government, I will miss Brendan. He helped me to think about big-picture issues relating to creativity, complexity and change. He encouraged me to run my own race and to believe in my own instincts and skills—a gift I have come to understand he gave to many others as well. Brendan had a wisdom that I miss. He felt like a wise leader and a wise friend. So, when I have doubts or anxieties about my work and my choices, I try to ask myself: 'What would Brendan do?' It is an act of imagination, but imagination is also a source of power.

Brendan reminded us of the crucial role that imagination plays in our work. Imagination helps us to break free from the current set of possibilities and envisage new ways of being and moving forward. Brendan wanted to encourage our nation's strategic imagination, but imagination is also relevant in scholarship and thinking more broadly because it fuels creativity, helps us to better understand complexity and is useful in trying to navigate change. That sounds to me like a strategic use of time and resources.

---

15   On file with author.

6

Imagination and policy

Dennis Richardson

This chapter is the transcript of an interview conducted with Dennis Richardson, former secretary of the Department of Defence (2012–17). It discusses his time working with Brendan Sargeant and the role of strategic imagination in Australian defence policymaking. Questions and comments from the interviewer are in bold. The transcript has been lightly edited for ease of reading. Where useful additional context has been added, it appears in square brackets, [ ].

Very few people ever rise to become associate secretary of a major government department, let alone secretary. What led to Brendan's rise to that position?

Certainly in terms of Brendan's part it was his abilities. He had a very interesting background. He was in Defence. He went off and worked in finance. He worked in Centrelink. So, Brendan, by the time he was a deputy secretary and in charge of strategic policy and intelligence, had well-grounded experience across government and outside policy areas. He had experience in managing parts of government that were largely administrative, process driven and program oriented.

The position of associate secretary in Defence [held by Brendan from 2013 to 2018], when I was there, was in part that of a chief operating officer. His focus was more management rather than policy. He had been in the key policy job as deputy secretary of strategic policy and intelligence and he applied for the associate secretary job, and he got it for two reasons. One, because of his broad experience across government. And it was clear that he was able to take on the challenges of oversight in the personnel areas, the IT [information technology] areas, the other parts of Defence that make the system go around. Plus, he also had a sharp policy mind. You had an associate secretary also with a policy background. So, Brendan was promoted to associate secretary in about 2013 or 2014, and it was very much because he could wear dual hats. Very versatile.

So, Brendan had policy expertise and knew Defence, the management skills and had been around various parts of government, but he also had that background in English literature and linguistic interests. Did you see that playing into the way he did the job?

It played into the way he saw the world and the way he saw countries. He was interested in culture, in literature, in the way he was. To some extent, he sought a deeper understanding of countries than, if you like, merely looking at the end, analysing their strategic circumstances and policies, he could see what sat below those policies.

Did you see that as a strength for his contribution?

Yeah and when I first worked with Brendan, he was deputy secretary of strategic policy and intelligence, he was largely responsible for the *2013 Defence White Paper*. He was the principal author of that and that had two things in it that were of significance. First, it was the first really big government document that articulated the concept of the Indo-Pacific and it was also the Defence White Paper that committed Labor to spending 2 per cent of GDP [gross domestic product] on defence. Labor had got into strife by taking defence spending down to 1.58 per cent of GDP. And they were hammered incessantly because of that. The White Paper came out in May of 2013. In the leadup to the September general election of 2013, Stephen Smith as foreign minister was eager to neutralise national security as an issue, hence the commitment to 2 per cent of GDP.

The Indo-Pacific was very much what we'd had for quite a while. We'd had either one or both of our foreign and defence ministers from Western Australia. And the Western Australians do sometimes see the world a little bit differently to other parts of the country and that is perfectly understandable. They look out on to the Indian Ocean and you had Smith, you had David Johnson, you had Julie Bishop, going back to 1969, you had Freeth [Gordon Freeth, minister for external affairs], who lost the seat in 1969 because of comments he made about the Russians in the Indian Ocean. But you've had [Kim] Beazley as defence minister in the Hawke government. So, you've had quite a few people from Western Australia—Linda Reynolds and Andrew Hastie. Quite a few people from Western Australia, for whatever reason, they've been defence and foreign policy types. And I think it's natural if you're from Perth. You just don't see the Asia-Pacific, which, if you're in Western Australia, and you're talking about the Asia-Pacific, you're really cut off from that. And it doesn't really reflect your part of the world. And it doesn't really reflect the way you see half of your own country. So, the Indo-Pacific sort of brought that together.

Brendan played a big part in conceptualising that. He didn't originate it. That was as much as anything else political. But Brendan played a very important role in conceptualising it and articulating it within a proper policy framework. And that's to some extent the significance of the *2013 Defence White Paper*, which he was the principal author of. He had his policy background and all of that. So, he was able to contribute to that in a way in which other associate secretaries would have found difficult.

Does the process of writing white papers suggest some limits to this idea of strategic imagination if it ultimately results in a document that must reflect the government's views very closely and enable day-to-day work to occur?

It does, but Brendan had imagination. He was that sort of person. Brendan would have displayed imagination regardless of where he worked in government. He was a creative person. He had a creative mind. Some people have those types of minds. Imagination is important—everywhere. For instance, the 9/11 Commission in the United States, what did it say? It said the biggest single failure of the US intelligence community in the leadup to 9/11 was, quote, 'the failure of imagination'. A failure to imagine that something like that could happen. The inbuilt assumptions that attacks on US interests would be primarily offshore in countries with a limited security capability. Brendan was the sort of person who could see beyond those strictures. You put interests of poetry, literature and culture together and, for the most part, you will have a creative person. Those who lack imagination or whatever, perhaps like myself, have a more limited focus on something that might be called policy. To have real strategic imagination, you need an interest that takes you beyond the discipline framework of something called policy.

Do you see the need for strategic imagination shifting depending on the area? You've worked in defence, diplomacy, intelligence, etcetera. Do they call on imagination in different ways or does one have more of a demand for it?

Imagination is probably lacking in most countries. When it comes to any of those areas, occasionally you see real flashes of it. You see military imagination in the way Ukraine has fought its war, fought the invaders [from] Russia. Now, you could argue that Russia's invasion of Ukraine lacked imagination. Ukraine's defence demonstrates a heck of a lot of imagination apart from anything else. And in intelligence, particularly when you're up against terrorists and people like that, terrorists are limited only by their imagination. There was nothing to ever stop a terrorist driving a car along a footpath or a truck along the road, killing dozens of people, as we've seen over the past 15 years. Now, the means to do that has existed for decades. It didn't happen, you could argue, because of a lack of imagination. You know, not the imagination you want to see demonstrated, but you can argue that terrorists are limited only by their imagination.

That's the same with intelligence analysts. When it comes to making judgements about other countries and the like, to some extent, the study of foreign and strategic policy can serve to limit your imagination. It widens your knowledge, whether you then become captured by your knowledge and whether the mere existence of that knowledge limits your imagination is an interesting question, because you can be extraordinarily knowledgeable and lack imagination. What was unusual in Brendan's case was the fact that he had both the knowledge and the imagination. He was very curious. He always sought knowledge. He always had books on the go. And he normally had books on the go that were not directly relevant to what he was working on. More often than not when I went into his office, there would be books sitting on the table or a desk. It would be something quite unrelated to what he was working on. And I think that's what fed his imagination.

Does that suggest that if we need more imagination, we cannot train for it or get government to do better at creating people with imagination? That it is more about the talent that is out there already in the community and finding it?

There's a lot to be said for that. You can use the word imagination, but a critical ingredient anywhere in government is critical thinking … and, to some extent, you need an element of imagination for critical thinking.

After 9/11, I was in ASIO [Australian Security Intelligence Organisation]. I got in someone who was teaching philosophy at Melbourne University to run a course on critical thinking. We kept that going for a few years because critical thinking is lacking across government in all policy areas. And that's a little bit different to imagination, but to some extent it is connected. I don't know whether you can teach imagination, but you can certainly draw people's attention to the need to think outside established norms, the need to think beyond convention. For instance, if you're looking at our challenges today, you need to think that countries might not necessarily behave or do what you will assess. I'm not sure you can teach people to think and look beyond conventional thought. But I think imagination— real imagination—is something innate to the individual.

When Brendan was at SDSC he often talked about his time in the department with you as a partnership. And from the outside you and he are quite different people with different styles. How did that partnership work? Or what made it work?

Brendan's not here to say how he would describe that. So, you need to bear that in mind that this is just my view. I had a lot of time and respect for Brendan. I would like to think that he had a pretty free hand with me. That's the way I'd like to think about it; whether he would see it in that way, I don't know. But he was so versatile. For instance, he was one of the few people in government whom you could put in charge of a Defence White Paper and you could just leave it to him, as in 2013. And, at the same time, he was the same person whom you could have overseeing the engagement with and subsequently the implementation of the First Principles Review. So, one year a very strong policy focus with a Defence White Paper. The next year, he's engaging with a committee, which is looking at the fundamentals of Defence structure, how it works and how it's administratively arranged.

And Brendan's one of the few people who could have done both jobs equally well. There was nothing unusual about our relationship in the sense that we often talked, we had very few differences. Inevitably you get some [differences]; you wouldn't be human if you didn't. But he was someone who you could have them with. He had great interpersonal skills, too, so he could take on difficult jobs and work his way through the system because he by and large had the confidence of both the civilians and the uniform in Defence. That's central. You've got to have the confidence of both or a clear majority of both. And Brendan had that. He had the capacity for diplomacy, the art of getting someone to do it your way, and Brendan very much had the art of people doing what he wanted. But I don't think they always realised that it was what he wanted. I think they often thought it was their own doing.

What about differences in personal styles? From the outside you seemed quite different?

We had very few differences. We were different personalities. I can be more impetuous than Brendan. I could be more volatile than Brendan. However, I don't take emotion-based decisions and, second, I don't take decisions when I'm volatile. I simply don't. And Brendan, of course, was always very calm. By and large, very measured … he could sense the room very well. He could understand the different perspectives within a room and steer his way through to an outcome for the room. So, he was good at all of it. And he had a very deep understanding of Defence. He had a deep respect for the ADF [Australian Defence Force] and that's important. If you're occupying a senior civilian position in Defence, you can't see the ADF as your enemy. You have to see them as your colleagues and it's not to say you don't have differences. That's not to say you can't be critical, but that respect has to come through and I think it did with Brendan.

If in 10 years some future Defence graduate is reading this book, what would you want them to understand about Brendan and your time leading Defence?

In the time we were there, we had, what, two white papers? We had four prime ministers: Julia Gillard, Kevin Rudd, Tony Abbott, Malcolm Turnbull. We had four Defence ministers: Stephen Smith, David Johnson, Kevin Andrews and Marise Payne. We had a number of junior Defence ministers.

We ended up with two cabinet ministers in both Marise Payne and Christopher Pyne, as he was appointed a cabinet minister responsible for defence industry. So, we had a lot of political churn. We had the First Principles Review, which was about reviewing the fundamentals of Defence. There was a big push from the Defence Materiel Organisation to set itself up as a separate entity altogether. That would have been nuts, but anyway, there were people who wanted to do so. There are a lot of changes in the way that part structured itself and work which remains in place today. As a result of the First Principles Review, the key point is One Defence, which, if you like, goes back to the decision in the 1970s to create a single department out of five and, to some extent, that journey continues. Takes a long bloody time and then on, then on.

You had two white papers, you had decisions relating to the rebuilding of the Australian Navy, you had decisions on submarines. You had decisions on the frigates. The selection wasn't made when I was there, but the decision [was made] to have new frigates and to have the continuous ship build, the offshore patrol vessels, all of that. The decisions [were made] relating to the Air Force, the F-35 had been made a long time before but when they were going to come in, Land 400, etcetera.

So, you had a lot of big decisions in terms of military capability, structure and functioning of the department and the policy parameters set out in white papers. So, those were the three big overriding things. We gave a lot of attention to the civilian workforce. We established for the first time the Defence Civilian Committee, which exists today. There had not previously been a committee that was dedicated to the civilian workforce. All the committees were either purely ADF oriented or they were theoretically integrated, which meant 90 per cent of the effort was ADF. We tried to give a lot of focus to the professionalisation of the civilian workforce.

What about the relative power of the Department of Defence as an organisation over this time? Many have written about the Department of Foreign Affairs struggling for power and money compared with Defence in recent decades. How did that change during your time with Brendan?

Different parts of government have power through different means. The Department of Prime Minister and Cabinet has power because it's working to the head of government and heads that whole of government. Treasury has power because it reads the economy. Finance has power because it controls how much money everyone else gets. Defence has power by virtue of its size. Now it doesn't have a lot of power in peacetime by virtue of its responsibilities, but it's the sheer weight of it. If Defence sits there and doesn't do much, that in itself is an exercise of power, and Foreign Affairs has power. I think through the fact that many things in government now have external dimensions.

But whether Foreign Affairs or Defence is more powerful than the other at any one time in part is a function of the personalities of ministers. When was the last time we had a foreign and a defence minister with a profile in seniority of who we've got now? We've got a Deputy Prime Minister

[Richard Marles] heading up Defence. We've got Penny Wong heading up Foreign Affairs. Richard Marles is the most senior member of the Right in government. He could bring down the government at any point if the Right and Left fractured. Penny: good mind, close to the prime minister. A real thinker and all of that. And when was the last time you saw a foreign minister give a statement to the National Press Club in which he or she articulates the broad foreign policy strategic framework within which a week later the defence minister announces the results of the *Defence Strategic Review*? We've had cooperative relationships in the past between foreign and defence ministers, but I can't recall the last time we had both a foreign and a defence minister with the political strength and importance of who we currently have.

When I read Brendan's writings on strategic imagination, he often implies it is a responsibility for the highest levels. Do you think that makes sense? That, in addition to managing people and policy, we expect leaders to have that imagination? Or do you think it can come from other parts of the organisation?

It can come from anywhere in the system. The degree to which it manifests itself in policy decisions and outcomes is very much dependent on the top. The top can foster imaginative thinking by encouraging it and making it clear they work at it. So, I agree with Brendan on that. But if you're an SES [Senior Executive Service] officer and, indeed, if you're a director and if you have strategic imagination, then it's a question of how successful you are in selling ideas and the way you sell them.

What does strategic imagination mean to you? How do you understand it?

Strategic imagination to me is thinking outside the box. It is thinking about Australia's interests in ways that draw from more than your traditional military and foreign policy strengths. It's your capacity to bring in different arms of government, working together, particularly in the way you might engage [with] another country. It is being able to look over the horizon and see the possibilities of what might be emerging beyond the established wisdom.

For instance, in the late 1990s, early 2000s, if you had said, 'Look, China's economic miracle inevitably at some point is going to wash over into military modernisation, that is going to create a China quite different to what it is today.' You might not see a President Xi or any of that, but you might say power balances are going to change. Whether that would be strategic imagination in the late 1990s, early 2000s, I don't know. I don't know whether you would class that as an example, but not too many people were saying that going back X number of years.

The trouble with the word imagination is that it implies seeing things beyond what they are currently. For instance, is it strategic imagination to see the possibilities of India or Indonesia in a way that is counter to the accepted wisdom? Is it lacking strategic imagination to therefore say, well, it's never going to change? Or is it strategic imagination to say, yes, India is the way it is today. Brendan would have been interesting on that, because of his knowledge of the literature and culture. Or he might have had a view that this will change over time.

Or for Indonesia: I don't see Indonesia as necessarily remaining the same Indonesia as [it has been over] the last number of years. I see Indonesia as being potentially quite different. A country of 260 million people does not like a country of 1.4 billion telling it what to do. They don't like that country of 1.4 billion encroaching on it. They have a strong sense of being Indonesian. They have a strong sense of their own nation and country. And how you can work with that beyond the framework of ASEAN [Association of Southeast Asian Nations], I don't know. Is that about boldness? Is that about imagination? How do you define imagination? Is it simply being different? Or is it seeing possibilities that no-one else sees? I don't know.

Do you think this is a concept that works for Australia? I mean, we often see ourselves as quite pragmatic.

What have been the big four elements in our approach to the world since the Second World War? It has been not necessarily in this order, but it has been: one, a strong ally with a country much more powerful than our own and which has global weight. Second, engagement in the region. Way before Paul Keating said the word 'engagement', this really goes back to [Robert] Menzies. There's a photograph on the wall in Defence of a young Megawati Sukarnoputri [former Indonesian president and daughter of Indonesian's first president, Sukarno] sitting on Bob Menzies's knee. I mean, it really goes back. So, engagement in the region and the importance of the region to Australia go back to before the war. The third thing has been a commitment to international institutions. The rhetoric around the United Nations varies between the two parties but, ultimately, they've tried to engage. And the fourth thing has been a push for more liberalised trade, because we're a trading nation.

Those four elements have been there since the Second World War and they manifest themselves in what we like to do as a country. We like to get the big boys at the table. And we'd like to be at the table. So, what do you have to do? When I joined [the Department of] External Affairs in 1969, we had the Commonwealth Heads of Government meeting and that was it. Then you had the whole creation of APEC [Asia-Pacific Economic Cooperation] in Seoul in January of 1989, then that developed under Keating into the APEC leaders meeting. You had our strong push, led by [then foreign minister Alexander] Downer to be seated at the beginning of the East Asia Summit. [John] Howard had an ambivalent view, however, Downer said we need to be there from the beginning.

As we moved through 2008, it became clear that the US would need to bring together a group of leading economies against the backdrop of the Global Financial Crisis. And the debate was whether it would be a G13 or 14 or whether it would be a G20. And no-one in Washington who argued for G13 or 14 had Australia in the mix. Rudd pushed very, very hard for a G20. Not only through the US itself, but through the UK and through others. Arguing that the G20 was an established forum, therefore, it made sense for the leaders of that established forum to come together rather than create a new forum. So, you have very much a consistency of approach. APEC, East Asia Summit and G20. And what does that give us? For the first time in our history, we sit down three times a year with the leaders of Indonesia, Japan, Korea, China, etcetera. And we sit down a couple of times a year with India; we sit down at least once a year with the leaders of France, the UK, Germany, South Africa, Saudi Arabia, Türkiye, etcetera.

The way we've imagined our global interests and the way we've imagined the input, the importance, of the type of international forums we've wanted, the tables we've wanted to be at and who we've wanted to be at the table with us, I don't think we've done too badly. And it's been not knowingly and consciously bipartisan, but it has been bipartisan. All those things were done without any domestic controversy, or party-political differences, reflecting the underpinnings of our foreign policy approaches.

One last question: how will you remember Brendan?

One, you remember his warmth. You remember his depth of intellect and it's not only his depth of intellect. It is diversity of intellect. Brendan had a diverse mind. Brendan was not mono-focused in his intellectual pursuits. And I think that is a secret to strategic imagination. It's the interest in poetry, the interest in literature, the interest in culture, combined with his deep knowledge of strategic issues, combined with a sense of Australia. All of that comes together to create his strategic imagination.

I doubt whether he would have even written about strategic imagination without his interest in poetry, culture and literature; I very much doubt it. His diversity of intellectual interests was the secret to his strategic imagination.

7

Thinking about strategic imagination

Ian Hall

Until recently, 'strategic imagination' was a concept more often discussed in the pages of the *Harvard Business Review* than in strategic studies. Business gurus and management consultants have long argued that imagination is central to good strategy. As Bruce D. Henderson, the legendary founder of the Boston Consulting Group, once put it, 'imagination and logic make strategy possible'. 'Without them,' Henderson added, 'behavior and tactics are either intuitive or the result of conditioned reflexes.'[1]

This argument is more relevant to Australian strategic studies than we might appreciate, for two reasons. First, across our broad region, states both big and small evince different—and perhaps also increasingly divergent—'strategic imaginaries', and we must understand them well if we are to secure our interests.[2] Second, our region and our world are changing fast, and Australia must become more imaginative in the approaches it takes to securing our national interests.[3]

---

1   Bruce D. Henderson, 'The Origin of Strategy', *Harvard Business Review*, November–December 1989, 140, hbr.org/1989/11/the-origin-of-strategy.

2   On regional strategic imaginaries, see Jochen Prantl and Evelyn Goh, 'Rethinking Strategy and Statecraft for the Twenty-First Century of Complexity: A Case for Strategic Diplomacy', *International Affairs* 98, no. 2 (2022): 443–69, doi.org/10.1093/ia/iiab212.

3   For a call for more imagination in Australian strategy, see Michael Fullilove, 'Australia, India and the Indo-Pacific: The Need for Strategic Imagination', 2nd Atal Bihari Vajpayee Memorial Lecture, Ministry of External Affairs of India, 25 December 2021, www.lowyinstitute.org/publications/australia-india-indo-pacific-need-strategic-imagination.

Today, as Brendan Sargeant argued in his important essay, Australia 'faces a challenge it has never experienced before—a changing strategic order … occurring in conjunction with a change in the biophysical environment, of which climate change is the most visible manifestation'.[4] It confronts this challenge, moreover, with less relative power than it once had. In the 1980s and 1990s and even into the 2000s, Australia could use its weight—as well as its skill—to impose its will, acting like a regional Achilles. But those days have gone. Now and into the foreseeable future, Sargeant suggested, Australia 'needs to be more like Odysseus': resourceful, creative, perceptive, cunning, deceptive when required and, above all, imaginative.[5]

Getting there will not be easy. We must look more closely at what 'strategic imagination' involves, how we might do 'strategic imagining' better and what resources we need to do it well. Sargeant rightly observed that 'our capacity to envisage and prepare for a future crisis can be constrained by the limits of our strategic imagination' and the 'quality of the imagination that responds to that challenge determines the shape of the strategy that follows'.[6] For the most part, however, his Centre of Gravity Series Paper focused on Australia's past and present 'strategic imaginaries'—what he called the 'contours of the Australian strategic imagination'.[7] Sargeant left open the issue of how we might, in the course of strategic policymaking, harness imagination better and go about imagining something different. So, this chapter picks up where his left off. It aims to define 'strategic imagination' and to suggest how it might be done better, given how central imagination is to strategy, as business gurus like Henderson recognised. To do that, it draws on the literature on the role of imagination in science, which explores, among other things, how imagination is used to advance knowledge and how to harness imagination more effectively to generate better understandings of the world.

---

4   Brendan Sargeant, *Challenges to the Australian Strategic Imagination*, Centre of Gravity Series Papers 58 (Canberra: Strategic and Defence Studies Centre, The Australian National University, 2021), 3, hdl.handle.net/1885/233085, sdsc.bellschool.anu.edu.au/experts-publications/publications/8022/centre-gravity-series-challenges-australian-strategic.

5   ibid., 12. On the contrast between Achilles and Odysseus as strategists, see Lawrence Freedman, *Strategy: A History* (Oxford: Oxford University Press, 2013), 22–27.

6   Sargeant, *Challenges to the Australian Strategic Imagination*, 4.

7   ibid., 6–10.

Scientific imagination

The common-sense definition of imagination is the act of envisaging something beyond the bounds of our immediate perception. But beyond that understanding, there is a great deal of argument about exactly what imagination entails, how and why it occurs, what function it performs and what uses it has, among many other things. Indeed, philosophers have distinguished (at least) 12 different 'conceptions of imagination' used in the social and natural sciences.[8] For the sake of what follows, I am going to try to keep things simple and distinguish between 'creative' and 're-creative' imagination—that is: 'combining ideas in unexpected and unconventional ways' versus 'an ability to experience or think about the world from a perspective different from the one that experience presents'.[9] This allows us to differentiate between creative and re-creative strategic imaginations, both of which are arguably needed and useful, but are nevertheless distinct.

Recent work on imagination in science provides some indications of why, how and when these kinds of imagination—creative and re-creative—are important in producing better understandings of the world around us. This literature challenges the long-held view that imagination has no proper role in science. For much of the twentieth century, philosophers of science neglected imagination, arguing, like Karl Popper, that science generates knowledge by the rigorous application of proper method. Theories are tested against systematically collated evidence and, if they are shown to be false, discarded. Where those theories came from was not a concern of such philosophers—nor should scientists waste their time thinking about it.[10]

From the 1960s, this view was challenged—notably, by historians of science like Thomas S. Kuhn. These challenges opened the way to explorations of the scientific imagination. Kuhn argued that distinguishing between theories and observations was harder than Popper suggested. What we look for when we search for evidence, he suggested, is shaped by the theories

---

8   Leslie Stevenson, 'Twelve Conceptions of Imagination', *The British Journal of Aesthetics* 43, no. 3 (2003): 238–59, doi.org/10.1093/bjaesthetics/43.3.238.

9   Shen-Yi Liao and Tamar Gendler, 'Imagination', in *The Stanford Encyclopedia of Philosophy*, edited by Edward N. Zalta (Stanford: Stanford University Press, Summer 2020 edn), plato.stanford.edu/archives/sum2020/entries/imagination/. Liao and Gendler take this distinction from Gregory Currie and Ian Ravenscroft, *Recreative Minds: Imagination in Philosophy and Psychology* (Oxford: Clarendon Press, 2002), doi.org/10.1093/acprof:oso/9780198238089.001.0001.

10   Karl Popper, *Conjectures and Refutations: The Growth of Scientific Knowledge*, 2nd edn (London: Routledge, 2002).

we have about what we expect to find. Kuhn posited that what he called 'normal science'—everyday 'puzzle-solving'—takes place within 'paradigms' consisting of interlinked theories about how the world works, which shape what scientists look for and how they think about the evidence they gather. These paradigms do not, of course, last forever; periodically, they collapse, to be replaced with new ones. This happens when scientists discover sufficient anomalies in the evidence to make them question the paradigm, as occurred, for example, in physics, when Isaac Newton's paradigm collapsed to give way to the theory of relativity, which better accounts for established facts.[11]

Kuhn's argument helped revive interest in scientific discovery and the role of imagination in that process—in what is sometimes termed 'epistemic progress'.[12] It allowed practising scientists to argue that the imagination was in fact central to this progress. Starting with the assertion that our 'knowledge of reality has ... an essentially indeterminate content'—that it is, in other words, a 'vision' of something we cannot presently demonstrate with the theories and facts we have—Michael Polanyi argued that imagination and intuition were means by which scientists established where problems with our knowledge are, which problems to tackle and how, and what means might be used to solve them. Scientists draw on 'thoughts of things that are not present, or not yet present—or perhaps never to be present' to perform these tasks. They imagine or intuit how the 'indeterminacies' in our understanding of the world might be explained, to introduce greater coherence into an existing vision or indeed to move to a different one.[13]

Today, Polanyi's view is widely accepted and most scientists acknowledge that imagination plays a role—and often an important role—in the advance of scientific knowledge.[14] Imagination is recognised as present in various aspects of scientific work, most obviously, perhaps, in models and in thought experiments used to represent aspects of reality or envisage alternative realities that might give us insights into our own.[15] Models can be understood as essentially fictitious simplifications of aspects of reality

---

11   Thomas S. Kuhn, *The Structure of Scientific Revolutions*, 3rd edn (Chicago: Chicago University Press, 1996). On the paradigm shift in physics, see pp. 72–73.

12   Alice Murphy, 'Imagination in Science', *Philosophy Compass* 17, no. 6 (2022): e12836, doi.org/10.1111/phc3.12836.

13   Michael Polanyi, 'The Creative Imagination', in *The Idea of Creativity*, edited by Karen Bardsley, Denis Dutton, and Michael Krausz (Leiden: Brill, 2009), 149, 156. The essay was originally published in 1966.

14   Michael T. Stuart, 'The Productive Anarchy of Scientific Imagination', *Philosophy of Science* 87, no. 5 (2020): 968–78, at 968, doi.org/10.1086/710629.

15   For a useful overview on which the rest of this paragraph draws, see Murphy, 'Imagination in Science'.

designed to better explain phenomena. Thought experiments, by contrast, are imaginary alternatives to real-world situations, used sometimes—but not always—to clarify our understanding of those situations. Models are a form of 'imagistic imagination', in other words, where we are asked to view something. And, by contrast, thought experiments are a form of 'propositional imagination', where we are asked to not just passively view but also actively explore a logic. This second kind of imagination is particularly common in theoretical work in the natural sciences, where arguments follow a supposition or set of suppositions that may or may not be grounded in the facts we have established about aspects of observed reality.[16]

Yet, while imagination is now recognised as central to scientific progress, there is also broad agreement that scientists are not free to let their imaginations roam wherever they like, even when using tools like thought experiments. There is a rough consensus that the scientific imagination must operate within certain boundaries to make positive contributions to the generation of new knowledge. The construction of a hypothesis about some difficult-to-explain process clearly involves imagination—namely, envisaging cause and effect that have not yet been observed. But such acts of imagination take place within limits—notably, the limits imposed by the known facts relevant to the issue at hand, by what the scientist knows about how other similar processes work, by our broader understanding of what is possible and impossible and by the dictates of logic. Moreover, scientists must clearly explain the grounding for whatever they have imagined: the assumptions they have made and the steps taken in arriving at their supposition. Finally, of course, whatever is imagined should then be tested against evidence in a rigorous and replicable way.[17]

Of course, not everyone agrees that the scientific imagination should be tightly constrained.[18] Famously, Paul Feyerabend argued that science would struggle to progress if the imagination was completely fettered to facts, existing theories and present methods and if scientists were unable to imagine the seemingly impossible.[19] But the points I want to take away from

---

16   Steven French, 'Imagination in Scientific Practice', *European Journal for Philosophy of Science* 10, no. 27 (2020), doi.org/10.1007/s13194-020-00291-z.

17   Deena Skolnick Weisberg, 'Is Imagination Constrained Enough for Science?', in *The Scientific Imagination*, edited by Arnon Levy and Peter Godfrey-Smith (Oxford: Oxford University Press, 2020), 251–52.

18   See, for example, Stuart, 'The Productive Anarchy of Scientific Imagination'.

19   Paul Feyerabend, *The Tyranny of Science*, edited by Eric Oberheim (Cambridge: Polity Press, 2011).

this discussion are that, in science, imagination is far from incompatible with rigorous thinking and there is no reason to think that it should be in either strategic studies or strategic policymaking.

Imaginative strategy

Indeed, when we look closely, we see imagination throughout strategic policy and strategic studies. Both the *creative imagination* and the *re-creative imagination* are perennial features. Using the first, strategists combine ideas, theories and evidence in different ways to imagine different scenarios or possible futures.[20] Using the second, they try to put themselves in the shoes of partners and adversaries, to envisage how they perceive challenges and opportunities.[21] Neither of these exercises is undertaken without limits, however: established facts, accepted theories, replicable methods and logic bound the best work in these areas.

Moreover, the *imagistic imagination* is widely employed, not least in strategic cartography, where maps are used in both official and unofficial publications to convey established or emerging strategic contexts, sometimes to dramatic effect. Recall, for example, Map 7.1, which appeared in the 2023 *Defence Strategic Review*. The map—or, more specifically, the projection—is apparently intended to illustrate the extent of the Indo-Pacific, Australia's centrality in that broad region, the salience of the maritime domain and the strategic significance of northern and western Australia.[22] It challenges the reader to imagine Australia's strategic situation and strategic potential in a different way to conventional views, which tend to focus our attention on a north–south axis running from China through South-East Asia and into Australia.

---

20   See, for example, Peter J. Dean, 'From Deft Diplomacy to Rebalancing Hard Power: Australia and Indian Ocean Strategic Futures', *Asia Policy* 16, no. 3 (2021): 34–39, doi.org/10.1353/asp.2021.0026.
21   See, for instance, Avery Goldstein, 'China's Grand Strategy under Xi Jinping: Reassurance, Reform, and Resistance', *International Security* 45, no. 1 (2020): 164–201, doi.org/10.1162/isec_a_00383.
22   Department of Defence, *National Defence: Defence Strategic Review 2023* (Canberra: Australian Government, 2023), 27, www.defence.gov.au/about/reviews-inquiries/defence-strategic-review.

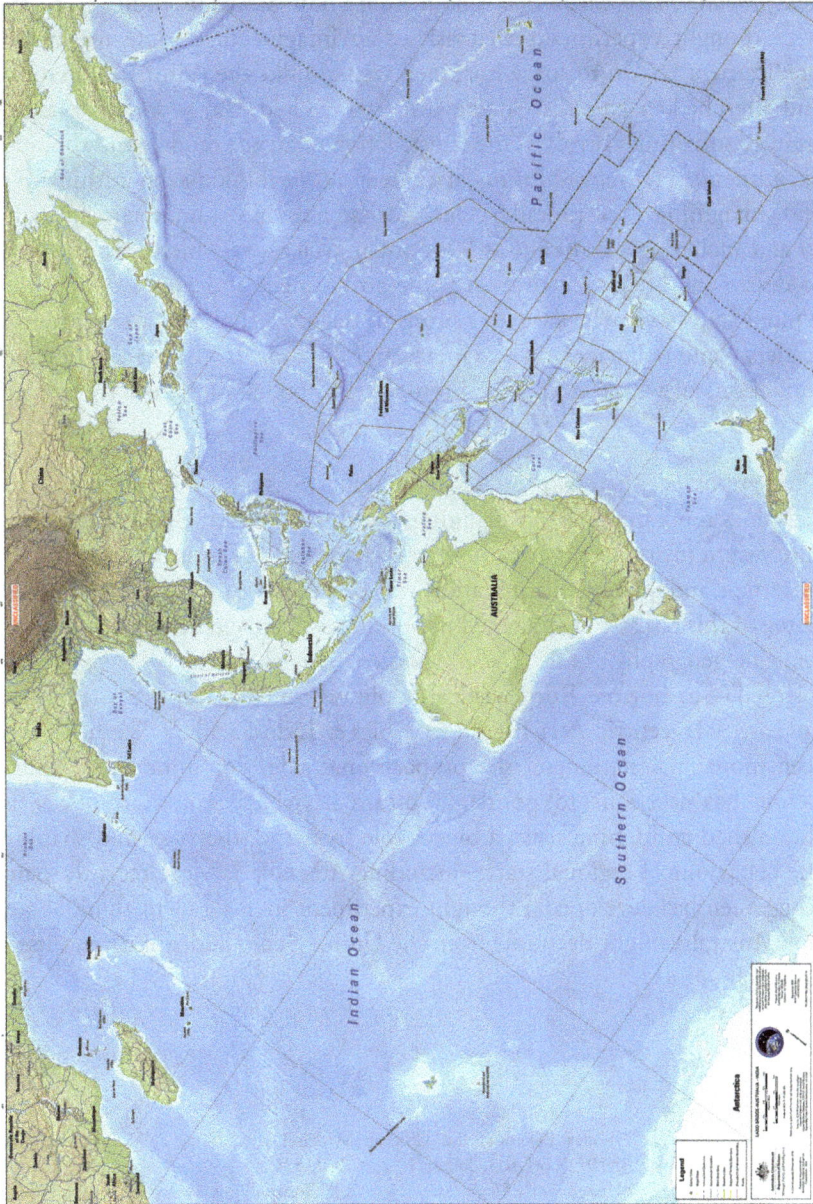

Map 7.1 The Indo-Pacific region

Source: Department of Defence, *National Defence: Defence Strategic Review 2023* (Canberra: Australian Government, 2023), 27, www.defence.gov.au/about/reviews-inquiries/defence-strategic-review.

The *propositional imagination* is no less common. Strategic studies is replete with thought experiments that ask us to imagine that some real-world predicament is akin to some imagined scenario like the prisoner's dilemma and the chicken game, to name just two.[23] Cold War work on nuclear strategy sometimes involved the construction of arcane models and thought experiments. Herman Kahn made a career out of thinking the unthinkable and imagining the morally—but not strategically—unimaginable, up to and including his infamous 'Doomsday Machine', which was designed to destroy all life on Earth even if the government and population of the United States were wiped out in a surprise attack.[24] Kahn's aim was to prompt readers—and policymakers—to more carefully consider the capabilities and limitations of weapons and the protocols and policies for their threatened or actual use.

Contemporary Australian strategic thinking does not need to go as far as Kahn's more outlandish imaginings—at least, not yet. But Sargeant was surely right to argue that our situation is changing, our future is increasingly uncertain and strategic imagination will be needed to meet the challenge. Some of this has already emerged in our imagistic imagination of Australia's strategic geography. As the *Defence Strategic Review* shows, we have already 'pivoted'—to borrow Rory Medcalf's phrase—our conceptual map from an East Asia–centric Asia-Pacific to a bigger Indo-Pacific.[25] We have also seen more imagination on the propositional side. For some time, Hugh White has asked us to ponder a future in which American power is diminished and China plays a bigger role in setting the rules and shaping the behaviour of regional states, including Australia.[26] More recently, Sam Roggeveen has developed a thought experiment inviting us to think about how Australia might decouple from the United States and still defend itself and its interests.[27]

23 Glenn H. Snyder, '"Prisoner's Dilemma" and "Chicken" Models in International Politics', *International Studies Quarterly* 15, no. 1 (1971): 66–103, doi.org/10.2307/3013593.

24 Herman Kahn, *Thinking about the Unthinkable* (New York: Horizon Press, 1962). On the Doomsday Machine, see Herman Kahn, 'The Arms Race and Some of Its Hazards', *Daedalus* 89, no. 4 (1960): 745–52.

25 Rory Medcalf, *Contest for the Indo-Pacific: Why China Won't Map Our Future* (Melbourne: La Trobe University Press, 2020).

26 See, for example, Hugh White, *The China Choice: Why America Should Share Power* (Melbourne: Black Inc., 2013).

27 Sam Roggeveen, *The Echidna Strategy: Australia's Search for Power and Peace* (Melbourne: La Trobe University Press, 2023).

Yet, more imagination is needed because the sheer number of challenges we now face is daunting. Australia presently lacks comprehensive strategies to uphold the integrity of our democratic processes in the face of a torrent of digitally enabled misinformation and disinformation, ensure prosperity amid the fragmentation of the multilateral economic order and the coercive practices of major states and, above all, somehow cope with the climate crisis already on us. What we have now are arguably piecemeal approaches, built up over time in response to particular challenges.

Conclusion

Sargeant was correct to argue that we will need imagination to formulate and implement the strategies we need, but we must also recognise that imagination on its own cannot produce good strategy. We also need knowledge, time for thought and an open conversation between scholars and practitioners. Scientific progress happens when informed scientists, up to date with the latest evidence and explanations, use their imagination to develop hypotheses that can account for the gaps in what the scientific community knows. This disciplined use of imagination requires a high degree of knowledge of the relevant constraints: of what is possible and what is not; of what has been established and what is still in doubt. Scientists acquire this knowledge through excellent mentors, adequate funding, time and—just as crucially—unfettered access to the latest data and scholarship produced across the world by their peers. Armed with all this, scientists can use their imaginations productively, targeting the puzzles that matter and bringing the latest knowledge to bear.

Strategic studies and strategic policymaking take place in different circumstances, with lower levels of knowledge about relevant constraints and considerable systemic inefficiencies. Strategists in universities and think tanks often lack access to the latest data about advanced weapons or the latest assessments of the intentions or capabilities of putative adversaries. Without knowledge of classified information, they must divert at least some effort, money and time to producing their own data and assessments, which may or may not be accurate. In parallel, strategic policymakers often lack access to the latest academic work, either because it is behind a publisher's paywall or because it is expressed in impenetrable language. Useful knowledge is thereby lost and effort wasted.

Stimulating the Australian strategic imagination—creative and re-creative—to help Australians cope with the challenges we face and may soon encounter must involve more than just appreciating the role that imagination can play in strategic thinking. Odysseus succeeded because he watched and learned from his experiences, because he had a great repository of knowledge about the world around him, because he had time to reflect and respond and because he accurately perceived the strengths and weaknesses of others, not just because he was cunning and resourceful. In Australia, however, our scholars of strategy are commonly starved of the knowledge they need by highly restrictive regimes of official secrecy, while our practitioners are starved of the time for reflection, as well as the insights that academic work can offer. Freeing Australia's strategic imagination and escaping the tendency to act simply on ill-grounded intuition or conditioned reflex must involve some creative thinking—and fast action—on both fronts.

8

The strategist as author

Andrew Carr

Wielding words

To be a strategist is to use words. From the generals of antiquity who briefed emperors about battle plans, through to the modern-day flood of books, reports and tweets about national security, strategists must identify, diagnose, discuss, consult, debate, define, persuade and promote their ideas about the world. This practical profession seeks compelling language not simply for the sake of eloquence but to achieve results. To be a strategist is to use words to try to move worlds.

In this chapter, I explore how words, both written and read, shape the role and capacity of a strategist.[1] Brendan Sargeant was a man who lived his life among words. At work, either in the Department of Defence or later at The Australian National University, his day-to-day responsibility was to consume deep in-trays of reports, notes, emails and briefs. At home, he relaxed by reading fiction and then, late into the evening, he would write— diaries, essays, books and poetry. All as a way of trying to grapple with the world. To talk with Brendan was to have a conversation not only with the man, but also with the literary world he carried with him. A chat might begin on the political controversy of the day and 15 minutes later Brendan would be explaining why Blake shows us a fresh world or how the ancient Indian epics operated at a scale unfathomable in the modern

---

1   Many thanks to Jonathan Lee for the research assistance he provided to support this chapter.

West. His daily climb through those mountains of words was his attempt to 'see what was worth seeing', to quote one of his favourite novels about Australia, Gerald Murnane's *The Plains*.

In this chapter, I look at three ways that words define the act of strategy. In part one, I look at strategy as a form of *sight*, of trying to capture a messy world and give it some cohesion and clarity on the page. To act strategically, we must first diagnose what the problems are and identify how we understand the trends, patterns and events around us. Only through reading and writing, reading again and writing again, can we effectively complete this task. In part two, I explore how written words can be a form of *experience*. Through reading the words of others, both historical and fictional, we can gain insight, empathy and wisdom that would not otherwise be accessible to us. We can live a thousand lifetimes on the page in order to better interpret the life we have to live in the flesh. In the final part of the chapter, I turn to strategy as a form of *imagination*. Once we have diagnosed the problems faced, strategists must think about the world as it could be, helping others to see that change is possible and the kinds of actions that might help to bring it about.

Strategists do not build the machines of war. They do not give the order. They do not fire the weapon. Instead, they wield words, giving reasons for why violence may be needed and what we intend to achieve through it. Only if their words are right, if their sight, experience and imagination are richly formed, can strategists help their societies to act in the world. In 1871 the French poet Arthur Rimbaud said:

> The poet must make himself a seer by an immense, long, deliberate disordering of all senses. He seeks in himself all forms of love, of suffering, of madness. He exhausts from them all their poison to keep only their essence.[2]

When I first read those words, I thought of Brendan and saw how much the strategist and the poet have in common. To see, to experience, to imagine— it's all just words, but on them, the fate of civilisations can turn.

---

2   Philip Hook, *Art of the Extreme 1905–1914* (London: Profile Books, 2021), 159.

Strategy — As a form of seeing

Some 4,000 years ago, humans began writing things down. What we owned and what we fought over were predictably the main topics. With this invention, our species obtained not only a new way of recording and transmitting information, but also a new way of thinking—one that provides a deeper space for consciousness and analysis. A spoken claim is always 'sponsored'; it is a product of the author.[3] During the Peloponnesian War (431–404 BCE), when Thucydides acted as a general in command of troops and a public advocate for military conduct, his words were filtered by his audience's regard for his authority and the context in which he spoke. However, when Thucydides the historian wrote down his thoughts about those same events, a space was created—'a conceptual gap between sentence and utterance'.[4] In that space, meanings and insights could emerge that allowed readers to test and explore and later generations to reinterpret and understand.

For the audience, a written text can be more directly interrogated than its spoken counterpart. Its logic can be explored step by step, its claims disputed, its context and purpose identified and overlaid on the words. Yet, the author benefits as well, as they can obtain a form of distance from the ideas and the context, revising and reconsidering to ensure the expression matches the intention.[5] Anyone who has struggled to find the right language, to work a draft again and again until it seems to say what you want, has experienced this space and its potential. By learning to write, humans gain access to a richer interior life than would otherwise be possible, a deepening of their consciousness and capacity for self-introspection and awareness of self.[6] Literary cultures have the ability not only to see the world but also, through this technology, the opportunity to see the world afresh. To write is to learn about the world. We use the distance offered between a thought and the written word to create new connections and re-examine our context.

---

3   Roy Harris, 'How Does Writing Restructure Thought?', *Language & Communication* 9, nos 2–3 (1989): 99–106, at 104, doi.org/10.1016/0271-5309(89)90012-8.
4   ibid., 104.
5   Walter J. Ong, *Orality and Literacy: 30th Anniversary Edition* (London: Taylor & Francis, 2012), 81.
6   Regina E. Fabry, 'Enculturation and Narrative Practices', *Phenomenology and the Cognitive Sciences* 17, no. 5 (2018): 911–37, doi.org/10.1007/s11097-018-9567-x.

The foremost example for strategists of this effort to think through writing is none other than Carl von Clausewitz's masterpiece *On War*. Written over decades and unfinished at the time of his death, *On War* demonstrates not only a writer whose views evolved as he worked, but also a writer who wrote in a very specific way to improve his capacity for thought. Clausewitz sets up competing ideas, pushing their logics to the extreme to understand their true essence. Hence, its essential, but often widely bemoaned, complexity.[7] Writing through opposing dialectics is how this otherwise obscure Prussian soldier developed two of his most important insights: that war is beset by friction and war is a form of politics by other means.

Like many of his time, Clausewitz had seen the rapid expansion of European armed forces and the growing devastation that Napoleon and his antagonists had wrought across the continent. This experience led Clausewitz to believe war had an intrinsic tendency towards the extremes. Yet, having outlined why this might be the case, Clausewitz then advances the opposite case: that the nature of war is always checked and bound. It is simply not possible for all parts of an armed force or an entire nation at war to be involved simultaneously. Nor is war a ceaseless drumbeat of conflict, even among those on the battlefield. There are pauses and respites, decisions to retire or delay. War both escalates and is impeded.

F. Scott Fitzgerald once said the sign of a first-rate mind is the ability to hold two opposing ideas simultaneously. Many would rebel against trying to sustain the justification for explaining war in such explosive and simultaneously bound fashions. Yet, by taking those ideas and placing them on the page, Clausewitz, and future generations of his readers, can gain the distance necessary to see that they actually adhere.

War may have an internal tendency towards extremes, but friction ensures it can never reach that totalising whole.[8] If war cannot be absolute, absolute military ambition is misaligned to the nature of war. The limits on war, the inability of war to reach its totalising whole, mean that some external force is always required to supply reason and purpose, justifying the effort to overcome friction, adapting to the extremes and making sense of the

---

7   Youri Cormier, *War as Paradox: Clausewitz and Hegel on Fighting Doctrines and Ethics* (Montreal: McGill–Queen's University Press, 2016), 5, doi.org/10.1515/9780773548497.

8   Carl von Clausewitz, *On War*, translated by Colonel J.J. Graham (New York: Barnes & Noble, 2004), 62.

slaughter. Only politics can fulfil that role. Because of war's essential tension between escalation and friction, war must ultimately be subservient to politics. War is politics by other means.

Clausewitz lays out his thinking on the page for all to see, but the experience of trying to use words to provoke thoughts, to then provoke the right words, will ring true to anyone who has written substantively. There are many tools for thinking, from the simplistic to the intricate. Most, however, boil down to one contribution: they direct your mind purposively towards a topic. Focused attention on a subject leads the bucking horses of the conscious and unconscious mind to pull in similar directions.

Writing, which requires us to give definite form on the page to what are often indefinite sensations in the mind, sustains and binds our thoughts, helping to slowly reveal their real nature. 'A word is a bud attempting to become a twig,' said the French philosopher Gaston Bachelard.[9] The American novelist and writer Flannery O'Connor once said, 'I don't know so well what I think until I see what I say' or, as a later author, Stephen King, bluntly put it: 'I write to find out what I think.'

Not everyone thinks through writing. Many today identify as visual thinkers, preferring metaphors and analogies, turning images around in their head, even whole scenes. Personally, I think through fragments of sentences: a partial phrase, description or pun that must be made whole. Often these remain just fragments. The translation onto the page as a full sentence reveals some break in the logic, context or rhythm that leaves it less than its original potential seemed to indicate. Other fragments make it to the page, but the context is wrong and, like valuable gems embedded in difficult rock, they must be carefully chipped away at, rewriting the start and end of sentences, moving these stones around in position, seeking new ways to reveal their shine.

This, too, can fail; it can result in long pages of nothingness. But even in that case, perhaps especially in cases of failed writing, we see productive thought. The phrase that too easily slips from the mind to the page is generally a cliché—a sentence of common use, a thought of banality that slips quietly in alongside our otherwise hard-won prose. As George Orwell

---

9   Quoted in Dorthe Jørgensen, 'The Philosophy of Imagination', in *Handbook of Imagination and Culture*, edited by Tania Zittoun and Vlad Glaveanu (Oxford: Oxford University Press, 2017), 19.

reminds us in his rules for good writing, we must always object to such easy insertions. The cliché represents the absence of thought, whereas the awkward phrase is often the bud of a fresh thought struggling to emerge.

The style and flow of those words can matter just as profoundly as their content, and often to the detriment of bureaucratic productions. To cite but a single example, in his biography of the US Cold War strategist George F. Kennan, John Lewis Gaddis observes:

> Not the least of the reasons Kennan succeeded as a strategist and a historian is that he used words well. There was passion, luminosity, rigor and originality in almost all of his prose, so much so that its vividness at times obscured the meanings he meant for it to convey. Had it not been for that—had Kennan written as most other Foreign Service officers did—the world might never have heard of him.[10]

What makes categorising good writing so hard is that writers can succeed by trying to close the gap between thought and representation as much as possible. Or they can succeed by deliberately keeping one at a distance from the other. What science and art seek from the written word is often very different. To tease out this distinction, we turn to the Australian art historian Robert Hughes, who observes:

> A sign is a command. Its message comes all at once. It means one thing only—nuances and ambiguity are not important properties of signs—and is no better for being hand-made. Works of art speak in a more complicated way of relationships, hints, uncertainties and contradictions. They do not force meanings on their audience; meaning emerges, adds up, unfolds from their imagined centres. A sign dictates meaning, a work of art takes one through the process of discovering meaning.[11]

Brendan Sargeant's strategic instincts were always of the art rather than the sign. His promotion of the 'Indo-Pacific' was as an idea that was not, but could be—a process of becoming, towards an unknown but hopefully beneficial new order. His concept of strategic imagination is equally open-ended—an attempt at grappling with the world rather than dictating to it. This reflected his deeply held belief that there was no single 'right' point on which we must stand when attempting to see the world. Rather, a multitude

---

10   John Lewis Gaddis, *George F. Kennan: An American Life* (New York: Penguin Group, 2011), 696.
11   Robert Hughes, *The Shock of the New: Art and the Century of Change* (Melbourne: Thames & Hudson, 1991), 325.

of perspectives is necessary, many of which can be found simply by looking at bookshelves nearby. They are the product of some long-ago author's struggle to think by turning ideas into symbols on a page. And we can be their beneficiaries.

Strategy — As a form of experience

Fiction, both written and read, can allow strategists to obtain experience, insight and empathy without loss of blood. Just as the shift from the spoken to the written word creates the distance for new forms of thought, so, too, the distance generated by fiction and imagination can create a fresh understanding of ourselves. As neuroscientist and philosopher Ian McGilchrist observes:

> [O]ne of the crucial functions of the imagination is to enable us to take various perspectives on the world: it enables us to 'see how it looks from over there'. This encourages a certain humility about how it looks from one's own perspective, and yet at the same time provides some reason for confidence in what one takes to be the case. Without imagination there can be no objectivity.[12]

According to cognitive scientists, something distinct happens when we read about imagined worlds. When in the realm of nonfiction, our brains work through their causal processes, focusing on 'action and their outcomes'; however, when we delve into fiction, our brains 'initiate simulation processes especially concerning the motives behind an action and thereby the protagonist's mind'.[13] Put another way, through fiction we learn how to view the world differently and begin to understand how other minds might take such views as normal and correct.[14] Charles Hill, in his book on strategy and literature, says that '[l]iterature's freedom to explore endless or exquisite details, portray the thoughts of imaginary characters and dramatize large themes through intricate plots brings it close to the reality of "how the world really works"'.[15]

---

12   Ian McGilchrist, *The Matter with Things. Volume 1: Our Brains, Our Delusions, and the Unmaking of the World* (London: Perspectiva Press, 2021), 395.

13   Ulrike Altmann, Isabel C. Bohrn, Oliver Lubrich, Winnifred Menninghaus, and Arthur M. Jacobs, 'Fact vs Fiction: How Paratextual Information Shapes Our Reading Processes', *Social Cognitive and Affective Neuroscience* 9, no. 1 (2014): 22–29, at 27, doi.org/10.1093/scan/nss098.

14   Fabry, 'Enculturation and Narrative Practices', 931.

15   Charles Hill, *Grand Strategies: Literature, Statecraft, and World Order* (New Haven: Yale University Press, 2010), 6, doi.org/10.2307/j.ctt1nq2n7.

This is a skill that matters profoundly for strategy. Andrew Marshall, one of the leading strategic minds of the twentieth century, argued that 'you just have to move away from either this vague "the Russians decided" or "the Soviets decided" or this more formal kind of "rational actor" model', and recognise the role of individuals, culture and organisational forms, if you are to understand how other actors operate strategically.[16] A classic example is deterrence. To deter, we need the other side to change their behaviour and decide against taking actions we do not want. While it is easy to focus on the many things we might first do, the better starting point is to ask to what the other side is likely to respond. To quote Marshall: '[T]he problem is finding out what is it that is distasteful, frightening, deterring to them? And that's an empirical issue.'[17] We cannot do that if we assume they think like us and we never try to see the world from their position. One way to 'see what is worth seeing', to gain the experience that enables such imaginative leaps, is through reading fiction.

Over the past decade, the strategy community has begun to embrace fiction. August Cole and Peter W. Singer have led the way through books such as *Ghost Fleet: A Novel of the Next World War*, which they see as contributing 'FICINT': 'an analytical tool … attuned to aiding in visualizing new technology and trends' in service of contemporary strategic problem-solving.[18] Mick Ryan, a former Australian soldier turned strategic commentator, rose to prominence with a nonfiction book, *War Transformed*, and then chose to make his second book a work of fiction, *White Sun War: The Campaign for Taiwan*. During his period leading the Australian Defence Force's professional military education environment, Ryan strongly encouraged others to read fiction.

Studies suggest readers of fiction are better at understanding personal cues, relationships and perceptions than most people, even those who heavily consume nonfiction material about the world.[19] What fiction offers is not just a different viewpoint, but also the space and legitimacy for that different view to be understood and not simply countered. As two psychologists observe in a study of reading and empathy, 'engagement with the thoughts and feelings of characters in fictional stories might be closely related to the

---

16 Jeffrey S. McKitrick and Robert G. Angevine, *Reflections on Net Assessment: Andrew W. Marshall* (Alexandria: Andrew W. Marshall Foundation and Institute for Defense Analyses, 2022), 59.
17 ibid., 15.
18 August Cole and Peter W. Singer, 'Thinking the Unthinkable with Useful Fiction', *Journal of Future Conflict* 2 (Fall 2020), 1.
19 Johann Hari, *Stolen Focus: Why You Can't Pay Attention* (London: Bloomsbury Publishing, 2022), 83.

processes by which individuals infer the mental states of people in the real world'.[20] The causal links are not yet sufficiently clear to demonstrate that we can build empathy by encouraging people to read fiction (empathetic people tend to naturally read more fiction), but the practice of encountering the minds of others is likely to offer benefits for strategists seeking to analyse others.

Active learning practices such as war games and the case method of teaching can also help us to gain experience and develop our strategic imagination. They create experiences that may not be otherwise accessible. Both allow us to play out scenarios and gain insight into the merits of our assumptions, as well as to recognise, through repeated exposure, the tensions that policymakers face and the skills and knowledge they require. A powerful example of this was the US Government's *Proud Prophet* exercise in the 1980s. This war game was on a scale unlike anything before (or probably since). It involved two full weeks, hundreds of participants, including the US secretary of defence Caspar Weinberger, and directly tested US strategy. In his account of the game, Paul Bracken observes:

> This game went nuclear big time, not because Secretary Weinberger and the Chairman of the Joint Chiefs were crazy but because they faithfully implemented the prevailing US strategy ... [A]fter Proud Prophet there was no more over-the-top nuclear rhetoric coming out of the United States ... The Reagan Administration switched gears.[21]

Strategic experience, perhaps even wisdom, had been gained, for a fraction of its usual price.

Strategy — As a form of imagination

All strategy requires imagination: to imagine how the world came to be, how it works today and how our actions may change it into something better tomorrow. None of these steps is easy. There has been a boon in

---

20   John Stansfield and Louise Bunce, 'The Relationship between Empathy and Reading Fiction: Separate Roles for Cognitive and Affective Components', *Journal of European Psychology Students* 5, no. 3 (2014): 9–18, at 15, doi.org/10.5334/jeps.ca.

21   Paul J. Bracken, *The Second Nuclear Age: Strategy, Danger, and the New Power Politics* (New York: Henry Holt & Co., 2012), 52–53.

studies of biases and psychological distortions over recent years,[22] so much so that it has resulted in a pushback, with some arguing that biases can help us err on the side of safety when dealing with the unknown.[23] All strategy depends on a set of heuristics—mental shortcuts that explain what are the most essential features of the world.

In the second half of the twentieth century, the globe-spanning and antagonistic relationship between the United States of America and the Soviet Union was framed as a 'Cold War' and 'strategic competition'. Today we are apparently in a 'new Cold War' that defines the messy relationship between the United States and the People's Republic of China, with their competition widely viewed as the 'defining feature of our region and time'.[24] Inevitably, such frames are countered by those who question the accuracy, logic or morality of seeing the world in a particular way.[25]

Frames often animated Brendan Sargeant's discussion of strategic imagination. He saw it as a tool for revealing the unconscious assumptions behind our concepts such as 'new Cold War' and 'Indo-Pacific'. Moments of crisis or confusion help reveal the contours of a country's strategic imagination. As Sargeant observed of Australia since the turn of the century: 'We have made border security a primary manifestation of sovereignty, notwithstanding the reality that sovereignty is traded every day in our interactions in the global community as we seek national benefit or to maximise our economic and geostrategic position.'[26] So, too, he considered geography, time, technology and nostalgia as essential features of the Australian strategic imagination.

22   See, for instance, Daniel Kahneman, *Thinking, Fast and Slow* (New York: Penguin Books, 2012); Ronald R. Krebs and Aaron Rapport, 'International Relations and the Psychology of Time Horizons', *International Studies Quarterly* 56, no. 3 (2012): 530–43, doi.org/10.1111/j.1468-2478.2012.00726.x.
23   Dominic D.P. Johnson, *Strategic Instincts: The Adaptive Advantages of Cognitive Biases in International Politics* (Princeton: Princeton University Press, 2020), doi.org/10.23943/princeton/9780691137452.001.0001; or the earlier classic study Gerd Gigerenzer and Peter M. Todd, *Simple Heuristics That Make Us Smart* (Oxford: Oxford University Press, 1999).
24   Department of Defence, *National Defence: Defence Strategic Review 2023* (Canberra: Australian Government, 2023), 17, www.defence.gov.au/about/reviews-inquiries/defence-strategic-review.
25   Carol Cohn, 'Sex and Death in the Rational World of Defense Intellectuals', *Signs* 12, no. 4 (Summer, 1987): 687–718, doi.org/10.1086/494362; Ali Wyne, *America's Great-Power Opportunity: Revitalizing U.S. Foreign Policy to Meet the Challenges of Strategic Competition* (Cambridge: Polity Press, 2022).
26   Brendan Sargeant, *Challenges to the Australian Strategic Imagination*, Centre of Gravity Series Papers 58 (Canberra: Strategic and Defence Studies Centre, The Australian National University, 2021), 9, hdl.handle.net/1885/233085, sdsc.bellschool.anu.edu.au/experts-publications/publications/8022/centre-gravity-series-challenges-australian-strategic.

In Sargeant's account, countries imagine with reference to their history. Partly this is a function of language. Useful concepts are hard to dislodge from our phrasing, becoming the first blocks into which we try to slot new events. We may acknowledge the power of a new concept, but it has a much harder task convincing us that it is valuable against something that has worked before and slips easily to mind when we are asked to describe what is going on. As Sargeant observed of the regular invocations of alliance and self-reliance in Australian strategic documents, 'We avoid the arduous task of self-creation and instead deploy these clichés as a shield against our anxieties.'[27] The 'we' here is not casual phrasing. As scientists have increasingly sought to examine in recent years, communities, quite literally, think together.[28] The strategic imagination of a country emerges as the reflection of a thinking and talking community. In his monumental study *The Sociology of Philosophies*, Randall Collins shows that philosophy has always worked through active communities, not lone genius: 'There is no thinking except as aftermath or preparation of communication. Thinkers do not antedate communication, and the communicative process creates the thinkers as nodes of the process.'[29]

That need for communication to be in response to *something* represents a challenge with which future scholars of the concept of strategic imagination will need to engage. Brendan's writings often focused on strategic imagination as a mapping exercise, seeking to understand how his own country of Australia thought about and engaged with the world. Though Brendan had the policy experience and breadth of reading to knit together vast themes of identity, culture, history, politics and war in his assessment of Australia, others who seek to use the concept could slip up, since there are no clear boundaries of what subject would not be valid to include within a 'strategic imagination' assessment.

For strategic imagination to be most useful, it may need to be deliberately tied down within specific problem sets. When Australia engages with China, addresses climate change or refashions its relationship with the United States, what are the contours within these specific questions of relevance? The content here may be broad—for instance, demographics is essential to the China problem for Australia—yet there must be some locus to

---

27   ibid., 11.

28   Hannah Critchlow, *Joined-Up Thinking: The Science of Collective Intelligence and Its Power to Change Our Lives* (London: Hodder & Stoughton, 2022).

29   Randall Collins, *The Sociology of Philosophies: A Global Theory of Intellectual Change* (Cambridge: Belknap Press of Harvard University Press, 2002), 2.

keep it sufficiently focused: a framework that begins not with identity and narratives and then engages with the world, but that begins with the specific problems of the world and then asks how our identity and narratives help or hinder us in response.[30] Without such a reorientation, analysis of strategic imagination risks allowing an imaginative process that flees reality for the sunny hinterlands of self-pleasing stories about ourselves (of our greatness or villainy, depending on your political persuasion) and does not access the powerful imaginative tools to recombine ideas or gain fresh perspectives, as Ian Hall outlines in Chapter 7 of this volume.

Beyond the content of our imagination, Sargeant was also concerned with interrogating the capacity of a country to imagine. 'How are we to live in the Indo-Pacific in the 21st century … Is our vision of our future large enough to accommodate and respond to the scale of change that we are seeing?' he asked.[31] He went on, noting of Australia: 'Our policy and strategic documents repeatedly reference the "rules-based global order" and of the US Alliance as the foundation of our security … Yet the Indo-Pacific asks us: how long will this rhetoric, increasingly nostalgic in tone, make sense?'[32]

If writing can help us see, and reading can help us experience, how might we do better at imagination? One obvious well from which many political leaders have drunk deeply is poetry. In 1941, seeking to reassure a frightened nation, the incoming Australian Prime Minister, John Curtin, told readers of the *Sunday Telegraph*: 'For 20 years it has been my habit on Sunday nights to devote at least an hour to reading poetry … [E]very man should read poetry—for the good of his soul.'[33] As Toby Davidson recounts, during the war, Curtin regularly turned to 'Byron, the Bible, James Russell Lowell and Shakespeare', urging it on his fellow citizens for 'its uplifting mental and spiritual power which was vital to the development of the nation'.[34] Standing in Opposition in the parliament but united in a love of prose was Robert G. Menzies. Menzies also lived a life among books, with the heroes of Scottish and British history forming touchstones for his management of power. He also dipped into it for rhetorical purposes, reading poetry the night before a big speech to help improve his expression the following day.

---

30   Andrew Carr, 'Strategy as Problem-Solving', *Parameters* 54, no. 1 (2024): 123–37, doi.org/10.55540/0031-1723.3276.
31   Sargeant, *Challenges to the Australian Strategic Imagination*, 3.
32   ibid., 11.
33   Toby Davidson, *Good for the Soul: John Curtin's Life with Poetry* (Perth: UWA Publishing, 2021), 2.
34   ibid., 236, 377.

'Relying as I always did on the moment for the choice of language, it wasn't a bad thing to have a little bit of poetry in one's subliminal consciousness,' Menzies observed.[35]

Conclusion

In his book *The Tragic Mind*, journalist Robert Kagan observes: 'Forty years as a foreign correspondent have taught me that while an understanding of world events begins with maps, it ends with Shakespeare.'[36] To think strategically, we cannot limit ourselves to a knowledge of the facts of the world. They no more tell us how to organise them than they give us instruction on what we might do about them. Instead, good strategic thought is an endless process of trying to incorporate what we can verify and know with our ways of knowing and our experience of the world.

This can occur through the process of writing—a supposedly simple act of transcribing thought that we now can recognise as a form of thought itself. The distance between author and audience and between mind, pen and paper allows for a richness of consciousness and creativity that is distinct from other forms of communication.

So, too, strategists can benefit through the pursuit of experience via fiction. It is not a replacement for living and acting but reading can offer experiences and encounters that no normal life could provide. This helps us to see the world as others do and understand the nature of their world view, even if we still reject another's logic or morality.

And, ultimately, strategic thought relies on a sense of imagination. Not as unbounded daydreaming, but as a conscious part of how we seek to accumulate, organise and act on the facts as we encounter them. These are skills that have atrophied and are often decried in the West, yet they are, as modern science and ancient wisdom clearly tell us, essential to the highest arenas of human leadership. To think strategically begins with the capacity to imagine, to experience, to write. Only with words can we move worlds.

---

35   Quoted in Troy Bramston, *Robert Menzies: The Art of Politics* (Melbourne: Scribe, 2019), 177.
36   Robert D. Kaplan, *The Tragic Mind: Fear, Fate and the Burden of Power* (New Haven: Yale University Press, 2023), 1, doi.org/10.12987/9780300268737.

Part 2.
The practice
of strategic
imagination

9
Strategic imagination: Practice

One of the last books that Brendan and I discussed was Richard Rorty's *Philosophy as Poetry*. I had pressed my copy on to him, in part as a bridge between our two instinctive literatures: his, the poetic; mine, the philosophical. He was sceptical of the genre, but appreciated Rorty's insistence that imagination was essential for rationality. Rorty, as part of the great pragmatist tradition in American philosophy, offers a way of assessing ideas that is ripe for interrogating 'strategic imagination'. Instead of seeking concepts that try to directly 'mirror' reality (a doomed and artificial quest), Rorty urged that '[w]hat we call "increased knowledge" should not be thought of as increased access to the Real but as increased ability to do things—to take part in social practices that make possible richer and fuller human lives'.[1]

That is, as William James, a forerunner in the pragmatist school, put it: 'Grant an idea or belief to be true … [W]hat concrete difference will its being true make in anyone's actual life?'[2] Ideas are valuable in the same way machine tools are valuable. If they can make a practical difference for today's problems, we should adopt them. When they no longer serve that need, we should feel free to put them down. Strategic imagination must therefore demonstrate its assistance in helping us lead 'richer and fuller human lives' if it is to represent an increase to our knowledge and a sustainable intellectual tool for scholars and policymakers alike.

---

1   Richard Rorty, *Philosophy as Poetry* (Charlottesville: University of Virginia Press, 2019), 43.
2   William James, *Pragmatism and Other Writings* (London: Penguin Books, 2000), 88.

In this section, we apply that philosophical blowtorch to the concept of strategic imagination. Does it help policymakers and analysts to better understand and act within the world? What changes if we adopt this concept? Either through offering new ways of viewing the world or by helping us to act in distinct ways through its conceptual framework, how does it really matter?

In a beautifully written contribution in Chapter 10, Professor Roland Bleiker reflects on his time stationed on the border of South and North Korea and illustrates 'how aesthetic approaches to security can offer a form of strategic imagination' that is both practical and scholarly. It is so easy to see the seven-decade-long conflict on the Korean Peninsula through tired eyes, but Professor Bleiker helps show us just how easily we look but do not see. Adopting a different method, however—one very much in line with a strategic imagination mindset—we can gain fresh insights into structures of power and dynamics of conflict.

In Chapter 11, Tom Barber and Melissa Conley Tyler argue that Australia is in a moment particularly ripe for strategic imagination and discuss ways to improve imagination by bringing diverse voices together to overcome the traditional silos of policymaking. They highlight the work Brendan did through his official and informal help to support new ways of understanding Australia's place in the world and forms of policymaking. Complementing their assessment, Professor Rory Medcalf in Chapter 12 discusses the widely embraced concept of the 'Indo-Pacific' as a case study of strategic imagination in practice—a concept that both Sargeant and Medcalf played crucial roles in helping to establish and encouraging its now-global adoption.

Professor Stephan Frühling in Chapter 13 applies strategic imagination to the world Brendan knew best: Australian defence policy. He considers how one of the safest countries in the world must live partially in the world of imagination and potential threats if it is to create intellectual coherence within its policy choices. Finally, in Chapter 14, Robbin Laird, a leading global military expert, provides a northern hemisphere example, tracking how Nordic countries are reimagining their defence situation and approach given the war in Ukraine and aggression from Russia. By emphasising the direct words and actions of contemporary military officials and strategists, Laird highlights the challenge today's leaders face when trying to apply strategic imagination as a practical tool of statecraft. In strained moments such as these, the pragmatist's insistence that we should seek and value knowledge that makes a concrete difference is ever more powerful and compelling a credo.

10

Imagination and the Korean crisis

Roland Bleiker

When developing the concept of the 'strategic imagination', Brendan Sargeant had in mind the challenge of dealing with seemingly intractable conflicts.[1] Perhaps more importantly, he had in mind challenging strategic policy approaches that are so dominant and so entrenched that they are no longer able to offer innovative ways of understanding and dealing with these intractable conflicts. Or at least this is how I interpret Sargeant's call for a theory of the imagination: as a scholarly and practical call for innovative solutions in strategic thinking and defence policy.

This chapter illustrates how aesthetic approaches to security can offer such a form of strategic imagination. At first sight, this seems far fetched. Aesthetic approaches tend to be associated with art and literature and the kind of 'soft' humanities inquiries that are worlds away from the real and 'hard' world of security and defence policy. Not so, I argue. Aesthetics can be defined in a much broader manner in a way that is inherently political. It refers not only to practices of art—from painting to music, poetry, photography and film—but also, and above all, to the type of insights and understandings they inspire and engender. Aesthetics in this sense is about the ability to step

1   This research was supported by the Core University Program for Korean Studies of the Ministry of Education of the Republic of Korea and the Korean Studies Promotion Service at the Academy of Korean Studies (AKS-2021-OLU-2250002). I am grateful to Dhruba Adkhikari for valuable research assistance. I am also grateful to Andrew Carr and an anonymous referee for insightful feedback that helped me revise the chapter.

back, reflect and see strategic dilemmas and policies in a new way. It is about cultivating an open-ended level of sensibility about the political.[2] Once we do this, we might be able to recognise and address issues and problems that we otherwise cannot even see, such as security threats that have not been part of traditional defence thinking. This includes—to mention an obvious and well-recognised example—the strategic challenges that Australia and other nations face in relation to climate change.[3]

I demonstrate that aesthetic approaches can generate the type of imagination that Sargeant had in mind. I do so with a sceptical social science reader or defence policy expert in mind. Such a reader would normally expect that research should be evaluated based on the empirical validity of the results that are generated. Instead, I show that research that draws on the 'strategic imagination' can be evaluated in alternative ways. Rather than relying on predetermined social science criteria, the usefulness of scholarly insights can also be evaluated based on how they help us see old security problems in a new light. Making this claim is not necessarily controversial. Scholars have long argued that alternative knowledge practices, such as those linked to aesthetic insights, 'cannot always be verified by methodological means proper to science'.[4]

I empirically illustrate the usefulness of the strategic imagination by showing how visual autoethnography can reveal new and potentially useful insights into one of the most protracted conflicts in the world today: the one that has dominated the Korean Peninsula for more than half a century.

---

2   For definitions of aesthetics and discussions of its implications for politics and security policy, see, for instance, Franklin R. Ankersmit, *Aesthetic Politics: Political Philosophy beyond Fact and Value* (Stanford: Stanford University Press, 1996); Roland Bleiker, *Aesthetics and World Politics* (Basingstoke: Palgrave Macmillan, 2009), doi.org/10.1057/9780230244375; Roland Bleiker, 'Seeing beyond Disciplines: Aesthetic Creativity in International Theory', *Australian Journal of International Affairs* 75, no. 5 (2021): 573–90, doi.org/10.1080/10357718.2021.1992129; Aida A. Hozić, 'Introduction: The Aesthetic Turn at 15', *Millennium: Journal of International Studies* 45, no. 2 (2017): 201–5, doi.org/10.1177/0305829816684253.

3   Brendan Sargeant, *The Implications of Climate Change for Australian Strategic and Defence Policy in Relation to the Alliance and Pacific Island States*, Regional Outlook Paper No. 68 (Brisbane: Griffith Asia Institute, Griffith University, 2021), 1–17, www.griffith.edu.au/__data/assets/pdf_file/0027/1407447/RO68-Sargeant-web.pdf.

4   Hans-Georg Gadamer, *Truth and Method*, 2nd edn (London: Sheed & Ward, 1979), xxii–xxiii.

Autoethnography is an approach that breaks with convention by drawing on an author's own experiences to reimagine the world. Visual autoethnography uses photographs to do so. It is part of a long scholarly tradition that highlights the importance of visuality to how politics, including strategic issues, is seen, understood, conceptualised and implemented.[5]

I draw on my experiences working in the Korean Demilitarized Zone (DMZ), where I was stationed as a Swiss Army officer between 1986 and 1988. I employ my own photographs to examine how an appreciation of everyday aesthetic sensibilities can open new ways of thinking about security dilemmas. In so doing, I draw and expand on research I have conducted on this topic over the past couple of decades.[6]

The key argument I advance is that visual autoethnography as a form of strategic imagination can be insightful not because it offers better or even authentic views—it cannot—but because it has the potential to reveal how prevailing political discourses and practices are so entrenched that we no longer see their partial, political and often problematic nature. First, I show how a self-reflective engagement with my own photographs of the DMZ reveals the deeply entrenched role of militarised masculinities that transgress the border and shape security policies on both sides. When I first took my photographs three decades ago, I noticed everything about the DMZ except its strikingly gendered nature. As a military officer, and having grown up in a patriarchal society, I simply took for granted and accepted the militarised and gendered value system that surrounded me. This was the case in Switzerland but also when I arrived in the Korean DMZ. A self-critical look at my own positionality and my changing relationship to my own photographs over a period of three decades reveals how deeply entrenched militarised approaches to Korean security are and how much they are implicated in the conflict itself. Employing the strategic imagination would entail identifying the problematic aspects of these security patterns and looking for innovative solutions beyond them.

---

5   I have elaborated in detail on the definitions and relevance of autoethnography and visuality in previous works, including Morgan Brigg and Roland Bleiker, 'Autoethnographic International Relations: Exploring the Self as a Source of Knowledge', *Review of International Studies* 36, no. 3 (2010): 779–98, doi.org/10.1017/S0260210510000689; Roland Bleiker, ed., *Visual Global Politics* (London: Routledge, 2018), doi.org/10.4324/9781315856506.

6   Roland Bleiker, 'A Rogue Is a Rogue Is a Rogue: US Foreign Policy and the Korean Nuclear Crisis', *International Affairs* 79, no. 4 (2003): 719–37, doi.org/10.1111/1468-2346.00333; Roland Bleiker, *Divided Korea: Toward a Culture of Reconciliation* (Minneapolis: University of Minnesota Press, 2005); Roland Bleiker, 'Visual Autoethnography and International Security: Insights from the Korean DMZ', *European Journal of International Security* 4, no. 3 (2019): 274–99, doi.org/10.1017/eis.2019.14.

Second, I reflect on my photographs of everyday life in North Korea. I show how and why it is impossible to see the Korean conflict in neutral ways. Drawing on my positionality and photographs, I then reveal a reality that is different from prevailing strategic and public discourses, which depict North Korea as a grim and authoritarian state, solely responsible for the recurring nuclear crises that destabilise the region. I do not deny the massive human rights abuses that take place in the North or trivialise Pyongyang's nuclear program, but my photographs, subjective as they are, show that life in North Korea is far more complex and diverse. They also show that demonising North Korea as an irrational rogue state hinders our opportunity to understand why Pyongyang acts the way it does. Here, the strategic imagination would seek to comprehend what the world looks like from North Korea in an attempt to develop more effective security policies and diplomatic initiatives.

The need to rethink the protracted conflict on the Korean Peninsula

It is hard to find a protracted conflict that is more in need of strategic imagination than the one on the Korean Peninsula. Defence policies in and towards the two Koreas call precisely for what Sargeant advocated repeatedly: a 'larger conception of strategy, a richer discourse and a more searching questioning' that can help develop innovative polices and defence strategies.[7]

More than 70 years after the Korean War, the peninsula remains caught in an anachronistic Cold War stalemate. The spectre of war is never far away. At regular intervals there are major crises—often triggered by North Korea's nuclear ambition—that bring the region and the world to the brink of catastrophe. Not long ago, then US president Donald Trump publicly vowed to 'totally destroy' North Korea, before suddenly reversing course and adopting a more conciliatory stance.[8] Such crisis–détente cycles have taken place many times before without substantial changes to the dangerous security dilemmas that drive them.

---

7   Brendan Sargeant, 'Challenges to the Australian Strategic Imagination', *Australian Journal of Defence and Strategic Studies* 4, no. 1 (2022), 8.

8   Donald Trump, 'Remarks by President Trump to the 72nd Session of the United Nations General Assembly', New York, 19 September 2017, trumpwhitehouse.archives.gov/briefings-statements/remarks-president-trump-72nd-session-united-nations-general-assembly/.

Prevailing strategic approaches to security on the Korean Peninsula—by South Korea, the United States and other major powers—have had no success in solving the recurring nuclear crises or forcing regime change in the reclusive and autocratic North. Based primarily on military threats and economic sanctions, these strategic approaches often reinforced North Korea's nuclear ambition and further strengthened the authoritarian regime.

Today, the situation is as tense and as dangerous as ever. Recent scholarly literature on North Korea suggests that the peninsula will likely remain a highly volatile region that poses significant security risks. Sue Mi Terry, for instance, highlights that North Korea possesses the capability to launch nuclear attacks on US territory.[9] She and other analysts believe that North Korea is unlikely to give up its nuclear arsenal as this is the very base of the regime's survival. Nuclear weapons are for North Korea a 'military asset, an insurance policy, and a vast source of prestige all in one'.[10]

Many other scholars agree with this pessimistic outlook that identifies North Korea's nuclear ambition as the source of continuing tension. Jung H. Pak thinks North Korea's leader, Kim Jong-un, does not want a normal international security environment.[11] Instead, the hostile international environment serves his purposes well as it allows him to blame the United States and its allies for the country's economic hardship. His regime 'requires a hostile outside world to justify its diversion of scarce resources into military programs' to legitimise the mythical image of the Kim dynasty as the saviour of the North Korean nation.[12] This is why Pak advises the United States and its allies to aim for nothing less than the complete nuclear disarmament of North Korea. He stresses that 'the United States and its regional allies must undertake coordinated and consistent actions to convince [Kim Jong-un] that nuclear weapons make his survival less, rather than more, secure'.[13] But complete disarmament is unlikely to take place, in the opinion of many

---

9   Sue Mi Terry, 'North Korea's Nuclear Family', *Foreign Affairs*, September–October 2021: 115–20; see also Jaganath Sankaran and Steve Fetter, 'Defending the United States: Revisiting National Missile Defense against North Korea', *International Security* 46, no. 3 (2022): 51–86, doi.org/10.1162/isec_a_00426.

10   Terry, 'North Korea's Nuclear Family', 117.

11   Jung H. Pak, 'What Kim Wants', *Foreign Affairs*, May–June 2020: 96–100.

12   ibid., 100.

13   ibid., 104. See also Kelsey Davenport, 'Orchestrating US Engagement with North Korea', *Survival* 64, no. 2 (2022): 125–40, doi.org/10.1080/00396338.2022.2055831; Ian Campbell and Michaela Dodge, 'Deterring North Korea', *Survival* 62, no. 1 (2020): 55–59, doi.org/10.1080/00396338.2020.17 15065; Victor Cha and Katrin Fraser Katz, 'The Right Way to Coerce North Korea: Ending the Threat without Going to War', *Foreign Affairs* 97, no. 3 (2018): 87–100.

leading defence analysts. Toby Dalton and Jina Kim argue that the only way North Korea can be disarmed is through military action, but that is no longer a viable option.[14] Andrei Lankov, likewise, explains why North Korea's elite needs nuclear weapons and, as a result, is reluctant to embrace even Chinese-style reform.[15] North Korea's elite, Lankov stresses, will never voluntarily denuclearise because nuclear weapons are what allow them to keep at bay a hostile United States and its allies. The nuclear weapons are, in this way, a guarantee of the survival of both the current regime and its political elite.[16]

Introducing visual autoethnography as a method to review and rethink security

The protracted conflict on the Korean Peninsula is precisely one of those situations that beg the questions Sargeant[17] asked: How is it possible that so little has changed over so many years? Why have prevailing approaches to strategy and security not been able to find—and enforce—a lasting solution to the conflict? I now seek to show that strategic imagination can offer innovative ways of understanding and potentially approaching the security situation on the Korean Peninsula. Using what could be called 'visual autoethnography', I try to rethink Korean security dilemmas by reflecting on my own experience and drawing on photographs I took while in the Korean DMZ and travelling back and forth between South and North Korea.

14   Toby Dalton and Jina Kim, 'Rethinking Arms Control with a Nuclear North Korea', *Survival* 65, no. 1 (2023): 21–48, doi.org/10.1080/00396338.2023.2172847.

15   Andrei Lankov, 'The Perspective from Pyongyang: Limits of Compromise', *Survival* 63, no. 6 (2021): 107–18, doi.org/10.1080/00396338.2021.2006447.

16   ibid., 111; Edward Howell, 'The *Juche* H-Bomb? North Korea, Nuclear Weapons and Regime–State Survival', *International Affairs* 96, no. 4 (2020): 1051–68, doi.org/10.1093/ia/iiz253; Andrei Lankov, 'The Survival Strategies of the North Korean Elite', *Russian Politics & Law* 58, nos 3–4 (2021): 173–92, doi.org/10.1080/10611940.2022.2111940.

17   Chapter 2, this volume.

Plate 10.1 The author with North Korean officers, Panmungak, Joint Security Area, Panmunjom, 1986–88

Photo: Roland Bleiker.

Plate 10.2 The author with South Korean officers, Seoul, 1986–88
Photo: Roland Bleiker.

Between 1986 and 1988 I worked as a young Swiss Army officer in the Korean DMZ. I was chief of office of the Swiss delegation to the Neutral Nations Supervisory Commission (NNSC), which was established with the Armistice Agreement in July 1953 and was meant to supervise two clauses in the agreement that prohibited the introduction of new military personnel and weapons. The commission's neutrality was based on each side choosing two nations that did not actively participate in the war. The North opted for what was then Czechoslovakia and Poland. Switzerland and Sweden were selected by the South, formally represented by the United Nations Command. With the intensification of the Cold War, the idea of retaining current levels of military personnel and equipment became a farce. With its official purpose gone, the NNSC radically shrunk. By the time I arrived in 1986, the Swiss delegation consisted of only six people and its real purpose was informal: to establish links across the DMZ at a time when there were few meaningful interactions between North and South.

Being able to cross the otherwise hermetically sealed DMZ and travel back and forth between North and South was a rare privilege. At the time, the NNSC members were among the very few able to do so. Even today, the DMZ remains tightly sealed, so much so that crossing to the other side is still, as Suk-Young Kim points out, 'a high-stakes performative act'.[18]

Equally unique is the location of the commission where I worked and lived: the so-called Joint Security Area (JSA) in the border village of Panmunjom. It is where the armistice was negotiated and is the only place in the DMZ where the North Korean and South Korean soldiers face each other daily. The dividing line cuts right through a series of buildings, where the occasional meeting is held. Observation posts on either side are permanently guarded to try to carefully survey every move by the other side. The DMZ, however, is not a location or even a straight line. It is a 4-kilometre-wide and 250-kilometre-long buffer zone: a complex 'interface' where political, ideological, economic, geopolitical and military interests overlap and clash in ways that are both intranational and international.[19]

The DMZ is also a symbolic marker of the conflict and, as such, both represents and influences political dynamics. Press coverage of the conflict is often accompanied by photographs or films of the DMZ. But very few people have seen and experienced the DMZ, for it is largely off-limits to civilians on both sides. There are tourist trips to the DMZ, but they are limited, tightly controlled and carefully staged. As a result, and as Suk-Young Kim points out, 'most Koreans encounter the DMZ not as an actual physical space, but through mediated images: photographs, films and videos'.[20]

---

18 Suk-Young Kim, 'Staging the "Cartography of Paradox": The DMZ Special Exhibition at the Korean War Memorial, Seoul', *Theatre Journal* 63, no. 3 (2011): 381–402, at 383, doi.org/10.1353/tj.2011.0083.
19 Valérie Gelézeau, Koen De Ceuster, and Alain Delissen, eds, *De-Bordering Korea: Tangible and Intangible Legacies of the Sunshine Policy* (London: Routledge, 2013), 7–8, doi.org/10.4324/9780203084571.
20 Kim, 'Staging the "Cartography of Paradox"', 386.

Plate 10.3 South Korean soldier facing the military demarcation line, 1986–88

Photo: Roland Bleiker.

Plate 10.4 Military demarcation line inside the DMZ, 1986–88

Photo: Roland Bleiker.

I now use my photographs from life inside the DMZ, and from regular visits to North Korea, to attempt to offer different perspectives of the peninsula's security issues. I would like to stress upfront that I am in no way suggesting that my photographs offer unique insights or perspectives that are more authentic than those we see from prevailing press coverage. Rather, I use my photographs as tools to re-view, re-evaluate and reimagine the world. If they are representative, it is only of my positionality and of how self-reflective ruminations about this positionality can reveal existing political discourses and the power relationships they embody. In this sense, my photographs illustrate the situatedness of knowledge and, in so doing, are illustrations that stand in a conversation with the text that surrounds them. Visual autoethnography is, in short, an ongoing reflective process that uses positionality to reveal the often arbitrary but largely concealed construction of political discourses and practices.

The Korean strategic imagination I: Exposing militarised masculinities through visual self-reflection

The first autoethnographic insight I would like to highlight has to do with the militarised nature of the so-called demilitarised zone. The border between North and South Korea is often characterised as 'the most fortified area in the world'.[21] The ensuing security dilemmas are so deeply entrenched that any lasting solution cannot be found through prevailing strategic policies since they have constituted and are an inevitable part of the existing dangerous stalemate. An innovative way forward requires what Sargeant advocated in numerous policy settings: a 'reimagining of the role of strategic and defence policy'.[22]

---

21 Rachel Lee, 'UNC Allows Heavy Weapons in DMZ', *Korea Times*, 7 October 2016, www.korea times.co.kr/www/news/nation/2016/07/205_209010.html.
22 Sargeant, *The Implications of Climate Change*, 14.

Plates 10.5 and 10.6 'Northern' and 'Southern' soldiers in the JSA, Panmunjom, 1986–88

Photos: Roland Bleiker.

Militarism cuts right across the hermetically sealed dividing line. Consider, as a visual example, the Joint Security Area where the border runs through shared buildings and where North and South Korean troops face each other eye to eye. Military marching formations and salutes take on an explicitly performative dimension here as they are staged primarily for the other side to see. Look at Plates 10.5 and 10.6: insiders to the conflict can right away see a clash between two antagonistic and completely different worlds, epitomised by North and South, here represented by the US-led UN Command. But from a distance one can see more similarities than differences between these political enemies. All are soldiers marching in uniform and performing the same militarised ritual.

One key point struck me when I went through my hundreds of photographs of the DMZ: the almost complete absence of women. As a feminist scholar, I look at my photographs from back then and am stunned. There are only men in my photographs. There are South Korean men, North Korean men, Chinese men. There are Czech, Polish, Swedish and Swiss men. There are American men.

I had a hard time finding any photographs that feature women. One of the few I found was from a UN Command Military Armistice Commission meeting. Discontinued in the early 1990s, these meetings took place inside the barracks of the JSA, where the two sides met across the table from each other. The meetings rarely amounted to more than an exchange of prepared statements in which each side accused the other of violating the armistice. The meetings, too, were part of a militaristic performance and, as a result, were staged to a limited number of military personnel, press and other observers.

Plate 10.7 shows military personnel looking in on the 'negotiations', with US (UN Command) soldiers in the foreground and North Koreans in the background. The photograph sticks out because it is one of the very few featuring a woman. She is looking not at the meeting room but across the border to the northern side. I wonder what she thought while surveying this all-male world.

Plate 10.7 Meeting of the Military Armistice Commission, JSA, Panmunjom, 1986–88

Photo: Roland Bleiker.

On some level my observations are not surprising. Of course, one would expect soldiers in a militarised zone and, of course, one would expect that most, if not all, are men. The surprising observation, and the significance of visual autoethnography, has to do with my own experience and my changing relationship to the photographs I took more than three decades ago.

When I first arrived in the DMZ in 1986, I noticed everything except the absence of women and the gendered nature of the place. When settling into the JSA and crossing back and forth between South and North, I was struck by many of the things I saw: the stark political differences, the ideological hatred, the cultural diversity, but not the most obvious feature—the absence of women. I took this for granted. All my colleagues in the NNSC were men. All the soldiers and officers with whom I interacted were men, no matter on which side of the dividing line they were. It seemed normal to me, in part because I was in a military setting, in part because I grew up in a very patriarchal society, Switzerland, where women were granted the vote only when I was 11 years old, with some cantons holding out until well into my adulthood. I was conditioned by the environment in which I grew up. I was drafted into the army at 18 and, in an all-male environment, was trained how to march, salute, fire a gun, throw a hand-grenade and drive a tank. I was taught how to execute and obey orders, but not how to think critically, and particularly not about gender issues. Militarised values had been normalised and I accepted them as common sense without questioning—or even being aware of—the political values they entailed.

I now look back in bewilderment at my inability to see the obvious: the highly gendered nature of politics in the DMZ. This is precisely where the links between power and militarisation are at their most effective: in the construction of common sense, in societal discourse that defines what is accepted as normal and not, even if this construction is based on highly partial, exploitative and problematic foundations.[23]

This is also where visual autoethnography can provide political insights: in self-reflective accounts of our own experiences, including how our own views change in relation to visual representations of these experiences. It is, indeed, the confrontation with visual evidence that made me realise most acutely how my own positionality reflected political dynamics that were so naturalised for me—and I presume for many men around me—that I did not even recognise them. The fact that three decades had passed since I took the photographs adds to, rather than subtracts from, the potential of visual autoethnography. It is, in fact, the elapsed time that provides the opportunity of insight, for it is the changing relationship between me and my photographs that reveals the power of discourse to construct and mask power relations.

Plate 10.8 Flying in a US Army helicopter
Photos: Roland Bleiker.

23   Linda Åhäll, 'The Dance of Militarisation: A Feminist Security Studies Take on "the Political"', *Critical Studies on Security* 4, no. 2 (2016): 154–68, at 155, doi.org/10.1080/21624887.2016.1153933.

Plate 10.9 From inside a US Army helicopter, south of the DMZ
Photos: Roland Bleiker.

My experiences and my relationship with my own photographs show how and why the political consequences of the gendered and militarised nature of the DMZ go far beyond the immediate and obvious: men in uniforms, surveillance installations, barbed wire. Militarised masculinities are part of broader societal values. They shape collective attitudes and policy formation.[24] In the two Koreas, they reach far beyond the DMZ. They can be seen, for instance, in clusters of prostitution that pop up around US military bases in the South or in how military personnel interact in a more general way with the civilian population on both sides.[25] My entire experience in Korea was gendered, revealing what feminist scholars such as Linda Åhäll, Laura Shepherd and Annick Wibben have pointed out for so long: the need to theorise how militarised masculinities permeate all aspects of society, from the every day to foreign policy. They are located and gain key political significance in the clothes we wear, the films we watch, the national anthems we rehearse and the security policies we deem urgent and compelling.[26] It is in this way that militaristic values become, as Sargeant pointed out, about far more than defence policy: they are at the core of how national identity is constructed.[27]

Militaristic ways of thinking become elevated as the primary and seemingly most reasonable and compelling manner to address security issues. The result is that certain individuals and the values they espouse are given

24   Cynthia H. Enloe, *Maneuvers: The International Politics of Militarizing Women's Lives* (Berkeley: University of California Press, 2000), 1–34, 289, doi.org/10.1525/9780520923744.

25   See, for instance, Katharine H.S. Moon, *Sex among Allies: Military Prostitution in US–Korea Relations* (New York: Columbia University Press, 1997); Grace M. Cho, *Haunting the Korean Diaspora: Shame, Secrecy, and the Forgotten War* (Minneapolis: University of Minnesota Press, 2008). For North Korean context, see Sandra Fahy, *Marching through Suffering: Loss and Survival in North Korea* (New York: Columbia University Press, 2015), doi.org/10.7312/columbia/9780231171342.001.0001.

26   Åhäll, 'The Dance of Militarisation', 165; Laura J. Shepherd, 'Militarisation', in *Visual Global Politics*, edited by B. Roland (London: Routledge, 2018), 209–14, doi.org/10.4324/9781315856506-31; Annick T.R. Wibben, 'Why We Need to Study (US) Militarism: A Critical Feminist Lens', *Security Dialogue* 49, nos 1–2 (2018): 136–48, doi.org/10.1177/0967010617742006; Anna Stavrianakis, Jan Selby, and Iraklis Oikonomou, *Militarism and International Relations* (London: Routledge, 2012), 1–18, doi.org/10.4324/9780203101476; Anna Stavrianakis and Maria Stern, 'Militarism and Security: Dialogue, Possibilities and Limits', *Security Dialogue* 49, nos 1–2 (2018): 3–18, at 4, doi.org/10.1177/0967010617748528; Bryan Mabee and Srdjan Vucetic, 'Varieties of Militarism: Towards a Typology', *Security Dialogue* 49, nos 1–2 (2018): 96–108, at 97, 99–103, doi.org/10.1177/0967010617730948.

27   Sargeant, Chapter 2, this volume. For the classical text on this topic, see David Campbell, *Writing Security: United States Foreign Policy and the Politics of Identity* (Minneapolis: University of Minnesota Press, 1992).

greater authority to comment on—and make decisions about—questions of national security. This hinders both adequate scholarly understanding and the search for innovative policy solutions.[28]

The power to elevate militarism as the most logical and compelling way to understand and solve security issues is particularly pronounced in the Koreas. Both sides analyse the conflict in strikingly similar militaristic terms, even though they assign blame in opposing ways. Militaristic values also permeate the search for solutions, to the point where it is difficult to break out of a cycle of violence in which threats and counterthreats produce ever more dangerous standoffs. Solutions to the conflict that are not based on a tough defence posture tend to be dismissed as well intentioned and naive at best, and ethically problematic and dangerous at worst.[29] This is why challenging the prevailing militarised approach to strategy is difficult and rare. One of the exceptions is the women's movement in South Korea, which critiques entrenched practices of militarism both within South Korea and in its relationship with the United States.[30] But these and other dissident movements function at the margins of society and have not yet had a substantial influence on military policy and diplomatic negotiations.

The strategic imagination II: Seeing beyond prevailing security narratives

The second illustration of the power of visual autoethnography revolves around photographs I have taken during my many visits to North Korea. I would like to flag again, and upfront, that I am in no way trying to claim that these photographs offer authentic insights into a 'true' North

---

28   Aaron Belkin, *Bring Me Men: Military Masculinity and the Benign Facade of American Empire, 1898–2001* (New York: Columbia University Press, 2012), 4; Åhäll, 'The Dance of Militarisation', 160; see also Linda Ahäll and Laura J. Shepherd, *Gender, Agency and Political Violence* (London: Palgrave Macmillan, 2012), 155.

29   For a highly compelling and classical account of how militarised approaches to security frame politics in particular ways, see Carol Cohn, 'Sex and Death in the Rational World of Defense Intellectuals', *Signs* 12, no. 4 (1987): 687–718, doi.org/10.1086/494362. See also Belkin, *Bring Me Men*, 4–5.

30   Young-Ju Hoang and Noël O'Sullivan, 'Gendered Militarisation as State of Exception on the Korean Peninsula', *Third World Thematics: A TWQ Journal* 3, no. 2 (2018): 164–78, doi.org/10.1080/23802014.2018.1471359; Belkin, *Bring Me Men*, 47–76; Ihntaek Hwang, 'Militarising National Security through Criminalisation of Conscientious Objectors to Conscription in South Korea', *Critical Studies on Security* 6, no. 3 (2018): 296–311, doi.org/10.1080/21624887.2018.1424986.

Korea. Rather, they seek to highlight what Sargeant stressed: that 'any representation is partial' and the work of the imagination is precisely to expose and challenge this partiality.[31]

Plate 10.10 Man next to Kim Il-sung statue, Kaesong, North Korea, 1986–88

Photo: Roland Bleiker.

31   Sargeant, Chapter 2, this volume.

Plate 10.11 Hotel in Pyongyang, 1986–88
Photo: Roland Bleiker.

At first sight, the photos I have taken of North Korea very much reflect the dominant Western narrative of the country. There are lots of photographs of gargantuan statues and towers. Then there was the personality cult around the country's first leader, Kim Il-sung, which permeated all aspects of life, visually and verbally. Most rooms had a portrait of Kim and everything revolved around him.

Other photographs show extreme hardship: roads being built quite literally by hand by thousands of workers; assault tanks were the only machinery available to flatten the road. Big banners and loudspeakers would fire up the workers, who laboured away, often in extreme, sub-zero temperatures. This personal photographic evidence is, of course, amplified by what we know happens behind what is visible: the exceptionally ruthless treatment of anyone dissenting with the regime; the horrifying 'gulags' that are documented by accounts from defectors.[32]

32   Examples here include Barbara Demick, *Nothing to Envy: Real Lives in North Korea* (New York: Spiegel & Grau, 2009); Daniel Tudor, *Ask a North Korean: Defectors Talk about Their Lives Inside the World's Most Secretive Nation* (North Clarendon: Tuttle Publishing, 2018); Chol-hwan Kang and Pierre Rigoulot, *The Aquariums of Pyongyang: Ten Years in the North Korean Gulag* (New York: Basic Books, 2005); Jang Jin-sung, *Dear Leader* (New York: Simon & Schuster, 2015); Blaine Harden, *Escape from Camp 14: One Man's Remarkable Odyssey from North Korea to Freedom in the West* (New York: Penguin Books, 2013); Yeonmi Park, *In Order to Live* (New York: Penguin Books, 2015).

Plate 10.12 Woman collecting herbs in Pyongyang, 1986–88
Photo: Roland Bleiker.

Plate 10.13 Urban scene in Pyongyang, 1986–88
Photo: Roland Bleiker.

What we see here is one of the most authoritarian societies on Earth, a dysfunctional and irrational regime that revolves around a personality cult and an anachronistic communist ideology of self-reliance known as *Juche*. Massive human rights violations are part of this view, as is shocking economic mismanagement. North Korea here is the exception in a region that, over the past decades, has steadily reduced instances of mass atrocities and moved towards democracy and economic development.

This prevailing vision is perfectly captured by one of the most influential photographic essays of North Korea, entitled 'The Land of No Smiles'. Published by *Foreign Policy*, it features the work of Tomas van Houtryve.[33] David Shim puts this photographic essay in the context of broader visualisations of North Korea and highlights a prominent theme: the depiction of a country inhabited 'solely by distress, depression and desperation', a place without 'happy and cheerful people'.[34]

While confirming prevailing perceptions of North Korea, my visual autoethnography also challenges this dominant narrative. When I look at my photographs, I see far more than a grey and grim land of no smiles. Yes, there was poverty and oppression and despair. There are also a lot of smiles in my photographs: people going about their everyday life, including with seeming joy. Some of these smiles were staged, but many were not.

My photographs of North Korea, subjective as they are, reveal how the prevailing visual narratives of the North—which see it only as a grim and grey land of no smiles—are partial and biased. I do not claim that my photographs offer a more authentic take on North Korea. They do not. They inevitably reflect my experience and my aesthetic choices as a photographer. But my photographs, and the positionality they embody, nevertheless reveal something that is of political significance: both prevailing discourses about North Korea are selective and they are highly political in their selectivity. These discourses reflect the political positions they embody and, in so doing, say as much about the values of the viewers as they do about what is visualised: life in North Korea.

33   Tomas van Houtryve, 'The Land of No Smiles', *Foreign Policy* 172 (2009): 106–13.
34   David Shim, *Visual Politics and North Korea: Seeing Is Believing* (London: Routledge, 2013), 65, doi. org/10.4324/9780203746479; see also Shine Choi, *Re-Imagining North Korea in International Politics: Problems and Alternatives* (London: Routledge, 2015), 96–134, doi.org/10.4324/9781315761541.

Plate 10.14 'The Land of No Smiles I', Man'gyŏngdae, North Korea, 1986–88

Photo: Roland Bleiker.

Plate 10.15 'The Land of No-Smiles II', 1986–88

Photo: Roland Bleiker.

Significant consequences follow from recognising that prevailing visualisations of North Korea are partial. Images frame the world and, in so doing, circumvent not only what is being seen, but also how we—as a collective—perceive an issue and view it politically. Visuals construct common sense: they provide us with a view of the world that eventually becomes so accepted and self-evident that its arbitrary origins are no longer recognised.

The image of North Korea as a rogue state is so entrenched that we cannot see anything else: 'a rogue is a rogue is a rogue', as I put it a while ago. North Korea is, in short, the ultimate 'other': the communist and authoritarian state that defies the sociopolitical logic of the international liberal order, which stands still even after the collapse of the Soviet Union and even after other communist states such as China and Vietnam introduced major economic and political changes. Consider the main slogan rehearsed by US or South Korean troops in the DMZ: the notion that 'we' are 'forever in front of them all', defending freedom against the threat of evil communism north of the dividing line.

Plate 10.16 'Forever in front of them all', Camp Bonifas, UN Command, DMZ, 1986–88

Photo: Roland Bleiker.

This political and visual depiction of North Korea stubbornly persists, even in the face of contrary evidence. And such evidence abounds. These studies document, for instance, that everyday life in North Korea is far more complex than commonly assumed.[35] There are also studies that show how North Korea has acted largely in a rational and predictable manner. It might be an authoritarian relic of the past, but the mere fact that the country has survived against all the odds—a small and poor country surrounded by a hostile world—is testimony of how successful its leaders have been in manipulating larger players in international politics.[36] Despite this evidence, the prevailing stereotype of North Korea largely persists: that of an irrational, unpredictable and mad country. Mainstream press coverage commonly presents North Korea's leader, Kim Jong-un, as 'an unpredictable, unknown quantity capable of lashing out at other countries without reason'.[37]

Understanding Pyongyang's policy decisions as rational is not to deny that nuclear proliferation is a great danger and a major security problem in the region. Nor is it to justify the country's human rights violations. But appreciating alternative vantage points can help to both understand and predict North Korean behaviour. It might also be a way to find new solutions to entrenched political dilemmas. One can agree or disagree with North Korea's dramatic brinkmanship tactics, but one cannot ignore its deeply entrenched existence. Doing so could lead to dangerous miscalculations. At a minimum, it prevents us from recognising how Pyongyang could be using its last bargaining chip, its nuclear potential, as a way of entering dialogue with the United States and other key states. But despite numerous and obvious signs, and despite detailed and insightful studies of North Korea's previous negotiating behaviour, most Western decision-makers repeat the same mistakes they committed in the past: they believe that by demonising North Korea as an evil rogue state they can force Pyongyang into concessions. The result is not a solution to the conflict but a further escalation of threats and counterthreats.

---

35   Choi, *Re-Imagining North Korea in International Politics*, 13; Andrei Lankov, *The Real North Korea: Life and Politics in the Failed Stalinist Utopia* (Oxford: Oxford University Press, 2013); Patrick McEachern, *Inside the Red Box: North Korea's Post-Totalitarian Politics* (New York: Columbia University Press, 2010), doi.org/10.7312/mcea15322; Suk-Young Kim, *Illusive Utopia: Theater, Film, and Everyday Performance in North Korea* (Ann Arbor: University of Michigan Press, 2010); Demick, *Nothing to Envy*.
36   Lankov, *The Real North Korea*, xi. Two earlier studies making a similar point are Scott Snyder, *Negotiating on the Edge: North Korean Negotiating Behavior* (Washington, DC: United States Institute of Peace Press, 1999); and Leon V. Sigal, *Disarming Strangers: Nuclear Diplomacy with North Korea* (Princeton: Princeton University Press, 1998), doi.org/10.1515/9781400822355.
37   'Trump Will Need to Resist the Impulse to Hit the Twitter Trigger', *Australian*, 28 April 2018, www.theaustralian.com.au/news/world/trump-will-need-to-resist-impulse-to-hit-the-twitter-trigger/news-story/d9d245e22726cb92d00c21d4cc23d23f.

Conclusion: Visual autoethnography as strategic imagination

The purpose of this chapter has been to explore how my experience of working in the DMZ, and my own photographs from that time, can be used as a form of strategic imagination that sheds new light on the Korean conflict. As Sargeant pointed out, this strategic imagination inevitably entails—and must engage with—a tension between the imagination and the realities of the material world.[38] Embracing the strategic imagination does not mean one can ignore the empirical realities or simply make things up. But neither can one assume that empirical realities are just out there and can be represented without bias. Our representations of the world—and thus, by definition, the policies that emerge from them—are always partial and thus inevitably political in nature. It is in the tension between these two poles that a creative approach to strategy can find innovative solutions to security dilemmas.

I have tried to show how my own experiences and photographs can offer two types of insights into the security dilemmas on the Korean Peninsula. First, I demonstrated that visual autoethnography can reveal how militarised masculinities are so deeply entrenched that they are taken for granted and shape security policies in fundamental ways. Looking at my photographs of the DMZ today, I notice one thing above all: their strikingly gendered nature. There are virtually no women in them. What is particularly revealing for me—and politically significant—is that three decades ago, when I took these photographs, I noticed everything except the absence of women. I came from and was embedded in a context that rendered gendered systems of inclusion—and the problematic militaristic policies they facilitate— natural and largely invisible. My inevitably subjective experiences show how deeply embedded militarised masculinities are and how they shape all aspects of security politics on the peninsula. Innovative solutions to the existing security dilemmas must challenge these militaristic patterns and promote a form of strategic imagination that can offer genuinely new ways of solving conflict and securing peace.

---

38 Sargeant, Chapter 2, this volume.

Plate 10.17 Pyongyang, 1986–88
Photo: Roland Bleiker.

Second, reflecting on my positionality and my photographs of North Korea shows how prevailing Western strategic approaches and public perceptions are partial and highly political: they vilify the North and present it as an authoritarian rogue regime whose irrational leadership regularly threatens regional and world peace. While true on some level, these discourses are also partial and, more importantly, they present North Korea as a mad and irrational state. Visual positionality here offers pathways to appreciate the more complex nature of the Korean conflict and envisage innovative ways of understanding and addressing its security dilemmas. They could facilitate, for instance, an appreciation of how and why North Korea acts the way it does and, in so doing, lead to more informed strategic approaches.

There is no way a short chapter can outline in detail how strategic imagination can be used to re-evaluate the complex security situation on the Korean Peninsula. I have at best tried to offer two very short illustrations via a visual autoethnography. And I hope these illustrations have offered at least a convincing conceptual point in support of strategic imagination: that its usefulness should be judged not by the empirical accuracy of the insights that are generated but by the way they help us view entrenched security problems in a new light. Doing so is the precondition for finding innovative political solutions to conflicts that seem to have become intractable, like the one on the Korean Peninsula.

This is why the usefulness and power of visual autoethnography lie not in providing more accurate knowledge of empirical realities, but in the ability to reveal how prevailing ways of seeing, thinking and conducting security politics are so deeply entrenched and taken for granted that their often problematic nature is no longer recognised, yet alone discussed or addressed.

The broader lessons from my study suggest that scholarly work and policy recommendations based on strategic imagination should be pursued and evaluated by criteria that go beyond traditional social scientific validations. This is because strategic imagination is not about offering an accurate depiction of existing security dilemmas. It is about overcoming them. It is about reimagining the world around us, including the most pressing defence policy problems. Sargeant stresses this point: the 'quality of a country's strategic imagination may be judged by how it responds to the world—the space it creates for action'.[39] Opening such spaces breaks with existing habits and policy traditions. It is taking risks. A new strategy might be unproven and not yet empirically validated, but this does not render it invalid because, ultimately, the most crucial 'proof' will be how this policy 'might shape and therefore change the world as it is'.[40]

---

39 Sargeant, 'Challenges to the Australian Strategic Imagination', 10.
40 ibid., 9.

11

Australia in a new era: Why strategic imagination matters

Tom Barber and Melissa Conley Tyler

Introduction

In an era of unprecedented demand on Australian foreign policy—an era often characterised by 'polycrisis'—it can be a struggle to just maintain a heading, let alone chart a new course. But these headwinds, and the changes in tack they necessitate, are precisely why strategic imagination has never been more important: novel challenges require innovative solutions.

The late Professor Brendan Sargeant recognised that strategically imaginative approaches to contemporary challenges would be integral to Australia's future security and prosperity—in terms of the policies they produce, but equally, if not more importantly, in embedding the processes that produce them. He was concerned that a business-as-usual approach to foreign policymaking would 'inevitably result in a lack of imaginative capacity in our policy development and decision making'.[1]

---

1   Brendan Sargeant, 'Some Propositions about the World and the Australian Public Service', Submission to the 2019 Independent Review of the Australian Public Service, 24 July 2018, www.apsreview.gov.au/file/364/036f690d1fa436cd8113d4.docx?token=GY-xYRmv.

In his submission to the 2019 independent review of the Australian Public Service, Brendan identified a need 'to think about the whole policy ecosystem, not just the capability of the service itself'.[2] As a way of encouraging more strategic imagination, he recommended 'the use of "second track" vehicles to create a much more vibrant discussion around both the future (and current) policy context, and also on what constitutes good policy and implementation in this context'. It is against this backdrop that Brendan's key role in establishing the innovative Asia-Pacific Development, Diplomacy & Defence Dialogue (AP4D) should be understood.

In this chapter, we explore the challenge of expanding Australia's strategic imagination as championed by Brendan. We begin by looking at the changes in Australia's strategic environment in recent decades and identify why this demands more strategic imagination. We then explore why strategic imagination inertia tends to dominate during times of relative stability and shifts only during periods of crisis. Finally, we look at Brendan's involvement with AP4D as one way he actively encouraged and supported the generation of more strategically imaginative thinking through interdisciplinary collaboration for ambitious, future-facing ideas to better equip Australian policymakers for the decades ahead.

A new era

In his 2021 Centre of Gravity Series Paper, *Challenges to the Australian Strategic Imagination*, Brendan wrote:

> A country will possess a strategic imagination which will have evolved over time in response to the influence of geography, history, culture, and the many other tangible and intangible forces that go to create a community and its vision of itself.[3]

Like a fingerprint, each country's strategic imagination is uniquely shaped through collective experience: grand triumphs, spectacular calamities and everything in between. This amalgam of events, lessons and inputs cumulatively weaves a rich tapestry from which strategic imagination derives.

---

2   ibid.
3   Brendan Sargeant, *Challenges to the Australian Strategic Imagination*, Centre of Gravity Series Papers 58 (Canberra: Strategic and Defence Studies Centre, The Australian National University, 2021), 5, hdl. handle.net/1885/233085.

In Australia's case, its strategic imagination was predominantly formed in the colonial era. While there are signs that the more than 65,000 years of First Nations living culture is becoming a part of the national identity for Indigenous and non-Indigenous Australians alike—in addition to the decades of post–White Australia policy immigration that has produced a multicultural flourishing permeating the country's national character—it would be disingenuous to deny the Anglosphere antecedents of Australia's strategic imagination.

Since the Commonwealth of Australia was formed at Federation, it has had the benefit of being allied to the pre-eminent power of the day: first, the British and then, after the 1942 fall of Singapore and adoption of the Statute of Westminster, the Americans. This has meant that, from the end of World War II until recently (and particularly in the decades after the end of the Cold War), Australia inhabited an international order that largely accorded with its own interests and that was designed by allies and partners who broadly shared them, too. With US security architecture underpinning the stability required for international trade to flourish, scope for an Australian role in multilateral institution-building, rulemaking and norm-setting, and alignment between Australia's economic and security interests, '[t]he post-war order suited Australia perfectly'.[4]

The Australian penchant for cultivating a great and powerful friend has become a key animating idea of the national strategic imagination. The year 2025 marks the seventy-fourth birthday of the Australia, New Zealand and United States Security Treaty (ANZUS), meaning that Australians' familiarity with a time before the alliance with the United States is fast fading from living memory. This makes Canberra's tighter hewing to the United States as anxieties increase about China's rise somewhat understandable. In times of uncertainty people tend to stick with what they know; questioning and disruption of orthodoxies are generally a last resort.

There is wide agreement that Australia confronts a new era—one that is more contested than at any time since 1945. Successive policy documents acknowledge the deterioration in Australia's strategic environment and the implications stemming from it. Forecasting that Australia will 'face higher degrees of uncertainty and risk' within an international system buffeted by

---

4   Allan Gyngell, 'Australia and the Rules-Based Order', in *Australia and the Rules-Based International Order*, edited by Melissa Conley Tyler, Allan Gyngell, and Bryce Wakefield (Canberra: Australian Institute of International Affairs, 2018), 21, www.internationalaffairs.org.au/wp-content/uploads/2021/10/Australia-and-the-Rules-Based-International-Order.pdf.

'significant forces of change', the *2017 Foreign Policy White Paper* warns that Australia must 'seek security and prosperity in a region changing in profound ways'.[5] Describing Australia's region as 'under pressure' and noting how 'global challenges are interconnected and have a compounding impact', Australia's International Development Policy says that Australia faces 'the most challenging strategic circumstances in the post-war period'.[6] The 2023 *Defence Strategic Review* similarly underscores how 'Australia's strategic circumstances and the risks we face are now radically different' to those of the post–Cold War era, while advocating for 'a first-principles approach as to how we manage and seek to avoid the highest level of strategic risk we now face as a nation'.[7]

Explicit in these policy statements is that this new era demands more of Australia. Brendan recognised that this was easier said than done:

> Reflecting on my experience, I am struck by the degree of continuity in Australian strategic policy over many decades. I have also been struck by the operational focus of strategy as developed within Australian policy communities. We argue in policy and academic communities about how it has changed and what those changes mean, but the larger story is how it has not changed in its essentials over the past century. This begs the questions: why not?[8]

Strategic culture and continuity

A key impediment to thinking more imaginatively about strategy is the tendency for human systems to encourage path dependency—whether incidentally or by design. Just as an individual's personality is a function of their cumulative experiences over time, states also form strategic personalities. Brendan conceptualised Australian strategy 'as a series of interventions over

---

5   Department of Foreign Affairs and Trade (DFAT), *2017 Foreign Policy White Paper* (Canberra: Australian Government, 2017), 21–27, www.dfat.gov.au/sites/default/files/2017-foreign-policy-white-paper.pdf.
6   Department of Foreign Affairs and Trade, *Australia's International Development Policy: For a Peaceful, Stable and Prosperous Indo-Pacific* (Canberra: Australian Government, 2023), www.dfat.gov.au/sites/default/files/international-development-policy.pdf.
7   Department of Defence, *National Defence: Defence Strategic Review 2023* (Canberra: Australian Government, 2023), 23–24, www.defence.gov.au/about/reviews-inquiries/defence-strategic-review.
8   Brendan Sargeant, Chapter 2, this volume.

time in response to a changing external environment. The development and construction of these interventions occur within the context of previous interventions and ideas about Australia's relationship with the world.'[9]

During times when strategic circumstances are characterised by continuity rather than change, there is understandably little impetus for strategically imaginative approaches. As the adage goes, 'if it ain't broke, don't fix it'. Brendan considered the expression of the Australian strategic imagination in grand strategy as being 'relatively constant over the decades; at least, in my view, since the end of the First World War'.[10]

But as particular positions or ways of thinking become entrenched as conventional wisdom or dogma, they can ossify, becoming harder to challenge and think critically about.[11] Notwithstanding the value of a given approach in the period in which it was conceived, it nevertheless remains a product of its environment, and the more that context evolves, the more likely it is that its pertinence will diminish.

For contemporary Australia, this contextual evolution is happening fast. Whether it is the materialisation of global power shifts, the agglomeration of imbalances in Earth's biosphere or the acceleration of the rate of change wrought by technology, the new era in which Australia finds itself today compared with previous decades is not just changed but novel. In Brendan's words:

> [T]hese system-wide changes are interacting with each other and have compounding effects which creates the strategic environment which Australia really hasn't had to deal with before. So it's an enormous challenge. And I think that that presents a challenge for Australia in terms of how we operate in the region, how we contribute, how we exercise leadership and what role we will play in responding to these enormous changes which we are seeing.[12]

Brendan recognised that the scale of these changes presents a challenge in terms of not only how to respond, but also how to conceptualise: '[P]olicy is a secondary discussion. The first discussion is, what's driving the way you

---

9   ibid.

10   Brendan Sargeant, 'Burning Bright: Defence Policy, Strategy and the Imagination', *Australian Army Journal* 3, no. 3 (2006): 67–86, researchcentre.army.gov.au/sites/default/files/aaj_2006_3.pdf.

11   Allan Behm, *No Enemies No Friends: Restoring Australia's Global Relevance* (Perth: Upswell Publishing, 2022).

12   Sargeant, in David Pembroke, 'Australia's Place in the Asia-Pacific', *Work with Purpose Podcast*, Episode #59 (Canberra: Content Group, 23 May 2022), act.ipaa.org.au/ipaa-podcast/australias-place-in-the-asia-pacific/.

think about policy?'[13] Lamenting the 'narrowly framed' nature of Australia's strategic policy debate, he warned that we have 'only begun to comprehend the implications that flow from the major changes now occurring in the Indo-Pacific'.[14] He expressed this as follows:

> One way of thinking about strategy is to consider it as preparation for a future crisis. Yet, our capacity to envisage and prepare for a future crisis can be constrained by the limits of our strategic imagination, even as the crisis becomes visible and demands a response. My central proposition is that a strategic challenge of any magnitude is first a challenge to imagination.[15]

For Brendan, formulating policy responses to the challenges of the new era without updating the thinking behind such decisions was imprudent due to the questionable efficacy of solutions conceived of under different strategic conditions. 'Nostalgia,' he wrote, 'in its sentimental attachment to and overvaluing of the past, its refusal or inability to understand contemporary realities, its refusal to respond to the future on its own terms, is a failure of imagination.'[16]

He thus impelled his fellow Australians—and not just the foreign policy elite—to exercise genuine strategic imagination to find ways to 'open richer ways of thinking about' the challenges facing Australia in the new era 'and, in some circumstances, [open] new pathways for action'.[17] During a May 2021 public lecture, Brendan said:

> The quality of the imagination that responds to that challenge determines the shape of the strategy that follows. An understanding of the relationship between strategy and imagination can deepen our understanding of what strategy is and how we might assess the utility of strategy in specific circumstances.[18]

---

13   Quoted in Robbin Laird, 'Strategic Imagination: Meeting the Challenge', *Defense.info*, 6 July 2021, defense.info/re-thinking-strategy/2021/07/strategic-imagination-meeting-the-challenge/.
14   Sargeant, *Challenges to the Australian Strategic Imagination*, 5.
15   Quoted in Robbin Laird, 'Events, Policy Making and Strategic Imagination', *Defense.info*, 28 May 2021, defense.info/re-thinking-strategy/2021/05/events-policy-making-and-strategic-imagination/.
16   Sargeant, *Challenges to the Australian Strategic Imagination*, 5.
17   Sargeant, Chapter 2, this volume.
18   Quoted in Laird, 'Strategic Imagination'.

Why is imagination hard?

Brendan was far from naive; his advocacy of strategic imagination explicitly acknowledged the difficulties of being strategically imaginative. Writing on past crises that ultimately involved shifts in Australia's strategic imagination, Brendan explained:

> Each crisis was a moment of discontinuity that required an act of imagination large enough to envisage a future different from the continuities mandated by the past, and powerful enough to generate a strategy sufficient to chart a path towards this future. Each was a moment of transition. Each represented an enormous challenge because responding meant understanding and overcoming the forces of continuity and all that they represent in tradition, culture, practice, and established and settled institutional relationships.[19]

A common denominator in the crises he describes is the risk and threat of conflict and it is during these 'rare moments in a country's history where a genuine choice must be made and action taken, [that] a country's strategic imagination becomes most visible'.[20] The tendency for strategic imagination to lie dormant and come to the fore only in times of crisis underlines why it is so hard; were questioning and critiquing one's core assumptions and views easy, it would not require crises to stimulate such thinking.

Orthodoxies generally exist for a reason: they work (or at least they worked in the past). So, it takes courage to challenge them in an environment where there 'is not much room for imagination ... because imagination is superfluous to the task of problem-solving'.[21] As Brendan put it:

> The dilemma for those who work in strategy, particularly in the face of the need to undertake major change, is how to construct a discourse that can step outside or challenge the form that has been created and that mandates certain approaches and limits.[22]

While strategic imagination is necessary to reshape the foundations on which to confront the challenges Australia faces in a new era, it must simultaneously confront deep-rooted internal tensions. These include that between a fear of abandonment and a desire for strategic autonomy;

---

19   Sargeant, *Challenges to the Australian Strategic Imagination*, 5.
20   ibid., 5.
21   Sargeant, Chapter 2, this volume.
22   ibid.

between fortress Australia and participation in the global community; between maritime and continental defence; between history and geography; and between validation through commemoration of participation in foreign wars and silence on the Australian frontier wars and Indigenous dispossession.[23] While these tensions are exactly the types of things that strategic imagination is suited to tackling, that does not make the task any easier. This in turn begs the question: how can we encourage and improve strategic imagination at a time when it has never been more important?

How can we improve imagination?

Imagination is inherently intangible and, by definition, unbounded. 'If we do not understand our imagination, we cannot understand ourselves', wrote Brendan in 2006, conceding that we 'barely understand it, and because of this we can be blind to the full meaning and dimensions of our policy and strategic thinking'.[24] He thought deeply on the topic over the intervening years, trying to better understand how Australia's strategic imagination could be stimulated constructively. That cogitation bore fruit, and Brendan suggested some options for how strategic imagination could be improved.

First, foreseeing how imagination could be misunderstood as a primarily individual task, he emphasised how it is also as much an issue of systems and ecosystems. He argued:

> A strategic imagination is an integrating force. Different elements relate to each other to create a whole greater than the parts. It is, to use a metaphor, a living and dynamic reality that changes as it both shapes and is shaped by the world.[25]

He envisaged a collective 'Australian strategic imagination' that was 'the outcome of the dialogue between imagination and the constraints of what we might describe as the material world in all its manifestations'.[26]

Brendan understood that the value 'of thinking about imagination and its relationship with policy and academic discourses in strategy, security and international relations is that it can illuminate the meaning and limitations

---

23 ibid.
24 Sargeant, 'Burning Bright'.
25 Sargeant, *Challenges to the Australian Strategic Imagination*, 5.
26 Sargeant, Chapter 2, this volume.

of the structures that we have built in these fields'.[27] He recognised how bringing together thinkers from across disciplines—each with their own traditions and idiosyncrasies—could encourage osmosis across disciplinary membranes and help break down intellectual silos to unearth meaning: '[D]ifferent theoretical frameworks offer insight, much as the light at different times of the day will allow us to see different aspects of the same landscape … [N]o single theory will exhaust all the possible meanings in a text.'[28]

It is no coincidence that Brendan was one of the key figures involved in establishing the AP4D, which is a platform for collaboration between the different international policy communities with the aim of encouraging better Australian statecraft.[29] He appreciated how such a model could stimulate strategic imagination by facilitating conversations between unusual coalitions and cultivating a constituency for more strategically imaginative thinking:

> [T]he reality is that we are all connected, that we all have multiple connections across public and private sector and other communities. And we need to be in the conversation with everyone because we are not dealing with isolated problems. We are dealing with whole-of-nation challenges, which will require whole-of-nation responses.[30]

A key driver of the formation of AP4D was the desire to shift current practices over time, with the overarching aim of stimulating a cultural shift in the way Australian foreign policy and its strategic goals are formulated in a more complex and contested era. Established by Bridi Rice and Richard Moore as a joint initiative of the Australian Council for International Development, the International Development Contractors Community, the Institute for Regional Security and The Australian National University, AP4D, from its inception, was envisioned as a platform for ideas generated and refined through collaboration. Its name was chosen to epitomise this: a dialogue between key international policy communities (development, diplomacy and defence being shorthand for the full spectrum of Australia's international policy communities). This distinguishes AP4D from traditional foreign policy think tanks in that is concerned not just with

---

27   ibid.; see also 'Stranger than Fiction: Imagination as an Instrument of National Security', *The National Security Podcast* (Canberra: ANU National Security College, 26 January 2023), shows.acast.com/the-national-security-podcast/episodes/stranger-than-fiction.

28   Sargeant, Chapter 2, this volume.

29   See the AP4D website: asiapacific4d.com/.

30   Pembroke, 'Australia's Place in the Asia-Pacific'.

policy-relevant knowledge production, but also, and even more so, with the *process* by which knowledge is produced at the intersection of different policy communities. As the inaugural chairperson's statement makes clear:

> No existing Australian forum deliberately brings together the discrete strands of foreign relations represented by the development, diplomatic and defence communities … This new partnership between our organisations was created on the collective agreement that greater strategic collaboration between the individual fields of foreign policy is required to help Australia address the unprecedented international relations environment it faces.[31]

AP4D was fortunate to attract early support from the Australian Civil–Military Centre and has developed into a genuinely tripartite initiative funded by the Department of Foreign Affairs and Trade and the Defence portfolio and housed at the Australian Council for International Development.

A core tenet of AP4D's work is advocacy for Australia to respect, resource and coordinate 'all tools of statecraft',[32] with the aspiration being a situation across Australia's international engagement where the whole is greater than the sum of its parts. An integrated whole-of-government, 'whole-of-nation'[33] approach to international strategy is not a panacea, but the process by which such an approach is instituted can allow policymakers to step out of constraints, re-evaluate risks and opportunities and chart a new course.[34] In its first three years, AP4D has connected more than 650 nongovernmental development, diplomacy and defence[35] experts from Australia and across the region, facilitating dialogue and producing more than 20 options papers on important topics in Australian foreign policy.[36] This suggests a nascent '3D' constituency is taking shape that is actively 'reimagining Australia's

---

31 Asia-Pacific Development, Diplomacy & Defence Dialogue, 'Inaugural Development, Diplomacy and Defence Dialogue: Rethinking Australia's International Relations', 5 November 2019, asiapacific4d.com/wp-content/uploads/2022/11/610a7eba5ec4173fc3990076_Asia-Pacific-Chairs-Statement.pdf.

32 Asia-Pacific Development, Diplomacy & Defence Dialogue, *What Does It Look Like for Australia to Use All Tools of Statecraft in Practice*, Options Paper (Canberra: AP4D, 2023), asiapacific4d.com/idea/all-tools-of-statecraft/.

33 Asia-Pacific Development, Diplomacy & Defence Dialogue, *What Does It Look Like for Australia to Take a Whole-Of-Nation Approach to International Policy*, Options Paper (Canberra: AP4D, 2023), asiapacific4d.com/idea/whole-of-nation/.

34 Melissa Conley Tyler and Richard Moore, 'Does Australia Need a UK-Style Integrated Review?', *The Strategist* (Canberra: Australian Strategic Policy Institute, 20 October 2021), www.aspistrategist.org.au/does-australia-need-a-uk-style-integrated-review/.

35 AP4D uses 'development, diplomacy and defence' as shorthand for the full spectrum of Australia's international relations communities—for example, including policing, international law, and economics and trade.

36 See the AP4D Options Papers, at: asiapacific4d.com/ideas/.

international relations'—a phrase deliberately chosen with Brendan's input. This situates strategic imagination not as a primarily individual task, but as a task of building systems and ecosystems across Australia's policy communities.

In many ways, the type of cultural shift AP4D endeavours to foster and strategic imagination are two sides of the same coin. AP4D's work is designed to enable contributors to use strategic imagination 'to conceive of a different order and a different Australia within that order',[37] as Brendan put it, by explicitly framing consultations and the resulting publications in future-focused terms ('what does it look like for Australia to …'). It takes the view that strategic imagination will be best fostered by bringing together expert views from multiple policy communities to attempt to answer such questions.

AP4D's work has been well received by policymakers as a valuable, timely and constructive contribution to promoting better Australian statecraft and outlining practical pathways to achieve it within the broader Australian foreign policy debate. In addition to ministers and shadow ministers launching papers, there has been bipartisan uptake of the idea that Australia must use 'all tools of statecraft' following briefings to hundreds of parliamentarians, advisors, officials and international engagement staff. The prime minister, the treasurer and ministers for defence, foreign affairs and international development and the Pacific (as well as shadow ministers and other policymakers and senior officials) are all on record using this type of language.[38]

The unclassified version of the *Defence Strategic Review*, released in April 2023, included a full chapter on the need for a whole-of-government and whole-of-nation approach:

> National Defence must be part of a broader national strategy of whole-of-government coordinated and focused statecraft and diplomacy in our region. This approach requires much more active Australian statecraft that works to support the maintenance of a regional balance of power in the Indo-Pacific.[39]

---

37 Sargeant, *Challenges to the Australian Strategic Imagination*, 5.
38 Asia-Pacific Development, Diplomacy & Defence Dialogue, 'Support for Respecting, Resourcing and Coordinating All Tools of Statecraft', *YouTube*, 15 August 2023, www.youtube.com/watch?v=rGD_v68HSUI.
39 Department of Defence, *National Defence*, 23–24.

And in a media release to coincide with the 2023 federal budget, the ministers for foreign affairs, trade and international development and the Pacific said that 'the Budget will make Australia more influential in the world, by investing in all elements of our statecraft including diplomatic power, trade and development'.[40] Budget Paper No. 1 stated that Australia's changing strategic environment 'requires new investments in diplomacy, development, defence and national security, at a time of increased fiscal pressure'.[41]

Australia's new International Development Policy likewise:

> recognise[s] that Australia's development program cannot deliver the outcomes we seek in isolation. All elements of our national power must be deployed to respond to the needs of our region—integrating development with our diplomatic, trade, economic, defence, immigration, sporting, cultural, scientific and security efforts.[42]

Other key policy documents to use such language include the *Development Finance Review*,[43] Southeast Asia Economic Strategy,[44] Cyber Security Strategy[45] and *Intergenerational Report 2023*.[46]

The explicit adoption of this type of framing in official policy documents would please Brendan, who was always clear that the goal for AP4D was better statecraft that reflected Australia's changed circumstances. There remains much work to be done, but some of the foundations for more strategically imaginative thinking have been laid thanks in no small part to Brendan's vision.

---

40   Penny Wong, Don Farrell, and Pat Conroy, 'Investing to Secure Australia's Interests in the World', Media release, 9 May 2023, www.foreignminister.gov.au/minister/penny-wong/media-release/investing-secure-australias-interests-world.

41   Josh Frydenberg and Simon Birmingham, *Budget 2022–23: Budget Strategy and Outlook*, Budget Paper No. 1 (Canberra: Commonwealth of Australia, 29 March 2022), 139, archive.budget.gov.au/2022-23/bp1/download/bp1_2022-23.pdf.

42   DFAT, *Australia's International Development Policy.*

43   Department of Foreign Affairs and Trade (DFAT), *Development Finance Review: New Approaches for a Changing Landscape* (Canberra: Australian Government, 2023), www.dfat.gov.au/sites/default/files/development-finance-review-2023.pdf.

44   Nicholas Moore, *Invested: Australia's Southeast Asia Economic Strategy to 2040* (Canberra: Department of Foreign Affairs and Trade, 2023), www.dfat.gov.au/sites/default/files/invested-southeast-asia-economic-strategy-2040.pdf.

45   Department of Home Affairs, *2023–2030 Australian Cyber Security Strategy* (Canberra: Australian Government, 2023), www.homeaffairs.gov.au/cyber-security-subsite/files/2023-cyber-security-strategy.pdf.

46   Department of Treasury, *Intergenerational Report 2023: Australia's Future to 2063* (Canberra: Australian Government, 2023), treasury.gov.au/sites/default/files/2023-08/p2023-435150.pdf.

Conclusion

In 2006 Brendan wrote:

> Imagination lives most powerfully in dreams, memories, barely conscious urgings, in those instincts that run deep through our lives and drive us to take what materials we can and fashion from them a world that defines us and in which we might be able to live. It is imagination that allows us to create, to turn visions, dreams and desires into something real enough to make us breathe differently and be able to say that we live in a place we have made our own. It is through our imagination that we connect with the world and create more meaning and more life out of the crude materials it gives us. This is a large definition, but imagination is a large thing, capable of spawning worlds.[47]

Brendan's own imagination spawned worlds—as this volume attests. As a founding member of the AP4D Advisory Group, Brendan's wealth of experience, his intellectual passion and the generosity with which he gave his time and imparted his knowledge were inestimable and were deeply appreciated by AP4D co-chairs Michael Wesley and Marc Purcell and by all the AP4D team. AP4D is proud to be part of Brendan's legacy.

---

47   Sargeant, 'Burning Bright'.

12

The Indo-Pacific as strategic imagination

Rory Medcalf

Professor Brendan Sargeant left a profound legacy for all of us who make, implement and analyse Australian strategic policy. The fullness of his gift to the nation ranges across an exceptional commitment to leadership, analysis and mentorship, from the Department of Defence to the wider policy community and the academy. He is not the only senior official to have made a mark beyond the bureaucracy. One element, however, that distinguishes the work of Brendan Sargeant was his embrace of the act of imagination as integral to strategy. This was accompanied by a disarming openness about the place of imagination in policymaking. Professor Sargeant's pioneering official work on the concept of the Indo-Pacific as a two-ocean regional framework for Australian strategy, articulated in the *2013 Defence White Paper*, merits examination and proper prominence.

To describe the Indo-Pacific as an artefact of strategic imagination is not to reject this construct as meaningless or 'not real'; quite the opposite. The single strategic arc of connectivity and contestation Brendan identified a decade ago is now the orthodox understanding among many countries, even (however tacitly) China. Looking ahead, Australia's great challenge, as Brendan argued in his later scholarly work, is how to learn to live in the Indo-Pacific. Accordingly, Australian policy thinkers and practitioners have the opportunity and obligation to build on his vision in developing a statecraft to suit this inclusive strategic environment. This account brings together a sense of Brendan's exceptional personal qualities, his championing of the idea of strategic imagination, a case for the validity of the concept of the Indo-Pacific and his place in foregrounding that in Australian policy. It concludes with a reminder of the unfinished business of shaping and implementing an Indo-Pacific strategy.

Strategic guru

Brendan's passing in February 2022 was a loss not only in the most personal sense to family and friends, but also to Australia's community of scholars, strategists and policymakers. He is rightly remembered for his intellect, integrity and commitment to public service, combined with personal kindness and decency, undergirded by a striking absence of ego—taken together, a set of qualities rare in the worlds of policy and academia alike. Professor Sargeant was widely respected as a leader and thinker across strategy and policy. His long career in the Australian Public Service culminated in leadership roles in the Department of Defence, as associate secretary and deputy secretary. His subsequent stewardship of the Strategic and Defence Studies Centre (SDSC) at The Australian National University remained, sadly, a work in progress at the time of his passing. His role as head of SDSC continued a fine tradition of practitioner-academic leaders combining seasoned policy judgement with scholarly rigour, but his mission to navigate this national institution to suit the challenges and opportunities of the 2020s remained incomplete.

However, one can imagine Professor Sargeant being quietly philosophical about his unfinished business, for there was something of the mystic about Brendan. He was a guru in the full Sanskrit sense: a leader, but also a guide and mentor, who saw it as his calling not didactically to show new generations the path, but to encourage them to find it for themselves. The visitor to Brendan's office—whether on the executive floor of the Defence Department on Canberra's Russell Hill or later in the Hedley Bull Building at The Australian National University—could not help but notice his collection of idols of Ganesha, the beloved elephant deity, remover of obstacles and god of beginnings, knowledge and success.

This was not just a reflection of his Indian family by marriage. Brendan's world view was informed by, among other wisdoms, elements of Hinduism: an appreciation of ambiguity and duality and an ethos of duty and acceptance. There is only so much we can do to change the world; it remains a demanding enough task to learn how to live with and leverage what is, including for a strategist, our geographic reality. Not that Australia's geography needs necessarily be a source solely of difficulty or anxiety. On the contrary, Australian policy should recognise and embrace the opportunities of being in a part of the world so connected with Asia, including a healthy respect for the cultures and perspectives of this region or, as Brendan would put it, learning to live in the Indo-Pacific.

Power and poetry: Awakening strategic imagination

One of Brendan Sargeant's most powerful intellectual contributions was his 2021 SDSC Centre of Gravity Series Paper, *Challenges to the Australian Strategic Imagination*, with an associated public lecture. Here is explicitly set out his conception of how imagination could usefully inform policy, with reference to the Indo-Pacific as a vision for Australia's strategic environment:

> How are we to live in the Indo-Pacific in the 21st-century? This is not first a question of policy or strategy. It is a challenge to strategic imagination. Not only do we need to imagine ourselves into what we might be, but also what the world might be. Is our vision of our future large enough to accommodate and respond to the scale of change that we are seeing?[1]

We will return to Brendan's 2021 manifesto presently, but first it is worth recognising that his identification of imagination as a foundation for policy was not some radical remaking of his outlook with the benefit of liberation from the exigencies of the bureaucratic life. Rather, he was carrying forward an idea he had first articulated as early as 2006 in a foray into the academic and public sphere while a serving Defence official. Brendan's essay 'Burning Bright: Defence Policy, Strategy and the Imagination', courageously put forward the idea that threat perception—and consequent deployment decisions—was informed by nothing less than 'the imagination of the nation, of the people and of the Department of Defence'.[2]

---

1   Brendan Sargeant, *Challenges to the Australian Strategic Imagination*, Centre of Gravity Series Paper 58 (Canberra: Strategic and Defence Studies Centre, The Australian National University, 2021), hdl.handle. net/1885/233085.

2   Brendan Sargeant, 'Burning Bright: Defence Policy, Strategy and the Imagination', *Australian Army Journal* 3, no. 3 (2006): 67–86, at 67, researchcentre.army.gov.au/sites/default/files/aaj_2006_3.pdf.

Only Brendan Sargeant, perhaps, could have accused an impersonal Defence bureaucracy of possessing such a thing as an imagination. Only Brendan Sargeant, without a doubt, could have enlisted William Blake's 1794 masterpiece of transcendental poetry 'The Tyger' as a cipher to explain the relationship between imagination and strategy. Kudos to the *Australian Army Journal* and Catherine McGregor for releasing this discipline-defying essay into the intellectual wild, where, along with the Centre of Gravity Series Paper, it should be essential reading for future generations of security practitioners and academics alike.

The 2006 and 2021 publications repay examination side by side, to show both continuity and evolution. Both legitimised imagination as integral to strategy, the identification of possibility, creating meaning, opportunity and life from imperfect materials, turning visions into 'something real' or, in the words of Lawrence Freedman, 'the ability to get more out of any given situation than the starting conditions would suggest are possible'.[3] The 2006 paper, written in the aftermath of the disastrous invasion of Iraq, was also focused partly on the perils of imagination: '[W]e are in the most danger when we allow our imagination to separate from those realities in the world that establish limits.'[4] The 2021 paper, in contrast, concentrated on the need for more creative and expansive thinking to prepare Australia for the problems of the Indo-Pacific—a two-ocean region of many powers lacking mature institutions and in the midst of instability and power contestation. Both analyses emphasised the relevance of geography in defining realistic Australian strategic objectives. The paradox of the Indo-Pacific is that Australia cannot escape the vastness of this connected strategic environment, even while our limited ability to shape regionwide outcomes encourages an emphasis on the near neighbourhood of the South Pacific and South-East Asia.

Mapping the Indo-Pacific

In barely a decade, the concept of the Indo-Pacific has travelled from relative obscurity to become a new orthodoxy in the statecraft of many nations and institutions around the world. Not only has Indo-Pacific rhetoric and thinking permeated Australian defence, foreign, geo-economic

---

3   Lawrence Freedman, *Strategy: A History* (Oxford: Oxford University Press, 2015), xii.
4   Sargeant, 'Burning Bright', 83.

and development policy across the political spectrum but, since the mid-2010s, a growing number of governments and international organisations have recast their Asia-centric engagement through explicitly Indo-Pacific strategies or, at the very least, formal statements by their leaders. Notable on the list are Japan, the United States, India, Indonesia, France, Germany, the United Kingdom, the Netherlands, the Republic of Korea, Canada, Taiwan, the Association of Southeast Asian Nations, the European Union, the North Atlantic Treaty Organization, the G7 and even, with unsurprising Pacific-centric caveats, New Zealand.

The Indo-Pacific situates Australia in a larger strategic system than the Asia-Pacific of the late twentieth century, or even more bounded regional conceptions such as Oceania or the East Asian Hemisphere championed in the mid-1990s by then foreign minister Gareth Evans. Its advocates see it as a practical reimagining of the world map to suit the problems of our time. The concept reframes an Asia-centric region to reflect growing connectivity and contest across two oceans, providing somewhat equal billing to the Indian and the Pacific oceans, driven in substantial part by China's (but also India's) expanding interests and influence across this maritime space. This vision is useful to many nations because it explains and encourages the balancing and dilution of Chinese power through an array of new partnerships across collapsed geographic boundaries. We thus have a metaphor for collective action—code for a pivotal region where China can be prominent but not dominant. In a global discourse often dominated by Beijing's transgressions and triumphalism, or simplistic narratives of US–China bipolarity, the Indo-Pacific idea offers a useful alternative.[5]

In explaining what the Indo-Pacific is (and is not), there is merit in addressing several of the standard criticisms of the concept: that it is all about containing China, that not all Indo-Pacific policy positions align and that ultimately it is an artifice.

Much of the controversy regarding the Indo-Pacific is based on the perception that this is effectively a code for the containment—or exclusion—of China. Such portrayals make superficial sense if they are limited to interpreting the earliest 'free and open' variants of Indo-Pacific strategy as promoted in 2016 by then Japanese prime minister Abe Shinzo or in 2017 by then US president Donald Trump, but even those versions, especially Japan's, left the door

---

5   This section draws on the author's previous work, in Rory Medcalf, *Contest for the Indo-Pacific: Why China Won't Map the Future* (Melbourne: La Trobe University Press, 2022), ix–x.

open to engagement with China.[6] More broadly, there are multiple versions of Indo-Pacific policy, most with a focus on connectivity and inclusion. The Indo-Pacific is about offering the choice of incorporating a powerful China into a regional order where the rights of others are respected and actively counterbalancing that power when those rights are not. After all, it has been the growth of China's wealth, power, interests and influence across two oceans—which Beijing calls the Maritime Silk Road—that has been a large impetus for this Indo-Pacific era. The Indo-Pacific idea has a maritime fluidity and a philosophically Asian duality; it is about incorporating the interests of the many, while marshalling the capabilities of the willing.

Another line of criticism is that different nations profess different Indo-Pacific visions and that this is an intrinsic weakness; in other words, the Indo-Pacific is a hollow concept precisely because its advocates do not entirely agree on balancing or containing China. This disregards the degree of convergence and mutual acceptance among many national and institutional visions. For example, the 2019 Association of Southeast Asian Nations (ASEAN) outlook focuses on connectivity and development and lists more than 14 principles, including, unsurprisingly, ASEAN centrality, as well as openness, inclusivity, rules, mutual respect and renunciation of the threat or use of force.[7] The Quadrilateral Security Dialogue (Quad) of Australia, India, Japan and the United States has often been presumed an Indo-Pacific initiative to balance and exclude China, yet its communiqués resemble the ASEAN list, underscoring a convergence of Indo-Pacific visions. Essentially, all such perspectives articulate that this is a region defined by: connectivity and contestation across two oceans; a status as the emerging global centre of gravity economically, demographically and strategically; a multipolar and maritime character; and a core place for South-East Asia, both geographically and through ASEAN institutions.

Perhaps the strangest objection to the Indo-Pacific idea is that it is precisely that—a work of the mind. In the words of a Chinese diplomat, 'there is no such concept as an Indo-Pacific in geopolitics'—as though, absurdly, the full menu of possible geopolitical frameworks has been carved in stone since the

---

6   For a sophisticated discussion of Japan's free and open Indo-Pacific strategy and how it was influenced by Australian policy and, in turn, influenced American policy, see Michael J. Green, *Line of Advantage: Japan's Grand Strategy in the Era of Abe Shinzō* (New York: Columbia University Press, 2022), especially pp. 105–61, doi.org/10.7312/gree20466.

7   Association of Southeast Asian Nations (ASEAN), *ASEAN Outlook on the Indo-Pacific* (Jakarta: ASEAN Secretariat, 2019), asean.org/wp-content/uploads/2021/01/ASEAN-Outlook-on-the-Indo-Pacific _FINAL_22062019.pdf.

dawn of time, leaving no flexibility or agency as the world changes.[8] In the case of Chinese policy, this opposition to the Indo-Pacific on the basis of its being an artificial construct derives overwhelmingly from the concern that it mitigates against China's interests as a way to accentuate India's role in the wider region and undercut the supposed centrality of China. In parallel, there has been a wariness in parts of the academy—conservative in its own way— to engage with this different mental map. After all, why supplant the Asia-Pacific, which had the virtue of being 'established'? Of course, this begs the question: established when, how and by whom? All regional definitions are to a least some degree artificial, although it must be said that the material facts reflected in the Indo-Pacific—of economic connectivity and civilisational interaction across the two oceans—have a pedigree of millennia. There was a time when the Asia-Pacific itself was novel (and incidentally resisted by China because it privileged the United States)—a useful framework for the second half of the twentieth century, to reflect the new and impermanent reality of relations between East Asia and North America mattering more than relations across Asia. The Asia-Pacific, the Indo-Pacific and Chinese leader Xi Jinping's imposed view that somehow a region makes best sense as a 'Belt and Road' centred on Beijing—all are mental maps that states consecrate or defy with political purpose. That is the point. They are acts of strategic imagination.

Brendan the navigator

However much its content and utility are contested, the prominence of the Indo-Pacific idea is clear. What is less well known is the vital role played by Brendan Sargeant in influencing Australia's Indo-Pacific outlook and, by extension, the impact of Australian diplomacy in encouraging the framework's wider adoption.

In the early 2010s, the Labor government under prime minister Julia Gillard was open to an active reimagining of Australia's regional environment. In the aftermath of the 2008 Global Financial Crisis, there was a growing awareness of fundamental shifts in economic weight occurring, particularly through the growth of the Chinese economy, with new patterns of trade, but also through the rise of other Asian economies. In terms of security risk, the Australian defence establishment was also awakening to the prospect of rapid Chinese military and especially naval modernisation—though not yet to the level

---

8   Ananth Krishnan, 'U.S. Created Indo-Pacific Concept to Bring in India to Contain China, Says Chinese Official', *The Hindu*, [Chennai, India], 15 December 2022.

of strategic competition that would manifest later in the decade. The *2009 Defence White Paper* under prime minister Kevin Rudd anticipated a need for Australia to expand its naval power and suggested that the north-east Indian Ocean would be of rising importance to Australian security as part of a 'wider Asia-Pacific region'—a foreshadowing of the Indo-Pacific.[9]

Subsequently, distinct new narratives of Australia's region were framed in two key documents: in late 2012, an 'Asian Century' white paper, accentuating economic opportunity; and a Defence White Paper in early 2013 that sustained the ambition of greater Australian maritime power while, in an unpromising fiscal context, was necessarily cautious on the spending commitments to get there. Both documents introduced a seemingly novel way of defining Australia's region of interest: not the Asia-Pacific (a received wisdom from at least the 1980s) but something called the Indo-Pacific. This received experimental treatment in the Asian Century document, before becoming a signature theme throughout the Defence White Paper. This was in large part thanks to a certain Defence deputy secretary for strategy, Brendan Sargeant. Government documents are inevitably the product of process, politics and many institutional inputs. Nonetheless, in this one, Brendan's authorial voice was clear and spoke to history:

> [A] new Indo-Pacific strategic arc is beginning to emerge, connecting the Indian and Pacific Oceans through Southeast Asia … India is emerging as an important strategic, diplomatic and economic actor … Growing trade, investment and energy flows across the broader region are strengthening economic and security interdependencies … Although the strategic environment will be shaped largely by the relationship between the United States and China, and by the rise of India in the longer term, the increasing number of influential Asian states means we are witnessing the evolution of a more complex and competitive order.[10]

So many of the ingredients of subsequent Indo-Pacific analyses and policies were presented: an emphasis on the sea lines of communication; a warning about strategic risk, maritime disputes and flashpoints; and a premium placed on partnerships and mini-lateral 'smaller or ad hoc groupings' in a mega-region where a middle power would increasingly struggle to project its voice and protect its interests.

---

9   As noted by Melissa Conley Tyler and Samantha Shearman, 'Australia's New Region: The Indo-Pacific', *East Asia Forum*, 21 May 2013.

10   Department of Defence, *Defence White Paper 2013* (Canberra: Australian Government, 2013), 7–8, www.defence.gov.au/about/strategic-planning/defence-white-paper.

The case for the Indo-Pacific was captured in maps that Brendan specially commissioned. An unclassified map portrayed the density of civilian shipping—containers, energy and resources—across the Indo-Pacific arc, graphically presenting the rising significance of the Indian Ocean and the South China Sea, alongside the more established traffic across the Pacific between East Asia and North America. It did not suggest a central place for Australia, but rather an inescapable position of proximity, especially to the regional core (and chokepoints) of maritime South-East Asia. It also reinforced the acute dependence of Australia's and other major regional economies on those sea lanes, with deep implications for national security and stability. According to Brendan, this first official Indo-Pacific map was initially controversial in parts of the Australian policy community and reportedly was met with some bewilderment among US officials still focused on the Middle East.[11]

It is worth emphasising that, although some American officials had already begun toying with Indo-Pacific terminology, the concept remained contested within the US system and would for some years yet. This is a reminder that the Indo-Pacific was not an artefact of US policy imposed on a reluctant Asia, but had authentic regional progenitors, including in India, Indonesia and Japan.

Within Australia, Brendan was one of several influential policy practitioners and voices, along with Department of Foreign Affairs and Trade (DFAT) secretary Peter Varghese, defence minister Stephen Smith, ambassador to the United States Kim Beazley, director-general of the Office of National Assessments Allan Gyngell and, outside government, this author. My own interest in developing the Indo-Pacific concept began when I was an intelligence analyst from 2003 to 2007, building on my previous three years' diplomatic experience in New Delhi, where I had focused on the potential for India as a strategic partner. I found myself observing changing patterns of economic connectivity, military capability and diplomatic coalition-building, including the establishment of the East Asia Summit and the abortive 2007 Quad meeting. Subsequently, a career change in joining the Lowy Institute provided a platform for patiently advancing an Indo-Pacific world view in the public debate. A significant moment was an invitation to give the inaugural SDSC Centre of Gravity lecture on this

---

11   As recounted by Brendan Sargeant to the author, in Medcalf, *Contest for the Indo-Pacific*, 282.

topic in 2012—the kernel of many later articles and eventually a book.[12] All along, there were frequent trusted exchanges of insights with colleagues inside policy who were thinking along similar tracks. Among them, Brendan Sargeant—through his intellectual agency and his act of imagination—was decisive in getting the concept over the line as formal policy in the *2013 Defence White Paper*, which was the first official document of any government to call the Indo-Pacific a region of strategic interest. His vision and his map therefore became iconic in the unfolding history of Indo-Pacific policy and have informed much subsequent policy cartography.

Horizon, limits and the challenge ahead

Brendan Sargeant was never comfortable with strategic or policy orthodoxy; he was a champion of contestability and debate. Just as he advanced the Indo-Pacific as an act of strategic imagination, so, too, he would have been among the first to ensure that the policy conversation should not stand still. Likewise, he would have remained focused on the practicalities as well as the vision, for implementing Indo-Pacific policy requires constant awareness of the limits of Australian resources and the need to leverage partnerships. His own writings imply the tensions within the rapidly arrived Indo-Pacific orthodoxy. The Indo-Pacific idea he cultivated in the *2013 Defence White Paper* was not some crude contrivance to contain Chinese power, nor was it a call for Australia to overextend its capabilities across a region too large for any single power to manage. He recognised the duality in the fact that the Indo-Pacific encompasses some features of a strategic system—notably, the reliance of China and other East Asian states on the Indian Ocean—even while each subregion would maintain distinct concerns and the security architecture was not a 'unitary whole'. Professor Sargeant called for Australia to learn to live in the Indo-Pacific, while being realistic about the limits geography places on our ambitions. This is not a contradiction but a duality. Managing this constant tension is a principal task for Australian statecraft and will require all dimensions of national engagement, including societal, economic and diplomatic as well as military. As Brendan said, all this begins as a challenge to imagination, and this is where the quality of imagination is vital. He leaves us all with work to be done.

---

12   Rory Medcalf, *Pivoting the Map: Australia's Indo-Pacific System*, Centre of Gravity Series Paper 1 (Canberra: Strategic and Defence Studies Centre, The Australian National University, 2012), hdl.handle.net/1885/228705.

13

Approaching Australian defence and strategic policy through strategic imagination

Stephan Frühling

Brendan Sargeant's writings on strategic imagination as a way to understand Australia's defence strategy and debates are as rich as they are brief. They leave a lot of tantalising avenues for further research, exploration and interpretation. As much as war and conflict are about the societies that wage it and weapons technology, ultimately, the motivation to use violence is a deeply human affair. Academic training in literature, classics or philosophy is thus both more useful for defence and strategic studies and more common among Australian Defence officials than one might think. But Brendan's writings still stand out in the very direct way he drew on his literary studies background to inform his thinking on Australian defence.

Brendan saw imagination—as well as the lack thereof—as a key element to understanding Australian strategy and policy. In his view, imagination underpins perception of the region, perception of Australia and the way strategy is developed and conceived. For Brendan, understanding imagination as a process and a contrast to reality and understanding Australia and the Australian imagination itself were thus crucial to understanding Australian defence policy past, present and future. This is most vividly illustrated in the parallels he drew in his speech at SDSC's fiftieth anniversary to Gerald Murnane's story of the study of 'Inner Australia'. Deeply steeped in Australia's strategic as well as literary history and traditions, this approach gave Brendan a basis for discussing Australia from a detached, analytical perspective that made any conversation with him on this topic stimulating, insightful—and often lengthy.

This chapter will examine the concept of strategic imagination in Brendan Sargeant's writings and explore it as a way of understanding past, current and future challenges in Australian defence policy. The long-term development of a defence force always deals with contingent developments—future conflicts that often never come to pass—which are inherently 'imagined' as possible future realities.[1] However, the chapter will also argue that Australia's strategic policy is unusually well suited to being understood through the prism of imagination and indeed the application of literary theory to strategic imagination, which Brendan so skilfully sketches in his writings.

As Brendan acknowledges in his PhD proposal, a conventional narrative of Australian strategic imagination has obvious material from which to draw. It reflects broader national debates about Australian identity as a part of an old empire or as a new settler community; of 'great and powerful friends', emancipation and independence; of tension between history and geography. In 1997, prime minister Paul Keating sought to draw a line under those debates, stating:

> No choice we can make as a nation lies between our history and our geography. We can hardly change either of them. They are immutable. The only choice we can make as a nation is the choice about our future.[2]

Approaching those debates through the lens of 'strategic imagination', however, makes it obvious that both Australia's geography and its history are anything but immutable, insofar as the significance of both lies in the way there are reimagined and reinterpreted in arguments about the nation's future. And, as Brendan lays out in his Centre of Gravity Series Paper, focusing on the role of imagination also provides a basis for asking how interpretation of both might—and should—evolve as strategic circumstances change.[3]

---

1   Stephan Frühling, 'Australian Strategic Guidance since the Second World War', in *A History of Australian Strategic Policy Since 1945*, edited by Stephan Frühling (Canberra: Defence Publishing Service, 2009), 9–10.

2   Paul Keating, 'A Prospect of Europe', Robert Schuman Lecture, University of New South Wales, Sydney, 4 September 1997, www.paulkeating.net.au/shop/item/a-prospect-of-europe---4-september-1997.

3   For a valuable recent reimagining of Australia's strategic geography, see Andrew Carr, 'Australia's Archipelagic Deterrence', *Survival* 65, no. 4 (2023): 79–100, doi.org/10.1080/00396338.2023.2239058.

Imagination is thus important, in an ontological as well as an epistemological sense, for policy because, as Brendan said in his speech on the fiftieth anniversary of SDSC, 'when you are confronted by a genuinely strategic decision … [it] is also a challenge to your self-conception, to your sense of who you are and who you might be. This is why strategic choices are hard.'[4] This statement is not just true, but also a useful antidote to the careless proliferation of the term 'strategic' in defence and political discourse. Indeed, it is a statement that arguably also holds true in reverse, in that a genuinely strategic decision will challenge a country's sense of what it is. Sweden's and Finland's recent decisions to join NATO, for example—and indeed the determination of the Ukrainian people to join the European community of nations in the Maidan Revolution of 2014—thus stand out as genuinely strategic in a way that decisions by few other countries have been since the end of the Cold War.

The need to take decisions that 'challenge … your self-conception' is mercifully quite rare. Australia has been—and remains—particularly blessed, or 'lucky',[5] in that regard. One could argue that there have been few if any such instances since the momentous events of 1788, which challenge Australia to this day: Federation in 1901 and the referendum of 1967 arguably being the most significant and, tellingly, mostly domestic decisions that formed modern Australia and its 'self-conception'.

In a defence context, prime minster John Curtin's decision to withdraw Australia's divisions from the Middle East in 1942 is one that perhaps turned out to be of more symbolic than practical consequence in the long term. I do not know whether Brendan had a hand in displaying the telegram of that decision in the Defence Committee room in the Defence building on Russell Hill, but I have no doubt that he would have approved. As he stated in his anniversary speech:

> When I reflect on the strategic history of Australia filtered through the development of the Defence organisation … what I hear is an ongoing conversation … about who we are … what sort of country we are and how we should participate in the world.

---

4   Brendan Sargeant, '"To See What Is Worth Seeing": Keynote Speech to the Strategic and Defence Studies Centre Fiftieth Anniversary Dinner, 21 July 2016' [Chapter 22, this volume].
5   Donald Horne, *The Lucky Country: Australia in the Sixties* (Melbourne: Penguin, 1964).

But, as he also cautioned:

> The institution will tell its own story if left to itself. The task of strategy is to make it listen and understand that the reality it sees itself as part of can have many dimensions and actually be something other than what it thinks it is.[6]

For Brendan, strategy is thus a struggle of imagination against reality (in his PhD proposal) or against experience (in his Centre of Gravity paper). This is a very rich approach, which has some parallels with the more common concept of strategy as a (falsifiable) 'theory of victory'.[7] But whereas the latter makes the concept of strategy abstract and systemic, focusing on the role of imagination highlights its human nature: strategy as a struggle between imagination and reality as lived experience is not just an intellectual exercise, but also a very personal and bureaucratic one. In that sense, it is a concept of strategy that is far more evocative and in sync with the two 'trinities' that Carl von Clausewitz argued are intrinsic to war: (the psychological effect) of hatred and enmity, probabilities and chance, and instrumentality and reason; and the people, military leadership and government.[8]

Importantly, imagination can be in contest with reality even if the latter has not 'falsified' underlying assumptions. Indeed, reality has been kind to Australia, so strategic debates are animated by imagination instead. In a comparative perspective, it is hard to avoid the impression that Australia's strategic debates about itself are perhaps so existential exactly because it has been spared existential crises where imagination crashed into reality. Australia was on the winning side in all the wars that mattered and when it was not, such as in Vietnam or Afghanistan, it carefully curates a collective memory that instead focuses on individual experiences and tactical successes. Domestically, while Australia has an evolving but unbroken history of government since 1788, France is on its fifth republic in the same time and Germany has had five or six national incarnations since Australian Federation. The experience of revolution that not only changes government but also profoundly affects every person's life trajectory is part of the living memory of many countries from Eastern Europe (as well as Portugal, Spain and Greece) to East Asia, Latin America and South Africa. The importance of imagination—including Australia's collective imagination of itself, its

---

6   Sargeant, 'To See What Is Worth Seeing'.
7   Stephan Frühling, 'Uncertainty, Forecasting and the Difficulty of Strategy', *Comparative Strategy* 25, no. 1 (2006): 19–31, doi.org/10.1080/01495930600639528.
8   Carl von Clausewitz, *Vom Kriege* [*On War*] (Stuttgart: Reclam, 1994), 42.

history and geography—for understanding Australia's strategic debates and policy is thus also a reflection of the *absence* of any lived experience of external or internal disjuncture.

In that sense, however, Australia's turn from forward defence to self-reliance and the 'Defence of Australia' in the 1970s was indeed a genuine 'challenge to the strategic imagination'. Australia had a hard time imagining a strategic future for itself different to the lived experience of working together with its 'great and powerful friends', the United Kingdom and the United States, in its own region. This was a challenge to Australian strategy not just because Australia had to imagine a different future, but also because the reality on which Australia's strategic view of itself was based was irrevocably changing: its allies reduced their commitments in South-East Asia and countries in the region—including Australia's own colony in Papua New Guinea—were gaining independence.

As Alan Thompson wrote in 1987, Australia entered this era with:

> organizational, structural and perceptual barriers to implementation of the defence of Australia itself … almost totally deficient in a capacity for strategic intelligence and assessment … commanders [who] were good tacticians, but by their role were precluded from strategy … [and] lacking in experience and knowledge of how to develop a national strategy that was more meaningful than shibboleths.[9]

Ultimately, as Brendan writes, 'a strong imagination asserts primacy over the continuities represented by tradition'[10] and this was certainly what happened in the case of the 'Defence of Australia'. As Thompson also wrote in 1987:

> Australia would have a fundamentally different approach to its defence if the likelihood of nuclear war between the superpowers were judged to be high. Exactly what that would have produced for defence policy is a fertile field for speculation. My own view is that we would have nuclear armed naval and air forces operating predominantly in the northern Pacific and a ground force able to help defend the Persian Gulf. But I am certain that Australia's defence would not contain a primary focus on meeting low level raids and harassments in Northern Australia.[11]

---

9   Alan Thompson, *Defence Down Under: Evolution and Revolution, 1971–88*, Working Paper (London: University of London Sir Robert Menzies Centre for Australian Studies, 1988), 5–6.
10   Sergeant, Chapter 2, this volume.
11   Thompson, *Defence Down Under*, 2.

In Brendan's concept, the strategy that evolved in Australia during the era of the 'Defence of Australia' can thus be understood as imagination unchallenged by harsh imposts of reality. The construct of the self-reliant 'Defence of Australia' was grounded in the historical memory of how limited US assistance had been in Australia's diplomatic and military conflicts with Indonesia over West Papua and during Konfrontasi. Ultimately, the edifice of Australia's strategic policy at the time was based on abductive logic—the logic of possibilities and imagination—rather than deduction from real threats or induction from operational pressures and experience.[12] Abductive logic underpinned the grounding of Australian strategic interests in geography,[13] as well as the approach to defence planning 'without a threat'[14] and reimagining Indonesia as the tough 'Kamarians' that Brendan still encountered the army fighting against four decades later.

Approaching the debates and policies of the time through literary studies thus seems highly apt. Brendan writes that '[i]magination creates worlds— "images or concepts of external objects not present to the senses"'.[15] Indeed, Australia's defence policy during the 'Defence of Australia' era was most peculiar as it was developed, described and debated through the meaning of abstract concepts—'self-reliance', 'Defence of Australia', 'warning'— that persist to this day. Or, in Brendan's words: 'The *1987 Defence White Paper* and the *2020 Defence Strategic Update*, for example, can merge in an uncanny ahistorical space to become one text with variation.'[16] Social scientists, including this author, tend to approach these as 'contested concepts', but there is no doubt that an approach based on the far more sophisticated structural literary theories that Brendan sketches in his PhD proposal would yield far richer, more interesting—and policy relevant— observations. For these concepts are not merely contested but also shift their meaning—or must be actively reinterpreted and redefined—to fit their

---

12   For a discussion of the logical underpinning of defence planning concepts, see Stephan Frühling, *Defence Planning and Uncertainty: Preparing for the Next Asia-Pacific War* (Abingdon: Routledge, 2014), 25–29, doi.org/10.4324/9781315818764.

13   Hugh White, 'Strategic Interests in Australian Defence Policy: Some Historical and Methodological Reflections', *Security Challenges* 4, no. 2 (2008): 63–79.

14   Paul Dibb, *The Conceptual Basis of Australia's Defence Planning and Force Structure Development*, Canberra Paper No. 88 (Canberra: Strategic and Defence Studies Centre, The Australian National University, 1992).

15   Brendan Sargeant, *Challenges to the Australian Strategic Imagination*, Centre of Gravity Series Papers 58 (Canberra: Strategic and Defence Studies Centre, The Australian National University, 2021), 4, hdl. handle.net/1885/233085.

16   Brendan Sargeant, Chapter 2, this volume.

context.[17] As early as 1979, Des Ball quoted a first assistant secretary in the Department of Defence commenting that the *Strategic Basis*, the most senior policy guidance document at the time, 'is the gospel; but it has as many interpretations as the gospel'.[18] Indeed, describing Australian defence debates as 'defence theology' is an analogy that is as fitting and common in the Australian context as it is rare and remarkable from the outside; the only other situation where the term received similar use was in northern hemisphere debates about (equally imaginary) nuclear strategy during the Cold War.[19]

To highlight the importance of imagination in making sense of Australian strategy after Vietnam is by no means to denigrate the importance of the achievements of that era. But it may help explain the subsequent struggles as the exigencies of reality reimposed their place as worthy contestants of the imagination. Indeed, one of the interesting questions about Australian strategic history is why, despite an ever-more frequent series of crises in the South-West Pacific, strategic policy guidance of the 1990s in the end so underestimated the importance of operations in Australia's inner neighbourhood before the deployment of the International Force East Timor (INTERFET) in 1999. The idea that 'the institution will tell its own story if left to itself' is certainly part of the answer. Those with a less geographically based concept of Australia's national interest would argue that the imagination that underpinned the policy consensus of the 1980s and 1990s had itself become a challenge to a more holistic imagination of Australia's security.

Certainly, if strategy arises from a contest of imagination and reality within the Defence organisation, that reality can thus also take the form of a new government and proactive minister! As esoteric as Brendan's approach may seem, it is rooted in a deep understanding of—and deep sympathy for—the Defence organisation itself:

---

17 Interested readers are invited, for example, to compare paragraph 2.21 of the 1987 White Paper with paragraph 3.30 of the 2020 *Defence Strategic Update*.

18 Quoted in Desmond Ball, *The Politics of Defence Decision Making in Australia: The Strategic Background*, Reference Paper 93 (Canberra: Strategic and Defence Studies Centre, The Australian National University, 1979), 1.

19 See, for example, the discussion on the exegesis of 'flexible response' in Ivo Daalder, *The Nature and Practice of 'Flexible Response': NATO Strategy and Theater Nuclear Forces since 1967* (New York: Columbia University Press, 1991), doi.org/10.7312/daal92104. French thinking about the principles and practice of strategic autonomy is the only other example of which the author can think, which, being rooted in both Cartesian thinking and the French imagination of the historical role of the *Grande Nation*, also proves the point.

> I work in an organization … that does many different things every moment of the day. It never sleeps. It never stops. It is relentless. It has its own imperatives and appetites. It has a personality and life independent of those people and organisations that contribute to its being. It is what it is and, in its deepest dreaming, has no desire but to be what it is.[20]

As much as strategy is a matter of international pressures and high policy, it is ultimately also something that arises from the contest of imagination and experience within that organisation, and one of the limits to strategy lies in the limits to imagination within the Defence organisation itself.

Brendan's approach based on imagination is so useful because it can ultimately encompass both these aspects of strategy; indeed, I would argue that he saw them as inseparable. Effective national strategy arises from—or is at least enabled by—the extent to which the Defence organisation can imagine a different reality. No-one impersonates this unity better than Sir Arthur Tange, who not only shaped strategic thinking in the Vietnam and post-Vietnam eras, but also created the modern Department of Defence.[21]

To be effective, strategic imagination must shape the organisation itself, exactly because this can set up clashes with its experience and inertia. Brendan has left little writing—at least in the public domain—about imagination and strategy within the Defence organisation and its relationship with national strategy. But a common thrust of the changes with which he was associated—from strengthened corporate planning and 'One Defence' and the fostering of a strong strategic centre and re-establishment of a contestability function, to the creation of a wider national security community—is that they all sought, in one form or another, to help the organisation question itself, rethink its own role and assumptions and thereby make it fit for future challenges.

What are those future challenges? 'Policy is as much about creating future worlds by describing them as it is about bringing those worlds into being through strategy,'[22] Brendan wrote. If strategy arises from the clash of imagination with reality (or experience), Australian strategy in the 1980s and 1990s was characterised by a surfeit of the former, and that of the

---

20   Sargeant, Chapter 22, this volume.

21   Sir Arthur Tange, *Australian Defence: Report on the Reorganisation of the Defence Group of Departments* (Canberra: AGPS, 1973).

22   Brendan Sargeant, 'The Pacific Islands in the "Indo-Pacific"', *Security Challenges* 16, no. 1 (2020): 26–31, at 30.

2000s and 2010s by a surfeit of the latter.[23] However, vacillating between creating intellectual edifices to guide preparations for ultimately imagined threats on the one hand, and satisfying the urgent demands of ongoing operations on the other, has left Australian strategy—and the Defence organisation—poorly prepared to imagine the role of armed force in shaping the international environment it faces today.

There was once a brief and intriguing time when the end of the Vietnam War was on the horizon and Australia imagined a less stable postwar region than it became, when Australia thus had to contemplate the need for a genuinely national strategy to secure its own region and security. Encapsulated in the 1968 and 1971 Strategic Basis papers, drawn up by the then interdepartmental Defence Committee that comprised not just the secretary of defence and service chiefs, but also the secretaries of the departments of Foreign Affairs, Prime Minister and Cabinet and Treasury, are sketches of a broad strategy of regional engagement in South-East Asia with economic, political, diplomatic and military dimensions, through which they prepared to address an imagined, unstable post-Vietnam environment that never came to be.[24]

'Grand strategy' in that sense does not come easily to Australia. In the Euro-Atlantic context, foreign, defence and economic policies of the late 1990s and early 2000s were dominated by a generational project of 'neighbourhood policy' to make Central and Eastern Europe ready to join the European Union and NATO—an undertaking institutionalised in NATO membership action plans and EU accession programs that sought to knit together what had been torn asunder by the Cold War and, before that, the end of the great empires after World War I. The author has vivid memories, after arriving in Australia from that region in the mid-2000s, of a distinct sense that there must be something he did not get, that he was missing something in Australian policy, of looking in the wrong places or looking for the wrong forms, when searching for Australia's equivalent program for its own 'Pacific community'. Even the Pacific 'Step-Up' remains defined almost solely by what it seeks to prevent and how, rather than by 'creating a future world' that it seeks to achieve (let alone as a shared project with the Pacific itself).

---

23   See also Andrew Carr and Stephan Frühling, 'Australia: The Limits of Pragmatism', in *Defence Planning for Small and Middle Powers*, edited by Tim Sweijs, Saskia van Genugten, and Frans Osinga (Abingdon: Routledge, 2024).

24   See Stephan Frühling, *Ghosts of Papers Past: The Strategic Basis Papers and Australian National Security Strategy in the Twenty-First Century*, Occasional Paper 3 (Canberra: ANU National Security College, 2012).

Brendan had a leading hand in the creation of the *2013 Defence White Paper* that introduced the concept of the 'Indo-Pacific' to Australian strategic guidance. 'The Indo-Pacific is as much a policy construct as it is a geographical reality, so how it evolves further will in part depend on how policy and academic communities build and use the idea,'[25] he wrote in 2020. It is easy to see how he was attracted to the concept of the 'Indo-Pacific'. Rooted as it is in economic and geographic realities but also an imagined community, the way it is open to interpretation and only takes form as a policy project as a new imagining of what used to be referred to as the 'Asia-Pacific' region makes it almost an embodiment of his definition of strategy, as a contest of imagination and reality.[26]

A key element in this is the role of the US alliance. 'Australia's management of the alliance since the Vietnam War through to the beginning of the Trump era responded to a strategic environment that was relatively stable and, in terms of potential crises, relatively low risk', Brendan wrote in 2021, and, in 'this context, Australia has managed its alliance relationship by establishing processes that enable it to maximise its discretionary decision-making capacity'.[27] Living memory or experience is not required to imagine a different form for the alliance, but it certainly can help. A key challenge for Australian defence policy and strategy today is that the time in which it actively sought to use its US alliances—ANZUS as well as the Southeast Asia Treaty Organization (SEATO), the latter of which was far more important than the former but is almost completely forgotten— to actively deter threats and shape our region is now well beyond living memory.[28]

---

25 Sargeant, 'The Pacific Islands in the "Indo-Pacific"', 26.

26 See Brendan Taylor, 'Contested Concept: Unpacking Australia's Indo-Pacific Debate', *Asian Politics and Policy* 12, no. 1 (2020): 71–83, doi.org/10.1111/aspp.12512.

27 Brendan Sargeant, 'Australia: Maximising Discretion in an Untested Alliance', in *Alliances, Nuclear Weapons and Escalation: Managing Deterrence in the 21st Century*, edited by Stephan Frühling and Andrew O'Neil (Canberra: ANU Press, 2021), 101–10, at 105–6, doi.org/10.22459/ANWE.2021.09.

28 The challenges themselves and their implications are well beyond the scope of this chapter but include the problems of integrating Australia's regional and the United States' global strategies, managing extended deterrence, limited appreciation of the role and importance of alliance institutions and the use of forward presence for deterrence. See Stephan Frühling, 'Australian Strategic Policy in the Global Context of the Cold War, 1945–65', in *Fighting Australia's Cold War*, edited by Tristan Moss and Peter Dean (Canberra: ANU Press, 2021), 11–34, doi.org/10.22459/FACW.2021.01; Stephan Frühling, 'The Fuzzy Limits of Self-Reliance: US Extended Deterrence and Australian Strategic Policy', *Australian Journal of International Affairs* 67, no. 1 (2013): 18–34, doi.org/10.1080/10357718.2013.748273; Stephan Frühling, 'Is ANZUS Really an Alliance? Aligning the US and Australia', *Survival* 60, no. 5 (2018): 199–218, doi.org/10.1080/00396338.2018.1518384; Andrew Carr and Stephan Frühling, *Forward Presence for Deterrence: Implications for the Australian Army* (Canberra: Army Research Centre, 2023).

As Brendan wrote:

> Australia needs to move towards a sense of strategic community in which participation enables and strengthens that community … But much of our strategic discourse has worked against the idea of a community of nations with shared interests and challenges that are of greater importance for the future than purely national concerns.[29]

Hence, there is 'an overriding imperative to recognise the reality of interdependence, and to acknowledge that giving expression in action to this interdependence may be a more pressing requirement than the traditional focus on the preservation of state sovereignty'.[30] Percy Spender would no doubt have agreed and, while Brendan wrote these lines in the context of Australia and the South Pacific, we can equally apply the same thought to the US alliance—or to relations with Japan and other countries in the Indo-Pacific.

As discussed at the start of this chapter, Brendan recognised the opposing poles of Australia's narrative of itself, such as independence and alliance, as important elements of our strategic imagination, but at the same time he saw a need to challenge what they should mean. Independence and alliance not as opposing poles of Australian strategic policy, but alliance as a prerequisite of independence—now there is certainly a challenge to the Australian strategic imagination! Close reading of, building on and further developing the ideas that we can find in Brendan's writings will no doubt turn up many more. Other readers of his works will no doubt come to different conclusions. But through the imagination that his writings kindle, Brendan's legacy will live on.

---

29 Sargeant, 'The Pacific Islands in the "Indo-Pacific"', 30.
30 Brendan Sargeant, *The Implications of Climate Change for Australian Strategic and Defence Policy in Relation to the Alliance and Pacific Island States*, Regional Outlook 68 (Brisbane: Griffith Asia Institute, Griffith University, 2021), 14.

14

Strategic imagination: The case of reimagining Nordic defence

Robbin Laird

I first met my friend and colleague Brendan Sargeant when I was working on the F-35 aircraft program. I had earlier worked on the Aegis combat system program and coined the phrase the 'Aegis global enterprise', referring to the possibility that if several allies operated the program, we would build a unique shared sensor capability. I suggested to Brendan that we would see in the future an even more powerful 'F-35 global enterprise'.

We talked at some length about the program and its unique qualities, which could create a new type of combat aircraft and sharing arrangement for data and command and control in the future. Ironically, I first came to Australia in 2014 precisely to write my first report for the Williams Foundation, dealing with airpower and its evolution and the unique contribution provided by fifth-generation capability.

That is in part what Sargeant was talking about when considering using strategic imagination to envisage a world in which, in this case, ubiquitous new technological capabilities would alter the defence landscape. But he clearly meant more than that. In a 2021 interview I did with him, we discussed the nexus of global shifts or crises and strategic imagination. This is what he emphasised:

> We need to be ruthless in our self-analysis, about our strengths and weaknesses, and who we are. We need to have a clear sense of the range of possible futures and the various responses that we may need to make. That is why I say a crisis is a challenge to imagination, a challenge to identity before it becomes a policy or a strategy challenge.[1]

Brendan underscored the importance of strategic imagination for reshaping defence and foreign policies when entering a new historical era, such as we are doing right now. As he noted in his Centre of Gravity Series Paper in 2021:

> A country will possess a strategic imagination which will have evolved over time in response to the influence of geography, history, culture, and the many other tangible and intangible forces that go to create a community and its vision of itself. A country's strategic imagination is a living thing, dynamic and evolving in contact with the world, and full of contradictions. In those rare moments in a country's history where a genuine choice must be made and action taken, a country's strategic imagination becomes most visible.[2]

We are in a new historical era

What Brendan and I discussed frequently by phone and in person was the fact that we had entered a new historical era. It was no longer an American-dominated 'rules-based order'. It was not an era for the spread of democracy but one in which multipolar authoritarian movements and states were becoming more prevalent.

What, then, did the liberal democracies need to do to preserve their way of life? What kind of alliance relationships made sense for Australia in the new situation? What kind of US leadership was possible? What kind of European dynamic would evolve from the growing impact of both China and Russia on the future of the European Continent?

---

1   Robbin Laird, 'Strategic Imagination: Meeting the Challenge', *Defense.Info*, 7 June 2021, defense. info/re-thinking-strategy/2021/07/strategic-imagination-meeting-the-challenge/.

2   Brendan Sargeant, *Challenges to the Australian Strategic Imagination*, Centre of Gravity Series Papers 58 (Canberra: Strategic and Defence Studies Centre, The Australian National University, 2021), hdl. handle.net/1885/233085.

Reimagining Nordic defence

I discussed with him what I thought was a good case study of the new era, what liberal democracies could do and the kind of American leadership that was possible. Frankly, I always work through case studies to general developments, for this is the only way that I can understand the details of general trends. He was focusing on India as his case study; I was focusing on the emergence of Nordic defence integration.

The strategic shift he was highlighting is clearly happening today in the Nordic region as the Nordic nations rather dramatically think through how to work together and how their alliances will change in the defence of Northern Europe in the face of threat, not only from Russia, but also from China.

My colleague Rear Admiral (retired) Nils Wang discussed in the autumn of 2022 how one should think about the 'new' geography of a Nordic defence that included both Sweden and Finland in NATO. He underscored that:

> for the first time in our lifetimes not only do the Nordic countries share common values but [they] will work within a common defence alliance. Although Sweden and Finland over the years cooperated more fully with NATO countries, they will now be fully integrated into NATO defence planning. That means they will look at their capacities compared with other NATO countries in order to have the right balance in the region. Now one needs to think in terms of defence of the North of Europe from Iceland to the Finnish and Norwegian borders.[3]

Finland and Sweden joining NATO changes how the defence of Northern Europe will work. There are three clusters of defence problems, each of which changes somewhat the key states in that cluster.

The first is a North Atlantic challenge associated with the Greenland–Iceland–United Kingdom gap. Here, Denmark, Norway and Iceland are the lead states in the region, but as Sweden reworks it air–maritime approaches it could be a player as well.

---

3   Rear Admiral (retired) Nils Wang, Interview with the author, 2022.

The second are the security and defence areas associated with the High North. In NATO until now, Norway has been the leader on these issues, but the entrance of Finland and Sweden provides significant opportunities for collaborative approaches.

The third area is that of the Baltic Sea and region. This area could see significant innovation. On the one hand, the Baltic Sea becomes a 'NATO' area as all the states that border it are NATO members, with Russia's entrance to the Baltic coming through the Gulf of Finland. Improvements to the security and defence of the Baltic Sea could be generated through innovations in maritime robotics and shared intelligence, surveillance and reconnaissance systems.

On the other hand, the defence of the Baltic states places the Nordic states as their strategic reserve along with Germany and Poland. An ability to project power in their defence through collaboration in ground capabilities and air–ground power through lift systems and innovations in ground manoeuvre forces will be significant in shaping an effective way ahead.

The point is rather straightforward: no defence problem has the same defence solution or the same lead state in shaping that solution. Each state can contribute assets to common defence problems, but each state could lead with an 'unbalanced' force structure—air versus maritime versus land systems—with that state's lead role within a particular 'defence cluster' within the overall defence challenges faced by the region.

How can we shape the most effective integrated force for the region given the different dense clusters and the ability of nations to emphasise their specific capabilities and contributions, and avoid unnecessary duplications of capabilities?

Several of the key security problems for the new era affect this region as well. How to defend offshore facilities from drone attacks? How to monitor undersea threats to infrastructure? How to defend undersea infrastructure?

The Nordic innovations in defence can intersect well with the innovations begun by the stand-up of the Second Fleet and Allied Joint Force Command Norfolk. This provides a case study of how key allies are reworking their defence and how the United States could craft a more realistic and appropriate contribution.

In fact, the re-establishment of the Second Fleet and the activation of the only NATO command on US territory clearly reflect the exercise of strategic imagination regarding North Atlantic defence before Finland's and Sweden's decision to joint NATO.[4]

In 2018, when US Navy Admiral John Richardson was the chief of navy operations, he commissioned the new Second Fleet. This was not a re-establishment of the fleet stood down by the Obama administration; it was a new approach to shaping maritime operations in the North Atlantic. The navy chief had a clear desire to re-establish a command that could address North Atlantic defence and, notably, the growing importance of coalition operations in the High North.

The Second Fleet is not a large command, certainly when compared with other numbered fleets. During the fleet's first three months, its commander, US Navy Vice-Admiral Andrew Lewis, worked with fewer than 10 staff to create the foundations of how the fleet should be established and how best to work its concept of operations.

Lewis described the process:

> We had a charter to re-establish the fleet. Using the newly published national defence strategy and national security strategy as the prevailing guidance, we spent a good amount of time defining the problem.
>
> My team put together an offsite with the Naval Postgraduate School to think about the way ahead, to take time to define the problem we were established to solve and determine how best to organize ourselves to solve those challenges. We used the Einstein approach: we spent 55 minutes of the hour defining the problem and five minutes in solving it. Similarly, we spent the first two and a half months of our three-month pre-launch period working to develop our mission statement along with the functions and tasks associated with those missions.

4   For a comprehensive look at the new commands in Norfolk as part of the strategic rethinking, which can be correctly identified as reflecting strategic imagination, see Chapter 8 ('It's Not My Father's Second Fleet', pp. 269–96) of my co-authored book, Robbin Laird and Edward Timperlake, *A Maritime Kill Web Force in the Making: Deterrence and Warfighting in the 21st Century* (Pennsauken: BookBaby, 2022).

> From the beginning our focus was in developing an all-domain and all-function command. To date, we clearly have focused on the high-end warfighting, but in a way that we can encompass all aspects of warfare from seabed to space as well.[5]

But the focus is not simply a new American command. The first operational NATO command on US territory, Joint Force Command Norfolk (JFC Norfolk) was also commissioned under Lewis. Structuring the new Second Fleet and JFC Norfolk under one commander signifies a clear focus on interoperability and shaping a credible twenty-first-century defence capability and infrastructure for deterrence and warfighting in the northern region.

The North Atlantic has returned as a core part of the defence challenge, but new relationships, new technologies and innovative concepts of operations are being shaped by the commands, under the leadership of Vice-Admiral Lewis.

Lewis's first deputy was a rear admiral from a distinguished navy family, John Mustin. Recalling his service with the Second Fleet, Mustin (who is now a Vice-Admiral and head of Navy Reserve) commented:

> As the 2nd Fleet Commander, Vice-Admiral Lewis clearly understands that we need to shape a new approach. When I was in High School in the 80s, my father was the 2nd Fleet Commander, so I can legitimately say that 'The new 2nd Fleet is not your father's 2nd Fleet.'[6]

That assertion is reflected in Lewis's current deputy and vice-commanders. On one side of Lewis's spartan office area is the office of Canadian Rear Admiral Steve Waddell, vice-commander of the Second Fleet, and on the other is the office of the deputy commander of JFC Norfolk, Rear Admiral Andrew Betton, of the Royal Navy, who was the first commander of HMS *Queen Elizabeth*. Those admirals, along with Norwegian, French and German admirals and a British commodore in the JFC, have tremendous command experience navigating some of the most challenging sea states in the world.

---

5   Robbin Laird and Ed Timperlake, 'Shaping a Way Ahead for North Atlantic Defense: The Perspective of VADM Lewis', *Second Line of Defense*, 26 May 2021, sldinfo.com/2021/05/shaping-a-way-ahead-for-north-atlantic-defense-the-perspective-of-vadm-lewis/.
6   ibid.

This advanced state of very senior defence collaboration is a key incubator for the shaping of new defence capabilities. The key role for cross-learning among allied navies is enhanced as well by the third command and has been incorporated into the Second Fleet.

The Combined Joint Operations from the Sea Centre of Excellence (CJOS COE) is the only NATO Centre of Excellence in the United States. It was established in 2006 and continued to exist while Second Fleet did not. Between the Second Fleet's stand-down in 2011 and its return in 2018, the CJOS COE worked hard to shape the way NATO-wide maritime operations would contribute to Atlantic defence and, in the wake of the events of 2014, focused on the coming reset of North Atlantic maritime operations. Admiral Lewis understood the importance of the centre in relation to the core operations of the Second Fleet, in terms of not just managing a NATO effort, but also the kind of distributed integrated force that must be shaped to deal with the new strategic environment.

A key change being addressed by the three commands under Vice-Admiral Lewis is the scope of the territory covered—namely, defence efforts in the High North. Establishing the new command in 2018, Admiral Richardson described the future scope of operations: 'A new 2nd Fleet increases our strategic flexibility to respond—from the Eastern Seaboard to the Barents Sea. Second Fleet will approach the North Atlantic as one continuous operational space, and conduct expeditionary fleet operations where and when needed.'[7]

The new operational area covered by the Second Fleet and synergistically shaped by the JFC-experienced admirals clearly includes the Arctic, the High North more generally and Nordic waters. Richardson highlighted that shift in this new approach and made clear the focus would be on projecting force: 'This one will be high-end, blue-water warfare using major elements of maritime power.'

Under the leadership of Vice-Admiral Lewis, the commands (for the two together really constitute the shaping of the new defence infrastructure) have pursued a very innovative approach to building capability. The Second Fleet was being shaped as new military capabilities were being generated

---

7   Robbin Laird and Ed Timperlake, 'Re-Crafting North Atlantic Defense: The Impact of the 2nd Fleet and Joint Force Command Norfolk', *Second Line of Defense*, 15 March 2021, sldinfo.com/2021/03/re-crafting-north-atlantic-defense-the-impact-of-the-2nd-fleet-and-joint-force-command-norfolk/.

on both the blue and the red sides of the equation. This command can leverage the practical capabilities that fifth-generation aircraft operating in the United Kingdom and the Nordic countries can deliver as well.

This will intersect most notably regarding common infrastructure, bases and sustainment decisions. A new era of significant innovation in Northern European and North Atlantic defence could be opening. In the summer of 2022, I talked with the admiral who led the initial efforts to re-establish the Second Fleet and stand-up JFC Norfolk about the impact of the Nordic innovations. For Vice-Admiral (retired) Lewis:

> With the changes in the Nordic region, there will be an opportunity, for JFC Norfolk to become a four-star command on an equivalent level with JFC Brunssum and Naples from a rank standpoint. We could also have a subordinate command physically stationed in the Nordic nations, that would have the effect of pulling the continents together whereas JFC Norfolk is stationed obviously in the continental United States.

> This would allow for significant innovation in thinking through how, in a practical sense, operations from east to west and west to east in the North Atlantic battlespace.[8]

The Finnish case

For years, there has been little room for argument that Finland is laser focused on how to defend its territory. The Finns have a long history of living with the Russians, including a century of being part of the Russian Empire itself (1809–1917). Knowing the Russians as well as they do, they are organised to defend when necessary their nation against their big neighbour.

Unlike others in Europe, Finland never bought into the idea of East–West peace lasting forever after the collapse of the Soviet Union. Indeed, just months after the dissolution of the Soviet Union, the Finns signed a $3-billion agreement to purchase 64 F-18 fighters—a major investment at the time, even as the world seemed ready to embrace a post–Cold War era.

---

8   Robbin Laird, 'The Way Ahead for Northern European Defense: Shaping the Future with Sweden and Finland as NATO Members', *Second Line of Defense*, 5 December 2022, sldinfo.com/2022/12/the-way-ahead-for-northern-european-defense-shaping-the-future-with-sweden-and-finland-as-nato-members/.

The F-18 procurement was a decision that underwrote enhanced Finnish sovereignty, while making a key tie with NATO interoperability, even as Helsinki threaded the needle between Russia and NATO for decades more. That legacy was echoed when Finland announced its decision on 10 December 2021 to buy the F-35 from the United States (and not the offering from close neighbour and militarily neutral partner Sweden), which clearly factored in the benefits of working more closely with key strategic allies to deflect Russian President Vladimir Putin's efforts to go back to a world in which 'Finlandisation' was a word.

With Finland officially joining NATO in April 2023, alliance members have begun planning how to integrate Finnish airpower into strategies to counter Russia. There is a base of knowledge from which to work: Finland has been participating in cross-border airpower training for several years with Norway and Sweden. Now it will be fully integrated with the other F-35 partners in the region—Norway, Denmark, Poland, the Netherlands and Belgium—along with other F-35 operators in the United States, the United Kingdom and Germany.

This means that when the Finns fly their aircraft, they will be part of a significant intelligence, surveillance and reconnaissance belt looking deep into areas of Russian interest and can provide command and control links to create a more integrated force response, dependent on national decisions. As I have written for years, the F-35 is not a traditional fighter aircraft; it is a flying combat system whose capabilities become magnified the more F-35s there are in the air. (Relatedly, the United States and the European F-35 partners must move more quickly on using the F-35 as an integrated force and its ability to deliver longer-range strikes against Russian targets in case of conflict.)

This means that Putin now faces a much more integrated and lethal force that can engage across the spectrum of conflict. Ironically, the Russians have skilfully generated Nordic defence collaboration and much closer working relationships with the Baltic states and Poland as well.

Given its location, Finland is a key state affecting how the Russians play the geopolitical game along their border with the NATO nations.

My travels to Finland and continuing discussions with Finns have taught me much about how they look at the evolving strategic situation. Their perspective and approach to defence modernisation were well articulated by Jukka Juusti, permanent secretary in the Ministry of Defence, in an interview conducted during a visit to Helsinki in February 2018.

Finland is clearly focused on mobilisation and security of supply as key foundations of national defence. And, as military transformation unfolds, these core capabilities become increasingly important to deal with the challenge identified in the Finnish defence policy document published in 2017: the threshold for the use of military force is lower and the time to respond shorter.

According to Juusti:

> If you look at the map of Finland, it's not an island but in practice we are an island. The vast majority of our trade is coming by ships. In that sense we are an island and this means that we have taken the security of supply always very seriously. It is the nature of Finland that we believe that we have to be able to take care of some of the most vital things by ourselves. That's the reason, for example, that security of supply is so important for us. For example, with regard to ammunition and those kinds of supplies, we have a lot of stocks here in Finland. Of course, with regard to some of the equipment we never can have enough in our own resources.[9]

Holding such a perspective means that Finns are unlikely to be shocked by current Russian behaviour. But Finland joining NATO, given its pragmatic view of the nature of the defence challenge, should push other NATO nations, including the United States, to get realistic about the depth of the defence challenge posed by Russia and China and the significance of the changes that must be made.

Indeed, the prospect of an integrated Nordic defence following on from their enhanced cooperation of the past few years can provide a significant stimulus for change in the approach taken to defence by both the United States and Finland's European allies.

---

9   Robbin Laird, 'Finland, in NATO and with the F-35, Forms a Powerful Challenge to Russia', *Breaking Defense*, 11 July 2022, breakingdefense.com/2022/07/finland-in-nato-and-with-the-f-35-forms-a-powerful-challenge-to-russia/#:~:text=That's%20the%20reason%2C%20for%20example,enough%20 in%20our%20own%20resources.

The Danish case

With NATO's expansion to include Sweden and Finland, how the Nordic nations rework their national security approaches and capabilities is a major challenge—and an opportunity. Denmark could play an important role in triggering innovative thinking and shaping Nordic integration.

The Kingdom of Denmark includes both Greenland and the Faroe Islands. As such, the kingdom's territory forms, in effect, the strategic rear for a Nordic integration effort—and requires their small navy and air force to operate over distances greater than a non-Dane might consider.

Because of its role in Greenland and the Faroe Islands, Denmark has reach in these important geographical areas as part of both North Atlantic defence and Arctic engagement. The Russians have expanded the perimeter of their defence capabilities in the Arctic and, in so doing, have raised concerns among the other Arctic powers. This is a core worry for the Nordic nations and an important consideration for their national and collective defence modernisation efforts.

As a result, linking communications inside the military, as well as between military and civilian authorities, is vital. This means the Danes have had to work non–line-of-sight capabilities for NATO's military data Link 16, which involves, among other things, ways to move Link 16 data over other networks.

Innovation in command and control now is a key part of the focus of Danish defence leaders and for shaping a way ahead for Nordic defence integration. In a 2021 interview I did with Major General Anders Rex, then head of the Danish Air Force and now in charge of the Danish Defence Review, he underscored how crucial command and control innovation is—using current technologies and not relying on some futuristic Joint All-Domain Command and Control world—for shaping integrability in the region. (While I believe joint all-domain command and control is clearly the future, I agree with Rex's point that we must work on enhanced capabilities with the current force.) Rex said:

> We need focus on both in parallel. Denmark does not have the muscle to shape the future of all-domain command and control, but we also need to drive the change—we need now to get the job done. What I have been focused on over the past couple of years is to make our force better now.

> We actually already have the capability to shape more effective networks of intelligence, surveillance and reconnaissance and [command and control] without significant investments. For example, we are leveraging the joint range extension application protocol (JREAP) that requires modest investments, and it is a way for us, our allies and coalition partners to build a modest combat cloud linking our data.[10]

When I visited Copenhagen in the summer of 2022, I had a chance to talk with Defence and industry officials in Denmark and it was clear there is a focus on innovations that could drive joint Nordic defence. That includes going beyond the command-and-control question to find other ways to work together. One issue facing Denmark's current defence review is that it was set in motion and is scheduled for release before Finland and Sweden accede to NATO. So, the challenge is to ensure that whatever changes are put in place during the domestic review do not get in the way of potential Nordic integration.

One area where we could see better integration regionally is on the water. The Danes are among the most innovative ship designers in the world. The Iver Huitfeldt–class frigate combines capability with affordability and the United Kingdom has adopted the Danish design for its new fleet of general-purpose frigates in a deal with Babcock International. With the clear need for Sweden, Norway and Denmark to expand their maritime capabilities in enhancing strategic depth for Nordic defence, Denmark is focusing on new ways to build a ship that can fit into a kill-web concept of operations or the ability of the ship to integrate with air and ground combat systems to deliver an integrated fire solution.

With Sweden facing a clear need to shift from its land-centric homeland defence posture and Finland also adjusting to a posture that provides for deep defence for the region, such Danish thinking could provide a trigger for shaping new and innovative ways ahead for Nordic defence innovation and integration.

---

10 Robbin Laird, 'Major General Anders Rex: Shaping Integratability', *Defense.Info*, 3 March 2021, defense.info/interview-of-the-week/major-general-anders-rex-shaping-integratability/.

The Norwegian case

In any reimagining of what Nordic defence looks like, Norway—a founding NATO state that served as the alliance's de facto lead in the High North—is a central player. Certainly, the template it has shaped in restructuring its defence since 2014 provides a central foundation for the way ahead. Yet, its role as the central player in NATO's Northern Europe defence strategy is changing as it becomes part of a much larger NATO area with the inclusion of Finland and Sweden.

But now that Norway is no longer the sole Nordic NATO leader in this key region, change should come. The focus will be primarily on not a conventional air–ground threat but an air–maritime and missile threat, which means Norway's investments in F-35 Aegis systems and the P-8, along with a joint purchase with Germany of new submarines, provide a solid template on which to build for the region. They are enhancing both active and passive defence systems for their bases and relying on sea bases as well.

For example, at the main F-35 base at Ørland, which I visited when it was being built in 2018, force protection is integrated into the design. In addition, they have moved their Quick Reaction Alert (QRA) base much further north, from Bodø to the Evenes Air Station. On 6 January 2022, the Royal Norwegian Air Force F-35s officially took over the QRA mission from the F-16. The P-8s will operate from Evenes as well.

Norway has also regenerated its 'total defence' concept to provide for mobilisation in case of crisis and conflict. As stated in its long-term defence plan published in 2018:

> The complexity of threats and risks requires stronger and more flexible civil–military cooperation. We will continue to build resilience and civil preparedness in order to strengthen the ability of the nation to withstand and recover from attacks and incidents. The defence of Norway is dependent on a modern Total Defence framework, which enables relevant civilian assets to support the national and allied defence efforts during peacetime, crisis and armed conflict.[11]

---

11 Norwegian Ministry of Defence, *The Defence of Norway: Capability and Readiness—Long Term Defence Plan 2020* (Oslo: Government of Norway, 2020), www.regjeringen.no/contentassets/7d48f0 e5213d48b9a0b8e100c608bfce/long-term-defence-plan-norway-2020---english-summary.pdf, 2.

The first test of the revised (from the time of the Cold War) total defence concept was the Trident Juncture NATO exercise held in Norway in 2018. I interviewed marines who participated in those exercises during a visit to 2nd Marine Aircraft Wing in North Carolina, US, and they recounted being supported by members of Norway's civil society as well as the host nation's military. It was clear when they were operating in Norway that it is a committed ally and the population is highly supportive of US Marine Corps operations, including providing real-time intelligence on the 'enemy' force. This was noted as a significant difference from US Marine Corps operations in the Middle East.

What we have seen already is that the chiefs of defence from the four Nordic countries have been working towards a plan for increased cooperation. The early focus appears to be twofold.

First, is a focus on how the region can work together to support allied reinforcements in a time of crisis. Until now this has been primarily a Norwegian activity, with the engagement of Denmark; now, there is a focus on how to use the entire region and to disperse forces including those that come from external allies in times of crisis. According to one source, the Nordic proposal to support reinforcements would be through the ice-free port of Narvik in northern Norway, Trondheim Fjord in the middle of Norway, the Gothenburg region in Sweden and the Esbjerg harbour in Denmark.

Second, the Nordic defence chiefs would like to see a new format for the Cold Response Exercise. Renamed Nordic Response, the focus would be on Nordic integration across the region. It would set in motion new large-scale exercises that could allow the region to coordinate their multi-domain efforts in air and maritime integration, with an eye beyond preparing for a ground–air assault from the Russians.

As one senior Nordic defence official told me recently:

> This is a chance to rebuild our defence together in innovative new ways. We don't want to prepare for the Cold War; we have to look at the challenges from not just the Russians but the threat from the Pacific as well.[12]

---

12   Robbin Laird, 'Re-Imaging Nordic Defense: The Norwegian Case', *Second Line of Defense*, 30 November 2022, sldinfo.com/2022/11/re-imaging-nordic-defense-the-norwegian-case/.

The context within which Norway will operate its forces and total defence changes significantly with the expansion of the operational territory for NATO forces with the inclusion of Finland and Sweden. But the refocus on defence begun by Norway in 2014 provides a solid foundation for doing so, and the role of the Nordic defence industry within the 'arsenal of democracy' will undoubtedly grow as well.

The Swedish case

Of the five Nordic countries, Sweden faces the longest journey towards a new regional defence approach but also has an opportunity for significant innovation in how it does so. It has the longest journey due to its unique and long tradition of neutrality in European defence and a history of navigating blocs in Europe and protecting its sovereignty. It has a significant chance for innovation because it can rebuild its defence forces within a wider context and has defence companies with a broader perspective that the country has not yet tapped to its full benefit.

The legacy of neutrality was seen in the Swedish experience of World War II. In John Gilmour's insightful book, *Sweden, the Swastika and Stalin*, he concluded: 'Sweden prudently looked after its own interests and spurned the tutelage of the self-interested and evidently untrustworthy combatants. The responsibility for Sweden rested in Stockholm and nowhere else.'[13]

What has changed is that Stockholm now sees its own interests as best served by enlightened participation and leadership in the two key alliances shaping modern Europe: the European Union and NATO. It is an accident of timing, and perhaps also history, that Sweden's presidency of the European Union is occurring in the same year as it will enter NATO.

Sweden holds the rotating presidency of the European Union precisely when the war in Ukraine and its significant ripple effects on security are centre-stage. And in preparing to join NATO it is increasing its defence spending and looking at the future direction of its defence policy in Northern Europe.

Sweden faces a double challenge. How can it lead a significant strategic rethink about the defence of the region and Europe? And can it do so by bold thinking in terms of a redesigned force structure?

---

13   John Gilmour, *Sweden, the Swastika and Stalin: The Swedish Experience in the Second World War* (Edinburgh: Edinburgh University Press, 2010), doi.org/10.3366/edinburgh/9780748627462.001.0001.

To be frank, Sweden has let its forces draw down to very low levels. Sweden began its rethink of its defence posture and structure in the wake of the initial Ukraine crisis in 2014. It was clear that the Swedish leadership woke up to the fact that being neutral did not mean it would not be at the centre of the fourth battle of the Atlantic given the nature of the new combat systems and the Russians lowering the nuclear threshold in their declaratory strategy and force acquisition. Neutrality is nice but not if your society is nullified by military action going through the region.

Notably, since 2014, Sweden has had a robust strategy of engagement with international partners in defence, even before its NATO application. For example, in 2017, the Aurora 17 exercise was the largest in Sweden in more than 20 years and was clearly intended to test Swedish defence capabilities against a larger, more sophisticated opponent.

The Aurora 17 exercise triggered a revival of their approach to total defence, so it involved about 40 Swedish agencies beyond the Ministry of Defence. And, in the runup to applying for NATO membership, a key element has been an emphasis on evolving their total defence or whole-of-nation approach, including the return of conscription. The total defence concept includes cyber-defence, mobilisation-enhanced approaches and, with coming into NATO, working out how reinforcements will operate from Swedish territory. But this is the third decade of the twenty-first century; what does mobilisation of society mean now?

There are several areas of innovation in which Sweden will be a key player in a more integrated approach to Nordic defence. The first will clearly be operations with Norway and Finland in the High North and working with non-Nordic allies. Notably, one of the recommendations of the Swedish Armed Forces Supreme Commander General Micael Bydén was to enhance Sweden's presence in the High North and find innovate ways to support force operations with regional allies.

A second area is clearly force mobility. Simply having a ground force that operates on its own territory is not enough; how will its ground forces operate with allies in forward defence of the region—notably, the Baltic? A third is to change how the air force and navy work together. The former has provided air defence for a small navy. As the air force and navy operate at greater distances, how will the combat platforms be outfitted and developed in the future?

Here, Saab's participation in the UK-led Project Tempest could lead to changes not only in the Swedish Air Force but also in those of its allies. Saab is one of the most significant, innovative and value-for-money defence firms in the West and will undoubtedly have an impact on a broader set of allies going forward.

The Swedish Navy has been focused on operating in the Swedish Archipelago, forward-leaning operations in the Baltic Sea and along the country's west coast. The navy will build on these efforts as it plays a broader role in providing strategic depth to the region, and will share more maritime defence interests with Denmark and Norway and could collaborate in shipbuilding.

And, as the Baltic Sea sees greater cooperation among the NATO allies who now surround the area (Finland, Sweden, the Baltic states, Poland, Germany and Denmark), how will they work together to deal with the Russians operating from the Gulf of Finland and Kaliningrad? How will Sweden approach maritime defence and security in this contested sea bordering Russia and directly confronting Russian maritime interests in the North Atlantic? The potential cross-national cooperation on joint intelligence, surveillance and reconnaissance and command and control could lead to significant innovation involving maritime unmanned systems.

In short, Sweden is at a crossroads. It can draw on its unique location and strengths to help shape a broader kill-web defence and security structure with its allies in the region. Finding ways to innovate in connecting land, air and maritime assets across borders and a crosscutting force able to operate from security operations to high-end ones could bring significant innovation. It would also show the kind of multi-domain innovation that nations working together and building integrated security and defence operations could do with the dynamic changes in technology that are on offer.[14]

Conclusion

The reimagining of Nordic defence along with that of Northern Europe within a reworked North Atlantic defence is a test of strategic imagination of the kind that Brendan Sargeant suggested was key to sound defence

---

14   For an examination of how to understand the nature and promise of a kill-web force, see Laird and Timperlake, *A Maritime Kill Web Force in the Making*.

thinking. When speaking to Nordic military leaders, it is clear the admission of Finland and Sweden to NATO is a key transformation point for the creation of new concepts of regional defence. Nordic countries had already been stepping up their level of integration after years of working together more closely based on NATO standards, but now officials have made plain that a true common defence for the region can be planned.

Sweden and Finland joining NATO is not simply an additive event. Rather, the prospect of Nordic defence integrability provides an opportunity for disruptive change to reset and recast how North Atlantic defence can be done. It is not just about how the United States manages the game; it is about how the Nordic countries work together to shape the game and to work out what the United States can usefully provide to Northern European defence, not the other way around.

Starting with geography, Norway and Finland will now represent a long land border with Russia. Sweden and the Kingdom of Denmark (including Greenland and the Faroe Islands) can stop focusing on immediate ground defensive needs and instead plan to provide regional defence depth by focusing on developing air and maritime capabilities.

This is especially significant for Sweden as it would represent a switch from decades of focus on narrowly considered territorial defence and an accompanying emphasis on its land forces, how its air arm works with its F-35 allies and the development of a new navy for extended defence in the region.

If any such depth transformation is to happen, non-Nordic NATO allies—particularly the United States and Canada—must rethink how they plan operations to reinforce Nordic defence, while the Nordic countries themselves shape greater capacities to defend themselves against Russia. Conflict among the nations is inevitable in this reworking and will test the ability of leaders to work together to reshape a sound defence policy in the region and beyond.

Part 3.
Remembrances of
Brendan Sargeant

15

Remembrance foreword

If most of this book has focused on the conceptual and practical significance of Brendan's idea of 'strategic imagination', in this final section, the remembrance element of this *festschrift* comes to the fore, allowing Brendan's colleagues at the Strategic and Defence Studies Centre (SDSC) at The Australian National University to focus on the person behind the ideas.

Brendan was known to many in SDSC for a long time before he formally joined The Australian National University in February 2018. While seeking time to think and write, he was too capable an administrator and too good a colleague to simply keep the bench warm. Within a few months, he was asked to take on a large administrative role and, just over a year later, in January 2020, he was appointed head of SDSC. The calmness and purpose with which he led the centre during the pandemic years endeared him to many. As you will see, each staff member saw something slightly different and connected in a distinctive way with him.

These pieces are the most personal of the book. Some contributors, such as Emeritus Professor Hugh White, Professor Jochen Prantl and Associate Professor Meighen McCrae, use their reflections to draw out wider lessons. Brendan was a teacher and a leader and there was much he still had left to teach and many things he had left to do. Other authors, such as Professor Evelyn Goh, Associate Professor Amy King and Professor Brendan Taylor, reflect by sitting in quiet gratitude with the memory of their time with Brendan Sargeant. He is dearly missed by us all.

16

Vale Brendan Sargeant

Evelyn Goh

On 13 February 2022, we lost a national asset, a valued colleague and a friend. I remain somewhat shell-shocked that Brendan Sargeant left us so suddenly, after only two years of his leadership at SDSC and at this important juncture in strategic affairs. Since 2018, he had brought a great deal to The Australian National University and, over the two years before his death, as SDSC head, he championed a comprehensive, refreshing and forward-looking brand of strategic studies that positioned SDSC and Australia well for the contemporary and future strategic challenges we face.

One of Brendan's most important legacies will be his genuinely inquiring and evolving strategic mindset, plus what he was beginning to do in terms of helping to bridge academia and strategic policy. As I tried to walk out from the academic side of the bridge, I always knew that Brendan was also walking towards me from the policy side and together we had a good chance of creating the fruitful connections that would not have been as creative and effective otherwise.

In the many conversations and email exchanges we had, Brendan continually grappled with the fundamental problem that, as he saw it, 'we have exhausted a line of thinking in relation to Australian strategic policy and we need to open up some new perspectives'. He was patiently but consistently addressing what he regarded as the key manifestation of this problem: 'an overvaluing of continuity as opposed to the need to imagine a different world and our place in it'. He addressed these issues in his May 2021 SDSC public lecture on strategic imagination, subsequently published as a Centre of Gravity Series Paper. Because he felt that 'we are at a point of crisis in our policy thinking', he expended immense energy bringing this to the attention of national leaders and assisting with various institutional reform processes. He also pinpointed a similar 'deep issue that afflicts SDSC': '[O]ur policy "style" no longer fits the environment we are in.' At the time of his death, he was systematically leading SDSC in a collective effort to address this problem.[1]

One of Brendan's priorities when he took over the reins at SDSC was to develop a strategy for our education programs and, in typical fashion, he went about this by facilitating SDSC faculty working with each other to take time to think through this on a 'first values' basis. One of his goals was for our graduate program to help build students' 'capacity to make integrating judgements about a situation to enable a course of action amid high levels of complexity and ambiguity'. For this, he felt that '[y]ou not only had to be clever, but you need to be able to think in certain ways which challenge both cognitive and emotional capacity'.[2]

With his immense experience of such challenges within government, Brendan was deeply encouraging of different scholarly efforts to develop helpful policy-pertinent frameworks and tools. Professor Jochen Prantl and I benefited from long conversations with him and Brendan took time to read our publications and learn our 'Strategic Diplomacy' diagnostic and policy tools, which we developed for addressing complex strategic policy problems.[3] A few weeks before his departure, Brendan reviewed our latest paper and congratulated us for making 'a very good case for a different approach to strategy and whole of system management'. He was realistic about the significant challenge posed by 'the cultural settings for the conduct of strategy [that] are at odds with the cultural implications of what the paper advocates', but characteristically bolstered us by saying that, 'as it travels into the world and through time, I hope it is like the grain of rice that is plucked from the bottom of the pyramid and helps precipitate that hardest [of] things to achieve, a change in mindset'.[4]

---

1   Personal correspondence, Brendan Sargeant to author, 31 May 2020.
2   ibid.
3   Jochen Prantl and Evelyn Goh, 'Rethinking Strategy and Statecraft for the Twenty-First Century of Complexity: A Case for Strategic Diplomacy', *International Affairs* 98, no. 2 (March 2022): 443–69, doi.org/10.1093/ia/iiab212.
4   Personal correspondence, Brendan Sargeant to Jochen Prantl and author, 24 January 2022.

Since 2019, Brendan and I exchanged occasional lengthy emails reflecting on the major strategic challenges of our age, including the diffusion of hegemonic power, the Covid-19 pandemic and climate change. Brendan found the last to be 'a very bleak subject' because he recognised it as 'the single overriding security and strategic issue of our time'—'a strategic force that dwarfs all others and will create the environment within which all other issues will be dealt with, if they are dealt with at all'. Brendan was aware that I shared this strong sentiment, partly because of our conversations and shared trauma about the Black Summer bushfires of 2019–20. We shared a consciousness that national security and strategy urgently needed to be reconceived to deal with these threats, which will recur with greater frequency and intensity. During our discussion about a paper I had co-authored on the great powers' environmental responsibility, Brendan observed: 'I think often about my [youngest] daughter Vidya, who if she lives to the age of her great-grandmother, will be alive in the year 2100. I wonder what sort of world is being bequeathed to her and her generation.'[5]

Many of us will be familiar with Brendan's very significant achievements in government and among Australian policy circles. Scholars at SDSC will additionally remember him as an intellectual force who held his own within academic settings. Brendan was always (too) modest about his educational training being in English literature rather than political science or strategic studies. But with his intellectual depth and breadth, as well as his deeply reflective mindset, Brendan contributed significantly to scholarly discussions. One example that is especially pertinent for SDSC is the remarkable keynote speech he delivered for the centre's fiftieth anniversary in 2016. Weaving together deep insights about Australia's strategic condition and history of strategic thought, Brendan asked: 'What are we doing when we do strategy?' His answer was that, fundamentally, we are having 'an ongoing conversation. It is a conversation about who we are. It is a conversation about what sort of country we are and how we should participate in the world.'[6] This was a powerful iteration from a respected practitioner that the foundations of national capabilities, operational commitments and foreign relations are ideational, socially constructed and necessarily evolving—a particularly crucial reminder for the current era of strategic transition.

---

5   Personal correspondence, Brendan Sargeant to author, 31 August 2021.
6   Brendan Sargeant, Chapter 22, this volume.

The other example is when Brendan spoke at the launch of my 2020 book with Professor Barry Buzan, *Rethinking Sino-Japanese Alienation: History Problems and Historical Opportunities*. Brendan's erudite commentary struck a chord with our large international and interdisciplinary audience, and he engaged effortlessly with the political science theoretical framework of the book. He also spurred us to think of more sophisticated ways to explore the relationships between historical experiences and contemporary and future international order. I found especially helpful Brendan's beautifully expressed idea that we ought to think about how 'the past is brought into the present as a weapon in the struggle between countries to establish priority', and his proposition that 'the struggle is in the present and the arena is the past, but the prize is the future'. As a geographer as well as a historian and political scientist, I was also inspired by Brendan's notion that supremacy is linked to the ability to 'occupy the space that the future implies and to determine what space others will have'.

The relationship between the past and the present/future was one of Brendan's intellectual preoccupations. Over the summer of 2021–22, he had been happily immersed in a project touching on the strategic relationship between Australia and India, ably assisted by his daughter Sita. In one of our last exchanges, he reflected on how Jawaharlal Nehru had been 'more acute than his Australian contemporaries in his understanding of the tensions between geography and Australia's colonial history, and our unwillingness to resolve the issue', remarking that this 'casts a different light on the strategic relationship, and the problem that I think we now have is that current policy is hampered by competing versions of the past'.[7]

Speaking personally, I must thank Brendan for two big-ticket items. First, he was instrumental in supporting SDSC and our head at the time, Brendan Taylor, to set up the Shedden Professorship of Strategic Policy Studies. He later told me that he had read my book on the United States' radical change of strategy towards China in the 1960s and 1970s and that, when consulted, he had supported my application because I would 'bring different ideas'. I hope I have been bringing different and helpful ideas since moving to Australia and The Australian National University in August 2013.

Second, I am grateful to have had the chance to befriend Brendan. He was not just an intellect, a visionary and a defence leader. He was also a genuine, honest and decent man. I learnt huge amounts from how he handled people

---

7   Personal correspondence, Brendan Sargeant to author, 18 January 2022.

and problems, and greatly enjoyed getting to know his wife, Vaidehi, and their family, too. I shall have very fond memories of the meals we shared and of their daughters reminiscing about spending significant time with Brendan in bookshops and libraries while they were growing up. Indeed, over the Christmas 2021 holidays, I had been enjoying Brendan's book *In the Path of the Elephant*, written for his children, but really, as he observed, 'a fable for children of all ages'.

Since February 2022, we have been finding ways to celebrate Brendan Sargeant's life. I hope that we will continue to build on these and other multifaceted aspects of his very significant legacy.

Thank you, Brendan, for helping us to see what is worth seeing.

17

Reflections on Brendan Sargeant

Amy King

Brendan Sargeant—as many other contributors to this volume have doubtlessly already remarked—was a rare figure in the field of defence and strategic policy. With his background and training in English literature and his ongoing practice of and deep respect for writing and language, Brendan approached the daily work of strategy and defence with phenomenal creativity. Brendan's conception of 'strategic imagination' was one such incredibly creative idea. When I first heard Brendan discuss 'strategic imagination', I was immediately hooked. Given my own research interests in how collective ideas shape countries' foreign policy and strategic choices, I felt that strategic imagination perfectly encapsulated the images, world views, narratives or intuitions that exist before, and deeply shape, the documents, plans and decisions that come later—those things that Brendan aptly described as the 'artefacts of strategy'.[1]

In his 2021 Centre of Gravity Series Paper, Brendan first began to excavate the sources of Australia's strategic imagination. To do so, he offered a set of powerful diagnostic questions that one might ask when trying to interpret the underlying assumptions, frames or other ideational constructs that shape a country's policy choices: 'What is excluded and for what reason?

---

1   Brendan Sargeant, *Challenges to the Australian Strategic Imagination*, Centre of Gravity Series Papers 58 (Canberra: Strategic and Defence Studies Centre, The Australian National University, 2021), 5, hdl.handle.net/1885/233085.

What are the constraints that it assumes and what are those that it has not understood or been aware of? What has been forgotten or not seen? What would other perspectives reveal?'[2]

These diagnostic questions allowed Brendan to interrogate some of the ideas that have historically bounded Australian strategic policy, as well as to see the constraints or blind spots created by those ideas. Brendan was especially clear on how certain forms of ideas—nostalgia, myths and collective memory—could lead to the failure of strategic imagination by foreclosing future ideas and alternative possibilities. Thus, for example, Brendan pointed to nostalgia about Five Eyes arrangements and Anzac mythology as ideas that were limiting Australia's ability to imagine strategic relationships beyond its traditional Anglo-American ones, or to think more creatively about the role that the Australian Defence Force could and should play in Australia's changing strategic environment.

But Brendan's diagnostic questions for strategic imagination were also powerful examples of the kinds of thinking he applied to all aspects of his professional life, including those beyond his own writing and practice of strategic policy. In 2019, the Coral Bell School of Asia Pacific Affairs— where the Strategic and Defence Studies Centre then led by Brendan is based—embarked on a major effort to address gender equality in its teaching, research, public engagement and organisational practices. Brendan was an active participant in these efforts, drawing on his own earlier experience with similar reforms in the Australian Department of Defence.

At an early schoolwide forum on gender equality, Brendan remarked that the graphs demonstrating the plunge in the number of senior women within the academy looked nearly identical to similar graphs on gender within Defence and the wider Australian Public Service. For Brendan, the only way to upend these numbers was to pursue deep structural and cultural change within the organisation and to require that individuals scrutinise their own individual biases and decision-making patterns. As someone with a proclivity to ask questions like 'what has been forgotten or not seen' and 'what would other perspectives reveal', Brendan was keenly aware of the need to be honest and humble about one's own biases, and of the ways in which collective decision-making could be improved when one listened 'to the quiet voice' or considered overlooked ideas.[3]

---

2   ibid., 5.
3   Brendan Sargeant, Chapter 22, this volume.

More than once, Brendan expressed to me the words 'it's all micro', by which he meant that he was optimistic that widespread structural and cultural change could occur as individuals began to change their behaviour over time. This aligned nicely with his view that '[s]trategic policy at the national level is a collective endeavour, the work of many people over time'.[4] Achieving that collective endeavour required getting the best out of many individuals, and this is where Brendan excelled. He was a fundamentally kind and decent person, honest about his own trajectory and lived experience and empathetic and trusting of others. He wanted people to do their best and rightly assumed that, with encouragement, they would.

But Brendan was also willing, when needed, to inject a sharp dose of reality or an alternative perspective to challenge the risk aversion or complacency that can arise in any collective endeavour. As academics, we deeply appreciated the value he saw in our slow, painstaking research and his recognition that our writing and teaching might help provide the policy world with some of those alternative perspectives or fresh doses of reality.

At the same time, we in the university were all the better for having Brendan's policy, governance and literary mindset make us think harder about our own risk aversion and complacencies. I am deeply grateful for the time we had with Brendan and for his contribution to our collective strategic imagination.

---

4   Sargeant, *Challenges to the Australian Strategic Imagination*, 3.

18

Reimagining strategy and statecraft for the future

Jochen Prantl

Crystal balls are a rare commodity in strategic policymaking. Yet, developing a structured and systematic way of imagining the future is more critical than ever in a strategic and policy environment that is undergoing transformational change.

The problem

Hyperconnectivity and power diffusion have triggered what the *Global Risks Report 2023* has called a cascading 'polycrisis', which cannot be confined to a single policy realm or scale of analysis.[1] Transnational diffusion of power makes power easier to obtain, but it also makes it harder to use and easier to lose.[2] Multiple policy challenges—war in Ukraine, pandemics such as Covid-19, climate emergencies, rising costs of living and inflation and disruptions in global supply chains—form a cluster of crises that mutually reinforce one another. There is a critical demand for diagnostic and policy frameworks to penetrate the fog of the future to be better prepared for

---

1   World Economic Forum, *Global Risks Report 2023* (Geneva: World Economic Forum, 2023), www3.weforum.org/docs/WEF_Global_Risks_Report_2023.pdf.
2   Moisés Naím, *The End of Power: From Boardrooms to Battlefields and Churches to States, Why Being in Charge Isn't What It Used to Be* (New York: Basic Books, 2013).

complex, overlapping international crises unfolding at multiple levels.[3] As such, today's survival challenges require a sea change and a new mindset in how governments imagine strategic scenarios and pursue policy planning. By reimagining contemporary strategy and statecraft, policymakers can win the prize of the future.

Cambridge theoretical physicist Stephen Hawking declared 23 years ago that the twenty-first century would be the age of complexity. Issue complexity puts state capacity to the test while the policy space from which to deliver public goods and policy outcomes has shrunk. According to the US National Intelligence Council's latest report, *Global Trends 2040*, there is a stark disequilibrium between the demand and supply sides of government.[4] This is a very serious problem that has spurred polarisation, populism, protest and internal conflict in a range of countries including the United States. Notably, the *Collins Dictionary* 2022 word of the year was 'permacrisis', highlighting the persistent and permanently difficult situation of government with no preordained outcome.[5] Thus, the need to develop strategies that are fit for purpose is very urgent indeed.

Embracing complexity

In the age of complexity, strategy is best understood as 'the art of creating power'[6] to regain and maximise policy space in the pursuit of statecraft. However, developing a shared understanding of the nature of the policy problem at hand and a shared imagination of the desired policy outcome precede any strategy. Strategic imagination helps to address cognitive biases generated by the human brain, which is fast and intuitive but error-prone, in making sense of the reality that surrounds us.[7] What we see tends to be biased by what we believe. However, a largely internalised foundation for attempts to give situations meaning and to suggest appropriate responses is deeply inappropriate in today's complex strategic and operational

---

3   See, for example, Jochen Prantl and Evelyn Goh, 'Rethinking Strategy and Statecraft for the Twenty-First Century of Complexity: A Case for Strategic Diplomacy', *International Affairs* 98, no. 2 (March 2022): 443–69, doi.org/10.1093/ia/iiab212.

4   See National Intelligence Council, *Global Trends 2040: A More Contested World* (Washington, DC: National Intelligence Council, 2021).

5   See Helen Bushby, 'Permacrisis Declared Collins Dictionary Word of the Year', *BBC News*, 1 November 2022, www.bbc.com/news/entertainment-arts-63458467.

6   Lawrence Freedman, *Strategy: A History* (Oxford: Oxford University Press, 2013), xii.

7   See Daniel Kahnemann, *Thinking, Fast and Slow* (New York: Farrar, Straus & Giroux, 2011).

environment. A reflexive reading of situations can lead to strategic scripts with predictable behaviour, which—if unchecked—could risk strategic failure. Strategic imagination helps to turn those intuitive judgements into persuasive arguments, especially for those situations that are complex and multifaceted. In sum, the key challenge of strategy is one of mindset, which begins with strategic imagination.

Strategic imagination necessitates embracing complexity, taking 'a crude look at the whole', as the Nobel laureate and physicist Murray Gell-Mann put it. This includes nurturing the skill of grasping the broader structures and patterns of the complex system within which specific policy problems are embedded rather than reducing them to a series of events to which policymakers must react. As the environmental scientist Donella Meadows stressed: 'Like the tip of an iceberg rising above the water, events are the most visible aspect of a larger complex—but not always the most important.'[8]

Strategic imagination generates a vision of the iceberg across time and space, facilitating a deep dive *into* and critical reflection *of* the mental models and paradigms underlying strategies. Looked at from the daily grind of strategic policymaking, three factors are essential to create a public service environment that is conducive to strategic imagination:

1. Knowledge workers who can operate across disciplinary and policy silos are in high demand. There is too great a tendency to frame and to respond to problems in their component parts rather than addressing them holistically.

2. Embracing complexity essentially boils down to the commitment to engage with the full iceberg of strategic policymaking. This goes well beyond the whole-of-government approach and includes public policymaking that accepts policy failure as a source of policy innovation.

3. Public policymaking needs an in-built learning infrastructure to allow for constant reassessment of policy solutions. Yet, this cannot be achieved without a paradigm change that encourages thinking outside the box, making mistakes and using that as an opportunity to learn and innovate.

Some of those prerequisite skills can be acquired through training. The main challenge, however, is a paradigm change in mindset and a willingness to operate outside well-established comfort zones as well as disciplinary and

---

8   Donella H. Meadows, *Thinking in Systems: A Primer* (London: Earthscan, 2008), 88.

departmental boxes and stovepipes. While policy co-creation—involving academia, the public service and civil society—is not a silver bullet, it goes a long way to help develop the strategic mindset and framework fit for purpose in the age of complexity.

The way forward

Brendan Sargeant's tragic passing prevented him from fully fleshing out the concept of strategic imagination and its application. While the various contributions to this *festschrift* reflect on Brendan's ideas, this can only be the first step. As Brendan noted himself, strategic imagination 'is a very abstract idea. It comes alive in context where it is visible through its manifestations and can be analysed in terms of its reality and consequence.' By deepening co-creation with the academic and policy communities, both domestically and internationally, we can test the reality and consequence of strategic imagination and bring it alive.

Inspired by Brendan Sargeant, policymakers should look to design initiatives that aim to generate content and capacity for the application of strategic imagination—an idea that sits right at the core of Australia's national interest. Such initiatives would bridge the gap between the academic quest for fundamental understanding of strategy and statecraft (how to develop cutting-edge ideas) and the quest for policy innovation in strategic policymaking (how to get things done). They would be a focal point for policy co-creation, to imagine strategic futures and to identify strategic opportunities, driven by the most critical of policy questions: *What is the policy space that Australia ought to imagine and occupy to fully realise its national identity in a strategic environment that gives the country less control over the future it wants to inhabit?*

Addressing this fundamental question requires the mobilisation of the best available academic and policy minds to co-create the content and the capacity to push forward the late Brendan Sargeant's pivotal thinking on strategic futures and statecraft. At the same time, it requires an investment in the next generation of policymakers and scholars to build capacity that is sustainable.

Remembering Brendan in this forward-looking way will put Australia in a very competitive position to reimagine strategy and statecraft with our eyes on the prize: the future we want.

19

The imagination of a bureaucrat

Hugh White

Imagination is an attribute that is not generally associated with the vocation of a bureaucrat. Indeed, to bring the two concepts together smacks of paradox, as though 'imaginative bureaucrat' is a contradiction in terms. Brendan Sargeant took delight in paradoxes and intellectual puzzles of all kinds, and this one in particular, and they framed his life's work. No-one better personified the interaction between the bureaucratic world and the imaginative life. He was the imaginative bureaucrat par excellence.

No-one who has had the pleasure of reading Brendan's writings on imagination and strategy or, better still, hearing him speak to these themes or, best of all, enjoying an hour's conversation with him about them will need to be convinced of the power of his imagination and his view of the centrality of the imagination in human affairs. They might, however, need to be reminded of Brendan's standing and authority as a bureaucrat—more formally, a public administrator—with all that these expressions convey. It is important that we do so, because we cannot do full justice to the delightful paradox that was Brendan Sargeant if we do not register that this person, whose imagination was of such power, breadth and sophistication, was at the same time a public administrator of exceptional probity, diligence, efficiency and competence, with a great practical flair for making things happen and making government work.

For those of us who had the pleasure of so doing, watching him at work inside government meant admiring how these two sides of his nature struck sparks off one another in a way that made them seem not paradoxical opposites but natural and mutually reinforcing partners. In his memory, one is prompted to think—as perhaps one should have done more carefully long ago—about how and why this was so. What is the role of imagination for the bureaucrat? Brendan would, I am sure, have offered a much wider, more thoughtful and also more playful answer to that question than I can give. But here are my reflections on this question, in four parts. You will forgive me for drawing examples from strategic policy and from the issues in strategic policy that have engaged me most in recent decades, but the reflections are equally applicable to other areas of public policy.

First, there is the capacity to imagine how things might be different. I half-remember a quote from John Maynard Keynes—a very imaginative bureaucrat—to the effect that the hardest thing for us to really grasp and understand is that the future is going to be very different from the past. Keynes was talking a century ago about changes in the way that national economics and the international economy were going to work, but the point applies more generally. We continually talk about living in an era of radical and unprecedented change, but we readily default to assuming the opposite: that the fundamentals of our situation will persist and hence no profound changes in our policies are required. It takes real imagination to see when this is wrong, and how it is wrong.

This kind of imagination was shown by the generation of Australian political leaders in the late nineteenth century who saw, at the apogee of British imperial power, that the distribution of wealth and power that had for a century defined the international system and Australia's place in it was passing, and that the future for us would be very different. This is the kind of imagination we need now as the distribution of wealth and power shifts again.

Second, there is the capacity to imagine how things might go wrong. I half-remember another line, this time from the late Owen Harries—another imaginative bureaucrat—who said to me once, claiming he was quoting someone else, that those who lack the capacity to imagine catastrophe lack the capacity to avoid it. That was a decade ago and we were talking about the risk of escalating rivalry between the United States and China leading to a catastrophic war. Many people then dismissed that risk as imaginary, so nothing was done to avert the escalation whose consequences we now endure. In the same way, many people today overlook the risk that war, if it happens, will cross the nuclear threshold and thus do too little to avoid it.

Third, there is the capacity to imagine how things could be done differently—that old policies and approaches, sanctified by time and use, can and should be abandoned when circumstances change and be replaced with new policies, perhaps radically different from the old ones. That requires imagination. How often have we heard, for example, that in the event of a US–China war over Taiwan, Australia 'has no choice' but to support America all the way. That statement—so obviously wrong—perfectly encapsulates the failure of this kind of imagination. So, too, more broadly does the claim we so often hear that Australia 'made its choice' to align itself with the United States long ago and there is no way we can change that today. As though policies cannot and should not change when circumstances do. But that requires imagination.

Fourth, there is the capacity to imagine how we, as a country, might be different—how we might change as circumstances change. This matters because big policy changes, the kind that are needed to respond to big changes in our circumstances, challenge our sense of who we are as a nation. This is true, for example, of the way we respond to the current transformation of the Asian strategic order. For most of us, Australia's alignment on this great issue with the United States, and with 'the West' more broadly, is a question not just of policy but also of identity. It expresses who we are, our essential nature as a nation, which we cannot imagine ever changing. Of course, that is wrong. Nations change like everything else and Australia has changed a lot over its short history. Just think of the changes in our racial composition, for a start.

We should not be surprised or alarmed that big changes in our foreign policy to meet big changes in our circumstances mean reimagining our identity as a nation. All the most important questions about how we relate to the world around us boil down to questions about how we see ourselves. So, as we encounter a fundamentally transformed Asia—transformed by the rise of not just China but also India, Indonesia and others—we must ask whether we still define ourselves to ourselves as a Western outpost or whether we can imagine ourselves differently.

This was, I think, the key message of Brendan's speech to SDSC's fiftieth anniversary celebrations. As he said then:

> When you are confronted by a genuinely strategic decision, or there is a genuine strategic change in the environment in which you are, the challenge is not just a challenge of how you might respond to that environment by taking various forms of action. It is also a challenge to your self-conception, to your sense of who you are and who you might be.[1]

---

1   Brendan Sargeant, Chapter 22, this volume.

20

Grappling with the past and present through imagination

Meighen McCrae

It was 6 pm and many of my colleagues at the Australian War College had departed for the evening. After spending the entire day reading, thinking and teaching about war, I needed a break. As was common whenever I walked back from the staffroom with a cup of tea, I could see Brendan Sargeant was still in his office, too. I gently knocked on his door and he welcomed me in. While he asked how teaching was going, the conversation soon turned to English literature, history and understandings of war.

This was a common pattern we had during these evenings. Brendan had a background in English literature and a deep interest in history. I had trained in both areas and had written a 32,000-word Master of Arts thesis on science fiction and British defence policy in the period leading up to the First World War. Between the two of us, we had plenty of ammunition to stay too late at the office musing on these topics.

We often discussed how the human brain can access the past and what tools the disciplines of history and English offer us to do so. I had gone back to thinking and reading about 'ways of war' and was in the process of working my way through *The First Way of War* by John Grenier.[1] I was caught up in the idea that an estimated 3.5 to 7 million First Nations peoples had lived in what is now Canada and the United States before first

---

1   John Grenier, *The First Way of War: American War Making on the Frontier, 1607–1814* (Cambridge: Cambridge University Press, 2005), doi.org/10.1017/CBO9780511817847.

contact with Europeans.[2] Thinking about population composition today, I was plagued by thoughts of 'where did they go' (even though, through the study of colonisation and this book, I knew the answer). You see, I grew up in Algonquin, Ontario, and while farmers often found arrowheads in their fields, I knew few First Nations people. Aware that these populations were savagely reduced by 35 to 80 per cent, I found it hard to understand the level of violence (and disease) that had to occur, let alone the mindset of those involved in enacting this violence.[3]

Brendan suggested I read Cormac McCarthy's *Blood Meridian*.[4] He was not the first person to make this suggestion, but something about the way Brendan talked about this book inspired me. McCarthy's portrayal of a band of renegades covering the American landscape in blood was horrifying, but somehow, in the context of Grenier's work, it opened this historical space in my mind. While McCarthy's imagery was repulsive, it was reading through the archival sources provided by Grenier and the way these depicted the systematic and intentional violence against First Nations non-combatants that made one question humanity.

I went back to Brendan for further discussion. As we were talking, he pointed out an Australian landscape painting in his office. 'Notice anything out of place with it?' he asked. I stood there wondering how to say politely that I am not that moved by landscape painting, and this was no exception. Likely sensing my ambivalence and confusion as to how the topic had suddenly taken a turn, he prodded, 'Where are the Indigenous Australians?' It was hard not to feel nauseated as we discussed the problematic nature of these paintings—specifically, the absence of Australian Indigenous peoples from these works. Brendan said they should be there given their sizeable population before colonisation. He reminded me that thoughtful consideration of landscape paintings was a good reminder of what once was.

He then lent me a copy of a critique of McCarthy's book entitled *I Meant to Kill Ye* by Stephanie Reents, which I promised to read to continue our conversation about the broad theme of colonisation. What interested me

---

2   Figures on these issues are highly contested. Suzanne Austin Alchon estimates the population at 3.5 million, whereas Russell Thornton estimates 7 million. Suzanne Austin Alchon, *A Pest in the Land: New World Epidemics in a Global Perspective* (Albuquerque: University of New Mexico Press, 2003), 147–72; Russell Thornton, 'Native American Demographic and Tribal Survival into the Twenty-first Century', *American Studies* 46, nos 3–4 (2005–06): 23–38.

3   Herbert C. Northcott and Donna Marie Wilson, *Dying and Death in Canada* (Toronto: University of Toronto Press, 2008), 25–27.

4   Cormac McCarthy, *Blood Meridian* (London: Picador Classics, 2015).

most about this work, again, was the human struggle and the resort to violence. I wrote my thoughts on post-it notes and placed them throughout the book. From my perspective, Reents did not understand violence and that weakened her critique. I looked forward to sharing these ideas with Brendan, but sadly that is where our conversation ended.

I have continued to think about our evening discussions. When I reflect on them, I think about the ways in which fictional writing can help us understand how war was experienced in the past. This has relevance to the societies in which we live today, which are built on, among many things, violence. To ignore this reality is to deny the experiences of others.

If I could speak to Brendan today, I would suggest he bring together some of his various ideas to push his exploration of the strategic imagination even further. In the introduction to his paper *Challenges to the Australian Strategic Imagination*, he writes that '[s]trategic policy at the national level is a collective endeavour, the work of many people over time'.[5] He also writes about a country as an imagined community. This raises an important line of inquiry. How has the role of violence shaped Australia and thus impacted who is involved in this collective endeavour?

The answers matter because Australia, like many other countries with a history of colonisation, cannot truly move forward until it addresses questions like these. Brendan comes closest to this idea when he discusses the problematic nature of the Anzac myth. Relying on this myth, he notes, is to persistently look backwards. In thinking about time and space, I would add that it is also essential, when thinking about Australia's strategic imagination, that we do not fail to look around us now, in the present, to see who is not being included in the 'we' of strategic imagination.

Brendan presented his work as a starting point for Australians to explore the potential of their strategic imagination. Given his support of gender equity and diversity principles both within the Strategic and Defence Studies Centre and the Coral Bell School more broadly, I suspect he would have woven together these concepts himself. As Brendan writes: 'Not only do we need to imagine ourselves into what we might be, but also what the world might be.'[6] If we can imagine, we can also imagine inclusively.

---

5   Brendan Sargeant, *Challenges to the Australian Strategic Imagination*, Centre of Gravity Series Papers 58 (Canberra: Strategic and Defence Studies Centre, The Australian National University, 2021), 3, hdl.handle.net/1885/233085.
6   ibid., 11.

21

Bridging the gap: Remembering Brendan Sargeant

Brendan Taylor

So, sing on,
Dear shut-eyed one, dear far-voiced veteran,
Sing yourself to where the singing comes from …

—Seamus Heaney, 'At the Wellhead'

Next to our beloved daughters—whose names frequently graced our conversations—the late Coral Bell was the woman about whom Brendan Sargeant and I spoke the most. This was a source of some comfort as Coral and her work were the one subject about which I felt I might have been slightly more knowledgeable than Brendan; he was, without question, the most well-read person I have ever met.

I am not sure whether Brendan and Coral knew each another. Given Brendan's longstanding association with the Strategic and Defence Studies Centre, there is a good chance they crossed paths. I first met Brendan in the mid-2000s at a dinner hosted by another Bell admirer and distinguished Australian strategic intellectual, Hugh White. The dinner was for first-year trainees undertaking the Department of Defence's graduate program.

Over the following two decades, Brendan became a regular presence at ANU dinners, including most notably at SDSC's fiftieth anniversary celebration. During that event, as the associate secretary of Defence,

Brendan graciously delivered a memorable keynote address. I had given him just a week's notice to prepare the speech because the then minister for defence had failed to respond decisively to a much earlier invitation, while Brendan's boss at the time, the normally supportive Dennis Richardson, was away on a work-related trip.

Brendan's and my strongest connection came through our shared interest in bridging the gap between the academic and policy worlds, which was an abiding focus for Coral Bell also. Aside from a short period in the Australian Department of Foreign Affairs very early in her career—during which she quickly tired of being a mere 'cog in the wheel' of government—Coral spent most of her life in academia. Yet, her scholarly preoccupations were always practical in nature and her work was, and remains, of relevance to policy practitioners.

Coral's work on crises and crisis management particularly intrigued Brendan. He often encouraged me to take a step back and examine crises from a strategic perspective. According to Brendan, practitioners excel in the mechanics of crisis management, but where the policy world benefits from academic insight is in conceptual frameworks, especially those that illuminate the long-term consequences of crises, which policymakers may not see.

Brendan's expertise in crisis management, honed over decades in government, was most evident during the Covid-19 pandemic. I vividly remember the late-night Zoom calls with Brendan and then director of the Coral Bell School of Asia Pacific Affairs Professor Toni Erskine. These calls, accommodating my unusual schedule due to home schooling and other commitments, were a source of great reassurance. Brendan's calm advice, wisdom and wealth of government experience were invaluable during those challenging times.

As The Australian National University grappled with the worst financial circumstances in its history, Brendan's command of the numbers became especially valuable. It was a command developed, no doubt, through those senior government positions he held, including in the Department of Finance. In one of his many contributions to The Australian National University, this expertise saw him appointed to a small group who provided budgetary advice to vice-chancellor Professor Brian Schmidt as he steered the university—expertly and empathetically—through the darkest days of the crisis. Brian's regard for Brendan was abundantly clear in the statement that he issued immediately following his passing: 'Brendan was not only a leader in his field—he was a true leader on our campus and a great friend to his colleagues, peers, our University and to me personally.'

However, Brendan's most significant contribution during this period was his capacity to do what he felt policymakers did not often do: take a longer view. As dire as the university's budgetary situation had become, he consistently stressed the need to look beyond the crisis and continue to invest in the next generation of scholars.

While Brendan held firm views on this and many other issues, he was never dogmatic. I recall a lengthy one-on-one conversation at his office in Defence in late 2012, when he was a deputy secretary. With the aid of a map on his wall highlighting the sea lines of communication on which Australia ultimately depends, Brendan introduced me to the Indo-Pacific concept that subsequently appeared in the *2013 Defence White Paper*. Significantly, this was the concept's first inclusion in an official Australian policy document, with Brendan as its lead author.

Several years later, however, after joining The Australian National University, he argued against its use in the Coral Bell School of Asia Pacific Affairs' new strategic plan, citing ongoing policy debates that made its adoption in the university context unnecessary.

Brendan was, at heart, a pragmatist. His work, as both a practitioner and a scholar, continued the long tradition of 'pragmatism' in Australian foreign and strategic policy. In his thoughtful May 2021 SDSC Centre of Gravity Series Paper, Brendan suggested that Australia should draw inspiration from Odysseus, a character in Homer's *Odyssey* known for his intelligence, cunning and resourcefulness, whose use of a wooden horse famously led to the fall of Troy.

It is in this context that Brendan's passing has left a significant void, particularly in the increasingly polarised Australian foreign and strategic policy debate, alongside the passing of other notable pragmatists such as Allan Gyngell and James Goldrick.

On a personal level, Brendan was someone to whom you could talk about literally anything. Knowing his background in English literature, I once confided in him my desire to read and enjoy poetry. His characteristically non-judgemental advice was, 'Just try reading it out loud.'

Thanks to Brendan, I finally developed an appreciation for poetry. Given our shared Irish ancestry—a fact of which I learned only during our final meeting just two days before his passing—it thus seemed fitting to include at the outset of this reflection a fragment from a poem penned by one of Ireland's finest poets, Seamus Heaney. I think Brendan would have liked that.

According to Celtic mythology, Brendan has returned home to 'where the singing comes from', joining Coral and the other legendary Australian strategists. However, the contributions to this volume illustrate that his legacy should not be confined to memory; instead, it provides a dynamic and enduring research agenda for all of us to carry forward.

22

'To see what is worth seeing': Keynote speech to the Strategic and Defence Studies Centre fiftieth anniversary dinner, 21 July 2016

Brendan Sargeant

It is a great privilege and pleasure to be here this evening to give the keynote speech at this celebratory dinner for the fiftieth anniversary of the Strategic and Defence Studies Centre.

Let me offer my congratulations on the centre's fiftieth anniversary. I think the conference topic, 'New Directions in Strategic Thinking 2.0', is absolutely the right question to be exploring.

It is good to see so many familiar faces here tonight. Some people here I have worked with and they have given me immeasurable help and guidance over the years. Others I know because I have read their work and pondered and learnt from it.

I speak for myself but also on behalf of Defence when I say that the SDSC has made a huge contribution to strategic policymaking in Australia over many years—a contribution of incommensurable value to Australia. From my perspective, it has enriched the policy environment and deepened understanding of the world we live in and the nature of the choices that we make as we find our way in that world. Long may it be so.

To speak before such an illustrious audience is a daunting prospect. I am very conscious that almost anything I might talk about is likely to be familiar ground to many in this audience.

I am not going to talk about recent Defence White Papers or the South China Sea or the emerging Indo-Pacific. If you are looking for advice on government policy, there are plenty of documents available. If you are looking for an expert commentary, there are people in this room better qualified than I.

What I would like to talk about is the importance of strategy and its value to large institutions—and most especially one I know intimately: the Department of Defence. But first I would like to digress with a couple of anecdotes to set the framework for my discussion.

Many years ago, I was haunting a bookshop somewhere in Little Collins Street in Melbourne, a bookshop that no longer exists and which sold books that were well beyond my price range at that time. I was there one day and I came across a book that had just been published. It was called *The Plains* by Gerald Murnane.

For some reason, I purchased it, spending more money than I could afford, and took it home and read it. It was one of those books that turns you five degrees off centre from the rest of the universe and gives you a completely different picture of the world. Nothing is quite the same after reading it. I think it is one of the great Australian books and it has never left me.

The story is simple enough. A young man who describes himself as a filmmaker decides to leave Outer Australia and journey to a place called Inner Australia. Inner Australia is the landscape of the plains where a vast and complex culture has been built and sustained by a wealthy landholding aristocracy. These landholders are patrons of the arts and sciences. They are obsessed by the landscape of the plains, which is their landscape. They devote endless resources to discover the true meaning of the plains, to get to an understanding of what they really are, for in knowing the world— their world—they will know themselves. They also know their quest is endless and perhaps futile.

The filmmaker meets these landowners and goes through a process of auditioning. Eventually he is employed by one of the landowners to be a resident filmmaker on his estate. The landowner expects nothing from this filmmaker but believes that he might one day be capable of 'seeing what was worth seeing'. The book then describes the filmmaker's life thereafter. Needless to say, no film is ever made, but the filmmaker goes into an endless and enriching exploration of the plains in this place called Inner Australia.

The book struck me with the force of revelation, for even though it was clearly a work of fantasy or speculative fiction, it described to me absolutely the reality of Australian culture in the world that I was living in. What I realised was that there is a world, but there are many different ways of describing it, and that these can create a richer sense of reality because the process illuminates what may not have been seen. The book is very rich and can be considered in many different ways, but the opposition set up between an Outer Australia, an Australia that is self-satisfied and feels that it knows reality, and an Inner Australia, where the culture is devoted to finding the meaning behind appearances, is worth reflecting on. I will come back to this, but I believe that the work of strategy is the work of this Inner Australia.

My second anecdote relates to my recent visit to Exercise Hamel, a large army exercise that took place in Cultana, a bleak and beautiful place in South Australia. I visited the exercise and had fun seeing what the army does when it is being itself.

In the exercise headquarters, the place where the exercise was managed, I saw a map on the wall that was very familiar to me—it hangs in my office—except that just north-east of the archipelago to our north was another country called Kamaria.

I spent some time contemplating this map, the geography and contours of this imaginary country inserted into a real world, and I remarked to one of my companions that there was an enormous amount of strategic policy history embedded in that simple map. One of the generals said to me: 'They're tough, those Kamarians, we've been fighting them for 40 years.'

What intrigued me, and continues to intrigue me, is how, in order to understand ourselves better, we construct an imaginary country against which we define ourselves and test our ideas.

I work in an organisation called the Department of Defence that does many different things every moment of the day. It never sleeps. It never stops. It is relentless. It has its own imperatives and appetites. It has a personality and life independent of those people and organisations that contribute to its being. It is what it is and, in its deepest dreaming, has no desire but to be what it is.

Most of my work is an attempt to help manage this vast enterprise. The practical reality of that is that I make lots of micro-decisions or supervise the work of others who also make decisions or provide advice to more senior decision-makers.

In this world strategy can be a distant reality—a quiet voice behind the noise and clutter of the daily routine. Yet, I never forget what one of my teachers once said to me: 'Listen to the quiet voice!'

The essence of my management task, which is also that of my colleagues, is to ensure that what this organisation does conforms to government policy and embodies in its activities the strategy that the government has signed up to in its policy documents. These include, most importantly, the white paper and the subsidiary documents that flow from it, such as the Defence planning guidance and the Australian military strategy.

What I have seen over the years is a continuing tension between the imperatives of the institution, its personality and its own desires—to speak metaphorically—and the requirements of government as expressed in policy and strategy. In this sense, strategy is the quiet voice that calls the organisation away from itself and requires that it look out into the world and respond accordingly. For this reason, the strategic policy function is central to organisational health and wellbeing and critical if the organisation is to remain relevant.

One of the features of the current environment is that there is an overwhelming emphasis—and rightly so—on sustaining operations. The challenge is to step back from this immediacy to reflect on the nature and meaning of the larger story that we are telling through what we do. The institution will tell its own story if left to itself. The task of strategy is to make it listen and understand that the reality it sees itself as part of can have many dimensions and actually be something other than what it thinks it is.

We do not have many strategists in Defence. That is not a bad thing, as long as we listen to what they are saying. This, I think, is the hardest part of working in a large organisation. It is developing the capacity to listen to the other voice—to journey into Inner Australia, so to speak.

What are we doing when we do strategy?

When I reflect on the strategic history of Australia filtered through the development of the Defence organisation, along with the successive documents to chart that development—primarily, white papers—what I hear is an ongoing conversation. It is a conversation about who we are. It is a conversation about what sort of country we are and how we should participate in the world. This conversation takes expression in the capabilities we build, our operational commitments and in our relationships with other countries.

I could trace the history of strategic thought over the time I have been associated with the Department of Defence. Its main narrative arc goes something like this: in the time after the Vietnam War, we started the process of thinking of ourselves as a strategic entity separate from the larger system in which we had participated since Federation. There were many debates, some still alive today. This thinking expressed itself in a policy and a strategy that were called self-reliance and had many dimensions in terms of how we organised the department, began the work of building the modern ADF and participated in the world.

This was essentially a nationalist project, and an important one. I also think it was part of a larger project of Australia rethinking its place in the world in the post-Vietnam era. The intervention in East Timor might be seen as an expression of that policy and strategy and the arena where its strengths and flaws were highlighted. It is a strategy that has never gone away.

Since Timor and particularly since 9/11, governments have pursued a fairly active engagement of the ADF in many different parts of the world. This reflects, I think, a sense that Australia has global interests and needs to support them, including through the use of the defence force. Our strategy in this context might be seen as a response to globalisation and an attempt to respond to some of the more malignant forces unleashed by globalisation in ways that support our national interests. Whether our strategy has been sufficient for the environment we are in is a debate for another time.

I see the recent white paper as a culmination of a journey that began decades ago in that it seeks to recognise that Australia is not only a country that lives geographically in the Indo-Pacific, but also has trading and national interests that extend across the world. How we balance the local with the global is an enduring tension in policymaking and strategy development. It is the location of most serious debates about defence policy.

So, I see our strategic thinking as partly the telling of a story about who we are and, more importantly, who we think we are. It is a story that never ends but will evolve and be reinterpreted over time as events occur and we respond. Most importantly, it is a story we tell through both what we say and what we do.

I am not one of those people who says that the current environment is more difficult or more challenging than the environment faced by our predecessors. I think that is simply being arrogant and historically myopic. Each time has its own demands, and every strategic challenge is new to those who have to face it. However, I do believe that we are in one of those moments in history where we are moving from one world to another. The strategic challenge before us is to make the transition successfully.

When you are confronted by a genuinely strategic decision, or there is a genuine strategic change in the environment in which you are, the challenge is not just a challenge of how you might respond to that environment by taking various forms of action. It is also a challenge to your self-conception, to your sense of who you are and who you might be. This is why strategic choices are hard and I think difficult for our institutions that can grow comfortable with a sense of things as they are.

It is also why doing the work of strategy is hard. And it should be hard—really hard—emotionally as well as intellectually.

Many of the contemporary challenges to security are also challenges that go to our sense of what sort of country we are and what we need to become. Some of these challenges have the potential to render the assumptions upon which we take action redundant or meaningless.

To take some examples:

- The assumptions that underpinned the current rules-based global order are increasingly being challenged and are increasingly challengeable.
- Military power is increasingly a commodity and the ability to generate strategic effects is being democratised. We have all seen what one person with a semiautomatic weapon can do.
- We cannot assume that all players in our strategic environment are rational or share our assumptions about how the world and conflict should be managed.

- It is not so easy anymore to distinguish between the world within our national borders and the world outside.

- We are seeing genuinely transformational technologies: cyber, quantum computing, autonomous systems and so on.

The task of strategy is more complex because it has to speak to many different realities and many different perceptions of what reality might or should be. It has to do this in a way that helps policy and decision-makers thread their way through to a course of action or decision.

Our response to these challenges, along with others that will emerge in coming decades, will change us. How do we understand and manage that change while also responding to what the world brings? Some of our choices will be constrained by our self-conception. We need to understand this as well.

What I worry about is whether we are truly seeing reality. Our institutional imperatives are, in my experience, so potentially powerful that they can blind us to aspects of the world that we live in. Do we prefer to be what we are rather than to consider what we need to be if we are to respond to contemporary realities? What are the costs of the choices that we might need to make, and do we really understand what those choices are? In a world of wicked problems—and strategic problems are all wicked—do we prefer our tried-and-true solution sets rather than seeing what is worth seeing?

When I looked at that map at Exercise Hamel and saw the country of Kamaria, I asked myself a question. In creating an imaginary country that we have used to define and test ourselves against, have we simply created another reflection of what we are and what we are comfortable with being?

When I think of that young man in that imaginary world of the plains commencing his lifelong journey to discover the true meaning of the plains—an impossible but necessary quest—I see it as a wonderful metaphor for the work that all of us do. I am most of all taken by the landowner's implicit request that he come to see what was worth seeing. The landowner understood that this might be the work of a whole lifetime.

Sometimes when I read the work of people who do strategy, including people at the Strategic and Defence Studies Centre, the practical administrator in me gets irritated because it just complicates my decision-making and

I prefer a smooth and easy life. It puts in front of me those most terrifying of all questions for an administrator: Have I got it right? Is what we are doing making sense? Do we really understand what we are dealing with?

When I am in a better, less harassed mood, I appreciate how valuable that work is. And I treasure it.

Sometimes I look at much of the writing on strategy and it is like wandering through a library of books about things that have never happened. Sometimes it is quite a strange experience to read these forlorn prophecies that have never come true. Yet, despite this, how important it is that we have these works of imagination, these documents of grim speculation and melancholy advice. They can be books of magic. Sometimes the writing of them ensures that what they talk about does not occur. They intersect with reality to help us understand that reality is more complex and more multidimensional and has more that is imponderable than we are ever quite comfortable with. They help us make choices that change reality.

This conversation, which we call strategy making, helps us understand the world around us and helps us understand the consequences of the choices that we might make or not make. It helps us change the world.

So, to the Strategic and Defence Studies Centre, let us have another 50 years of thinking and conversation and research.

Continue the great work of building a strategic conversation in Australia about who we are and what we might become.

Help us understand the choices and pathways that might take us there.

Help us to see what is worth seeing.

Index

Page numbers in **bold** text indicate images.

9/11 79, 81, 233
9/11 Commission 79

Abbott, Tony 54, 82
Abe Shinzo 163
Aboriginal *see* Indigenous Australians
academia xviii, xx, 4, 5, 66, 67, 68, 70,
    71–3, 74, 159, 160, 165, 203, 210,
    216, 226
ADF *see* Australian Defence Force
Aegis combat system program 181
aesthetics 6, 11–12, 116, 117–18, 119
Afghanistan 172
Åhäll, Linda 133
air power 181, 184, 188, 189, 192,
    193, 194, 196, 198
    Australia 83, 173
    Denmark 189, 191, 192, 198
    Finland 189
    Norway 189, 192, 193, 194
    Sweden 183, 189, 196, 197, 198
Aistrope, Tim 11
alliances
    ANZUS 147, 178
    AUKUS 25
    Australia–United States 24, 31, 32,
        43, 110, 147, 173, 178, 179,
        182, 219
    Australian 24, 25, 109, 147, 179
    Five Eyes 210
    Nordic states 183, 189, 193, 195

Quadrilateral Security Dialogue
    (Quad) 164, 167
Southeast Asia Treaty Organization
    (SEATO) 178
    see also collective action; European
        Union; NATO
Allied Joint Force Command Norfolk
    (JFC Norfolk) 184, 186, 187, 188
America *see* United States
Anderson, Joe (Burraga) 46
Andrews, Kevin 82
Ang, Yuen Yuen 74–5
Anglo-American 210
ANU *see* Australian National
    University
Anzac 25, 210, 223
    see also Australia, mythology about
        war
ANZUS 147, 178
AP4D *see* Asia-Pacific Development,
    Diplomacy & Defence Dialogue
Arctic 187, 191
    see also High North
armed force 24, 25, 102, 177
artificial intelligence 7
    see also cyber security
Asia 163, 164, 165, 167, 219
    Australia's relations with 26, 43,
        51, 94, 156, 161, 164, 166,
        173, 174, 177, 179, 219
    see also East Asia; South-East Asia

'Asian Century' 166
Asia-Pacific 79, 96, 163, 165, 166, 178
Asia-Pacific Development, Diplomacy
    & Defence Dialogue (AP4D) 146,
    153, 154–5, 156, 157
Asia-Pacific Economic Cooperation
    (APEC) 86
Association of Southeast Asian Nations
    (ASEAN) 85, 163, 164
Attorney-General's Department xviii
AUKUS (Australia, United Kingdom,
    United States) 25
Australia
    1967 Indigenous referendum 55,
        171
    Air Force 83, 173
    alliance with United States 24, 25,
        31, 32, 43, 96, 109, 110, 147,
        173, 174, 178, 179, 182, 219
    alliances 24, 25, 109, 147, 168,
        178, 179, 182, 210
    and China 23, 86, 94, 96, 109–10,
        147, 159, 164–6, 168, 219
    and nuclear arms 173, 175
    and role of geography 25, 26, 27,
        28, 31–2, 108, 160–1, 170, 206
    colonial 20, 21, 39, 41, 42, 44,
        147, 206, 222–3
    colonial mentality 41, 43, 44, 49,
        147
    community 20, 25, 31, 43, 48–50,
        59–60
    Constitution 39–63
    culture 22, 57, 104, 222, 231
    fear of abandonment 24, 151–2
    Federation 23, 39, 40, 44, 57, 62,
        147, 171, 172, 233
    foreign policy 24, 84, 86, 133, 145,
        148, 150, 153–5, 168, 219
    'fortress Australia' 22, 24, 152
    frontier wars 21–2, 25, 26, 44, 152
    geography and strategic policy 25,
        26, 27, 28, 94, 96, 152, 161,
        162, 168, 170, 173, 174–5

grand strategy 9, 20, 149, 177
history xvii, xix, 5, 22, 23, 25, 26,
    46, 47, 52, 56, 57, 60–1, 86,
    109, 152, 170, 171–3, 206,
    219, 223
in British Empire 20, 21, 22, 24,
    61, 147, 218
in international system 11, 13,
    27–9, 86, 96, 110, 116, 147–9,
    153–6, 163, 177, 218, 233
literature xix, xx, 4, 6, 22, 57, 100,
    106, 169, 230–1
maritime defence 24, 26, 28, 94,
    152, 166, 167
mythology about war 25, 26, 152,
    172, 210, 223
national identity 5, 20, 21, 22, 24,
    25, 42–5, 48–52, 63, 78–9, 87,
    109–10, 133, 147, 170, 171,
    179, 216, 219, 231
nationhood 26, 28, 31, 32, 49, 50,
    219
Navy 83
racism 43, 44, 54, 55–6, 59–61
reconciliation 45, 51, 58, 62, 63
referendum on Australian republic
    (1999) 37–8, 40, 41, 43, 55, 59
referendum on Constitution 39
regional relations 5, 32, 78–9, 84,
    85, 89, 90, 94, 148, 159, 161,
    162–8, 169, 177–8, 179
relations with Asia 26, 43, 51, 94,
    156, 161, 164, 166, 173, 174,
    177, 179, 219
relations with United States 109,
    147, 173, 174, 178, 219
reorientation of strategic policy 23,
    96, 110
republic, movement for 23, 37,
    39–63
security 20, 24, 25, 26, 78, 108,
    110, 145, 147–8, 156, 164,
    165–8, 175, 177, 205, 234
settlement of 12, 19–23, 24, 26, 50

shortcomings of strategic
  policymaking 27, 29, 109, 117,
  150, 173–4, 176–7, 203
silences 22, 23, 25, 49, 152
statecraft 153, 154, 155–6, 159,
  168
strategic environment 24, 27, 28,
  94, 108, 159, 161, 162, 166,
  178, 234
strategic environment, change to
  xx, 90, 146, 147–56, 170, 182,
  203, 210, 216, 219, 234
strategic identity 20, 22, 25, 173,
  179, 233
strategic imagination 61, 62,
  84–5, 87, 89–90, 94, 97–8,
  108–10, 116, 145–57, 160,
  168, 169–79, 203–4, 209, 216,
  218–19, 223
strategic policy xviii, 11, 20, 22,
  27, 28, 33, 62, 148–50, 159,
  169, 170, 176–9
strategic priorities xix, 94, 153
strategic thinking xviii, xix, 84, 85,
  94, 96–8, 109, 111, 117–18,
  150, 152–3, 159, 162–3, 169,
  176, 195, 205, 227, 233, 234
support for US alliance 25, 219
ties to United Kingdom 20, 25, 39,
  41, 42, 43, 48, 147, 173, 218
Voice to Parliament referendum
  (2023) 37–8, 44, 45, 47, 50,
  51, 52–63
White Australia policy 63, 147
see also Indigenous Australians
Australia, New Zealand and United
  States Security Treaty see ANZUS
Australian Army Journal 162
Australian Civil–Military Centre 154
Australian Council for International
  Development 153, 154
Australian Defence Force (ADF) 25,
  82, 83, 106, 210, 233
Australian Electoral Commission 48

Australian National University, The
  (ANU) 65, 76, 153, 206, 226
  Brendan Sargeant at xix, 5, 65, 99,
    160, 201, 203, 225, 226, 227
  see also Coral Bell School of
    Asia Pacific Affairs; Strategic
    and Defence Studies Centre
    (SDSC)
Australian Public Service xviii, xix, 3,
  5, 146, 160, 210, 216
Australian Republican Movement 41,
  42, 43
Australian Security Intelligence
  Organisation (ASIO) 81
authoritarianism 120, 121, 138, 140,
  141, 143, 182

Bachelard, Gaston 103
Ball, Des 175
Baltic region 184, 189, 196, 197
Baltic Sea 184, 197
Barents Sea 187
Bateson, Gregory 71, 72
Beazley, Kim 39, 78, 167
Belgium 189
Bell, Coral 225, 226
  see also Coral Bell School of Asia
    Pacific Affairs
Belt and Road initiative 165
Betton, Andrew 186
Bishop, Julie 78
Blake, William xviii, 3, 14–18, 20, 21,
  23, 27, 66, 99, 162
Bleiker, Roland 11, 116
Bloom, Harold 13, 14, 15, 23
Boyd, Arthur 40
Bracks, Steve 40
Britain see United Kingdom
British Empire 20, 44
  and Australia 20, 21, 22, 24, 61,
    147, 218
Burraga (Joe Anderson) 46
Bydén, Micael 196

Callinan, Ian 40
Canada 29, 163, 186, 198, 221
Canberra 47, 53, 160
Carr, Bob 40
Central Europe 177
Centrelink xviii, 77
China 129
    and Australia 23, 86, 94, 96,
        109–10, 147, 159, 164–6, 168,
        219
    and Indo-Pacific 159, 163–5, 168
    and NATO 183, 190
    as threat to Nordic nations 183,
        190
    'containment' of 163, 164, 168
    economy 74, 84, 165
    foreign relations 72, 86
    global power 14, 96, 163, 164–5,
        182
    Maritime Silk Road 163, 164
    military modernisation 84, 165–6
    policy 72, 165
    potential war with United States
        218–19
    reform 122, 140
    relations with Japan 14, 163
    relations with United States 66,
        108, 163, 166, 206
    relations with West 66, 86, 164
    rise of 66, 72, 147, 164, 219
climate change 7, 66, 90, 97, 109,
    118, 205, 213
Cold War 96, 104, 108, 120, 124,
    175, 177, 194
    'new' 108
    post 147, 148, 171, 188
Cole, August 106
Coleridge, Samuel Taylor 15, 17
collective action 22, 163, 204, 211,
    223
    see also alliances
collective imagination xvii, 68, 133,
    140, 146, 152, 172, 209, 210, 211
Colley, Linda 48

Collins, Randall 109
colonial Australia 20, 21, 39, 41, 42,
    44, 147, 206, 222–3
    see also Australia, settlement of
colonial mentality 41, 43, 44, 49, 147
colonialism 39, 42, 44
colonisation 60, 222–3
    see also Australia, settlement of
Commonwealth Heads of Government
    86
Commonwealth of Australia 39–63,
    147
Commonwealth of Australia
    Constitution Act 1900 39
communism 138, 140
connectivity 159, 163, 164, 165, 167,
    213
Cooper, William 46, 47
Coral Bell School of Asia Pacific Affairs
    xix, 210, 223, 226, 227
Cosgrove, Sir Peter 47
Council for Aboriginal Reconciliation
    58
Covid-19 pandemic 24, 201, 205,
    213, 226
creative imagination 17, 38, 91, 94
critical thinking 80, 81, 130–1, 149,
    215
Cruse, Ossie 45–6, 61
Curtin, John 110, 171
cyber security 156, 196, 235
    see also artificial intelligence
Czechoslovakia 124, 129

Dalton, Toby 122
Davis, Megan 50, 53, 57, 62
defence
    Australian maritime 24, 26, 28, 94,
        152, 166, 167
    community 33, 116, 118, 153–4,
        155, 165, 171, 175–7, 233
    'Defence of Australia' 173, 174
    maritime 183, 184, 185, 187, 192,
        193, 194, 197, 198

maritime and Indo-Pacific 163, 164
see also air power; Department of Defence
Defence Civilian Committee 83
Defence Committee 171, 177
Defence Materiel Organisation 82
Defence Strategic Review xix, 84, 94, **95**, 96, 148, 155
Defence White Papers see white papers
demilitarised zone see Korean Demilitarized Zone
democracy 43, 48, 49, 54, 55, 97, 138, 182, 183, 195
democratisation 234
Denmark 183, 189, 191–2, 194, 197, 198
    air force 189, 191, 192, 198
    navy 191
Department of Aboriginal Affairs 63
Department of the Attorney-General xviii
Department of Defence 38, 85, 162, 169, 171, 175, 176, 231
    and AP4D 154
    and China 165–6
    Brendan Sargeant at xvii–xix, 3, 4, 10, 77–87, 99, 159, 160–2, 166, 169–70, 175–6, 210, 225–6, 227
    Brendan Sargeant's speech to 229–36
    change in 33, 82–3, 210
    Dennis Richardson at 38, 77–87
    First Principles Review xviii, 81, 82
    ministers 78–9, 82, 83–4, 155, 167, 226
    'One Defence' 82–3, 176
    power of 83
    'Strategic Basis' papers 175, 177
    see also defence; white papers
Department of External Affairs 78, 86
Department of Finance 83
    Brendan Sargeant at xviii, 77, 226

Department of Foreign Affairs and Trade (DFAT) 83–4, 154, 167, 177, 226
    ministers 84, 155, 156
Department of the Prime Minister and Cabinet 83, 177
Department of Treasury 83, 177
Dibb Review see Review of Australia's Defence Capabilities
disarmament, nuclear 121–2
DMZ see Korean Demilitarized Zone
Downer, Alexander 86
Dubner, Stephen 74–5
Dutton, Geoffrey 41, 42
Dutton, Peter 45, 52–3, 57

East Asia 74, 96, 165, 167, 168, 172
East Asia Summit 86, 167
East Asian Hemisphere 163
East Timor 175, 233
Eastern Europe 172, 177
Einstein, Albert 69–70, 185
Erskine, Toni 226
Europe 102, 171, 182, 188, 189, 190, 195
    Central 177
    Eastern 172, 177
    Northern 183, 188, 193, 195, 197–8
European Union (EU) 163, 177, 195
Evans, Gareth 163

F-35 Aegis 193
F-35 aircraft program 83, 181, 189, 193, 198
Faroe Islands 191, 198
Federation (of Australian colonies) 23, 39, 40, 44, 57, 62, 147, 171, 172, 233
Feyerabend, Paul 93
fiction xix, 99, 100, 105, 106–7, 111, 221, 223, 231
    see also literature; poetry

Finland 171, 183, 184, 185, 188–91, 192, 193, 195, 196, 197–8
First Nations *see* Indigenous Australians
First Nations of North America 221–2
First Principles Review xviii, 81, 82
Fitzgerald, F. Scott 102
Five Eyes 210
force disposition 24, 25
Foster, Warren 45, 46
France 20, 86, 100, 103, 163, 172, 175n.19, 186
Fraser, Malcolm 40
Freedman, Lawrence 10, 162
Freeth, Gordon 78
French, Robert 60
frontier wars (Australian) 21–2, 25, 26, 44, 152
Frye, Northrop 29

G7 163
G20 86
Gell-Mann, Murray 215
gender 134, 210
    equality 51, 210, 223
    in Korean Demilitarized Zone (DMZ) 119, 129, 130–1, 133, 142
    see also militarised masculinities
Germany 86, 163, 172, 184, 186, 189, 193, 197
Gillard, Julia 82, 165
Gilmour, John 195
Global Financial Crisis 86, 165
Goldrick, James 227
Gorton, John 40
grand strategy 19, 20, 177
    Australian 9, 20, 149, 177
Greece 172
Greenland 183, 191, 198
Grenier, John 221, 222
Gyngell, Alan 24, 167, 227

Hanson, Pauline 52
Harries, Owen 218
Hastie, Andrew 79
Hawke, Bob 40, 78
Hawking, Stephen 214
Hayne, Kenneth 40
Heaney, Seamus 225, 228
hegemony 20, 22, 25, 34, 205
Henderson, Bruce D. 89, 90
High North 184, 185, 187, 193, 196
    see also Arctic
Hill, Charles 105
Hirst, John 49
history xix 1, 6, 29, 109, 110, 146, 151, 166, 182, 188, 195, 221, 234
    Australian xvii, xix, 5, 22, 23, 25, 26, 46, 47, 52, 56, 57, 60–1, 86, 109, 152, 170, 171–3, 206, 219, 223
    Australian foreign policy 24, 168
    Australian literary 169
    organisational 4
Hollingworth, Archbishop Peter 40
Homer xvii, 227
Horne, Donald 41, 42
Howard, John 26, 39, 40, 45, 59, 86
Hughes, Robert 104
human rights 120, 138, 141

Iceland 183
identity
    Australian national 5, 20, 21, 22, 24, 25, 49, 51, 52, 63, 109–10, 133, 147, 170, 216, 219
    strategic 20, 22, 25, 173, 179, 233
imagination
    and science 38, 66, 69, 90, 91–4, 97
    collective xvii, 68, 133, 140, 146, 152, 172, 209, 210, 211
    creative 17, 38, 91, 94
    're-creative' 38, 91, 94
    see also strategic imagination

India 2, 3, 85, 86, 99, 160, 163, 164,
165, 166, 167, 183, 206, 219
Indian Ocean 78, 163, 166, 167, 168
see also Indo-Pacific
Indigenous Australians 19, 21, 22, 23,
25–6, 39, 44–7, 49–63, 147, 152,
222
1967 referendum 55, 171
and truth-telling 45, 50, 53, 56,
59, 60–1, 63
makarrata 50, 56
Uluru Statement from the Heart 44,
45, 46, 49–50, 58, 61, 62, 63
Voice to Parliament referendum
(2023) 37–8, 44, 45, 47, 50,
51, 52–63
indigenous people 74
Indonesia 85, 86, 163, 167, 174, 219
Indo-Pacific xviii, xix, 31, 33, 78, 94,
96, 104, 108, 110, 116, 150, 155,
159–68, 178, 227, 230, 233
Institute for Regional Security 153
intelligence 33, 77, 78, 79, 80, 167,
173, 194, 197
intelligence, surveillance and
reconnaissance 184, 189, 192, 197
International Development
Contractors Community 153
Iraq 162

Jacob, François 68
James, William 115
Japan 14, 86, 163, 179
and Indo-Pacific 163–4, 167
and Quadrilateral Security
Dialogue 164
relations with China 14, 163–4
Johnson, David 78, 82
Joint Security Area (JSA) **123**, 125,
128, 129, **130**
Jomini, Antoine-Henri 38
Juusti, Jukka 190

Kagan, Robert 111
Kahn, Herman 96
Keating, Paul 40, 50–1, 56, 85, 86,
170
Keneally, Thomas 42
Kennan, George F. 104
Keynes, John Maynard 218
Kim dynasty 121
Kim Il-sung **135**, 136
Kim, Jina 122
Kim Jong-un 121, 141
Kim, Suk-Young 125
King George V 46
King, Stephen 103
Korea *see* North Korea; South Korea
Korea, North–South conflict 116, 118,
119–44
and United States 120–2, 129,
131, **132**, 133, 134, 140, 141
Korean Demilitarized Zone (DMZ)
119, 122, 124–5, **126**, 127, 129,
130, 131, **132**, 133, **140**, 142
Korean War 23, 120, 124
Kuhn, Thomas S. 91–2

Lankov, Andrei 122
Latin America 172
Lawson, Henry 43
Levine, Caroline 13, 14, 30–1
Lewis Gaddis, John 19, 104
Lewis, Andrew 185–6, 187, 188
literary
culture 99, 101, 211
theory 3, 12, 29, 170, 174
literature 3, 13, 18, 21, 22, 29, 30, 34,
79, 85, 87, 115, 117
Australian xix, xx, 4, 6, 22, 57,
100, 106, 169, 230–1
English xviii, 78, 205, 209, 221,
227
to inform strategic policy xvii, xviii,
12–13, 29, 38, 105, 169, 170,
174
see also fiction; poetry

London 39, 40, 41, 47, 48
Lowell, James Russell 110
Lowy Institute 167
Lyons, Joseph 46, 47

Machiavelli xix
Maidan Revolution 171
makarrata 50, 56
March, James 68–9
maritime defence 183, 184, 185,
    186–7, 191, 192, 193, 194, 196,
    197, 198
    and Indo-Pacific 163, 164
    Australian 24, 26, 28, 94, 152,
        166, 167
    see also naval; navies
maritime disputes 166
Maritime Silk Road 164
Marles, Richard 84
Marshall, Andrew 106
Martin, Roger 74
masculinity *see* militarised
    masculinities
Mayo, Thomas 62
McCarthy, Cormac 222
McGilchrist, Ian 105
McGregor, Catherine 162
McKenna, Mark 22–3
Medcalf, Rory 96, 116
Megawati Sukarnoputri 85
Melbourne xviii, 3, 230
Melbourne University 81
Menzies, Robert 40, 85, 110–11
Middle East 167, 171, 194
militarised masculinities 119, 127–34,
    142
    see also gender
militarism 119, 127, 129, 130–1,
    133–4, 142
Milton, John 14
Moore, Richard 153
Morrison, Scott 46
Mundine, Nyunggai Warren 52, 55,
    59

Murnane, Gerald xix, 6, 100, 169, 230
Mustin, John 186

Napoleon 102
NATO 163, 171, 177, 183–98
naval 165, 166, 173
    see also maritime defence
Naval Postgraduate School (US) 185
navies 186–7, 191, 196, 197
    Australia 83
    China 165
    Denmark 191
    Royal (United Kingdom) 186
    Sweden 196, 197, 198
    United States 185, 186
    see also maritime defence; naval
Nehru, Jawaharlal 206
Netherlands 163, 189
Neutral Nations Supervisory
    Commission (NNSC) 124, 125,
    130
New Delhi 167
New South Wales 46
New Zealand xviii, 25, 46, 147, 163
Newton, Sir Isaac 18, 73, 92
Nordic countries 116, 181–98
North America 165, 167
    see also United States
North Atlantic Ocean 183, 185–6,
    187–8, 191, 196, 197–8
North Korea 120–5, 127–30, 134–41,
    143
    nuclear weapons 120, 121–2, 141
    see also Korea, North–South
        conflict; Korean Demilitarized
        Zone; Korean War
Northern Europe 183, 188, 193, 195,
    197–8
Norway 183–4, 186, 189, 192, 193–5,
    196, 197, 198
    air force 189, 192, 193, 194
nuclear
    disarmament 121–2
    strategy 96, 107, 175

threshold 196, 219
war 173, 219
nuclear arms
and Australia 173, 175
North Korea 120, 121–2, 141

O'Connor, Flannery 103
Obama administration 185
Oceania 163
Odell, Jenny 70
Odysseus xvii, 90, 98, 227
Odyssey xvii, 227
Office of National Assessments 167
Olley, Margaret 40, 41
'One Defence' 82–3, 176
Orwell, George 103–4
'other', the 26, 140

Pacific 51, 155, 156, 163, 167, 173,
177, 194
South 162, 179
South-West 175
see also Indo-Pacific
Pacific Islands 33
Pacific Ocean 163, 166
Pak, Jung H. 121
Panmunjom **123**, 125, **128**, **130**
Papua New Guinea 173
'paradoxical trinity' 37, 38
Payne, Marise 82
Pearson, Noel 44, 51, 60
Peloponnesian War 101
Perkins, Rachel 62
philosophy 38, 81, 91, 103, 105, 109,
115–16, 160, 169
Plato 15
poetry xvii, xviii, xx, 3, 13, 14, 15, 18,
43, 79, 86–7, 99, 100, 110, 111,
117, 161–2, 227, 228
see also literature
Poland 124, 129, 184, 189, 197
Polanyi, Michael 92
'polycrisis' 145, 213
Popper, Karl 91

Portugal 172
positivist 18, 27
post–Vietnam War *see* Vietnam War,
post
postcolonial 44
Price, Jacinta Nampijinpa 52, 55,
59–60
Prince Charles 42
Prince Philip 40
Putin, Vladimir 189
Pyne, Christopher 82
Pyongyang **136**, **137**, **143**

Quadrilateral Security Dialogue
(Quad) 164, 167
Queen Elizabeth II 40, 43, 47

Reagan administration 107
realist 16, 22, 27, 28, 33, 37
reconciliation (in Australia) 45, 51, 58,
62, 63
're-creative' imagination 38, 91, 94
see also creative imagination
Reents, Stephanie 222, 223
referendums 45, 61, 62
1967 Indigenous 55, 171
on Australian Constitution 39
on Australian republic (1999)
37–8, 40, 41, 43, 55, 59
Voice to Parliament (2023) 37–8,
44, 45, 47, 50, 51, 52–63
Republic of Korea 163
see also South Korea
*Review of Australia's Defence
Capabilities* (Dibb Review) 31, 32
Rex, Anders 191
Reynolds, Linda 79
Rice, Bridi 153
Richardson, Henry Handel 22
Richardson, John 185, 187
Rimbaud, Arthur 100
Roggeveen, Sam 96
Romanticism 12, 14–18, 19, 21, 38
Rorty, Richard 115

Rowling, Myra xviii
Rudd, Kevin 82, 86, 166
Russia 78, 106, 191, 196
    and Europe 182, 183, 189
    and Finland 188–9, 190, 198
    and NATO 184, 189, 190, 197
    and Nordic nations 116, 183, 184,
        189, 191, 194, 197, 198
    and Norway 198
    and Sweden 197
    invasion of Ukraine 80, 116
    see also Soviet Union
Russian Empire 188
Ryan, Mick 106

Saudi Arabia 86
Sawczak, Peter xx
Schmidt, Brian 226
science 70, 71, 73, 97, 104, 109, 111,
    118, 156, 230
    and imagination 38, 66, 69, 90,
        91–4, 97
    cognitive 105
    complexity 6, 71
    'day' 38, 68, 69, 71
    mechanistic 19
    natural 73, 91, 93, 215
    'night' 38, 68, 69, 71
    political 73, 74, 205, 206
    positivist 18
    social science 66, 91, 118, 144,
        174
SDSC see Strategic and Defence
    Studies Centre
Second Fleet 184, 185, 186, 187–8
Seoul 86, **124**
Shakespeare, William 110, 111
Shepherd, Laura 133
Shim, David 138
Singapore 147
Singer, Peter W. 106
Smith, Stephen 78, 82, 167
social science 66, 91, 118, 144, 174
South Africa 86, 172

South China Sea 167, 230
South-East Asia 2, 94, 162, 164, 166,
    167, 173, 177
Southeast Asia Economic Strategy 156
Southeast Asia Treaty Organization
    (SEATO) 178
South Korea 86, 116, 121, 122,
    124–30, 133, 134, 140, 163
    see also Korea, North–South
        conflict; Korean Demilitarized
        Zone; Korean War
South Pacific 162, 179
South-West Pacific 175
Soviet Union 106, 108, 140, 188
    see also Russia
Spain 172
Spender, Percy 179
statecraft 22, 116, 162, 214, 216
    Australian 153, 154, 155–6, 159,
        168
Stevens, Wallace 15
Stockholm 195
Strategic and Defence Studies Centre
    (SDSC) xviii, xix, 6, 81, 160, 161,
        167, 169, 171, 201, 203–4, 205,
        206, 210, 220, 223, 225, 227,
        229–36
strategic 37
    Australian environment 24, 27, 28,
        94, 108, 159, 161, 162, 166,
        178, 234
    Australian environment, change to
        xx, 90, 146, 147–56, 170, 182,
        203, 210, 216, 219, 234
    Australian priorities xix, 94, 153
    autonomy 24, 151–2, 179
    capability 66
    cartography 94, 109
    challenges xvii, 26, 96, 118, 148,
        150, 161, 203, 204–5, 234,
        235
    competition 166
    crisis 9
    culture 22

experience 107
failure 210, 215
flexibility 187
framework for foreign policy 84, 154, 155, 227
history 26, 171, 175, 205, 210, 231, 233
identity, Australian 20, 22, 25, 173, 179, 233
intelligence 173
logic 25, 89
order 90, 219
problem-solving 106
review see *Defence Strategic Review*
risk 110, 147, 148, 151, 154, 165, 166, 178, 193, 213, 218–19
stability 9
studies 6, 27, 37, 38, 87, 89, 94, 96, 97, 98, 119, 169, 203, 205, 236
system 14, 24, 163, 168, 179
strategic imagination 79, 80, 84, 86, 87, 89–98, 100, 107–11, 142, 151, 159–68, 214–16
and defence policy xix, 116, 117–44, 146, 161–2, 166, 169–79, 181–98, 209, 232–4
Australian xix–xx, 9–34, 61–2, 76, 77, 90–8, 116, 145–56, 170, 175, 209, 223
Brendan Sargeant's conception of xvii, 1–2, 5–6, 9–34, 84, 87, 104, 108, 109, 117, 144, 146, 150–1, 162, 168, 182, 216, 223
concept 1–2, 6–7, 11, 37–8, 58–63, 104, 116, 157
practice 6, 84–5, 107, 115–16
strategic policy xix, 10, 24, 30–1, 33, 142, 218, 232
and Australia's geography 25, 26, 27, 28, 94, 96, 152, 161, 162, 168, 170, 173, 174–5
and history 25, 32, 169–70

and Indigenous Australians 25–6
and role of United Kingdom 25, 210
and US alliance 24, 25, 31, 32, 110, 173, 178, 210
Australian xviii, 11, 20, 22, 27, 28, 33, 62, 148–50, 159, 169, 170, 176–9
Brendan Sargeant's work in xii, xviii, 77–8, 120, 127, 203–11, 216, 217, 220
challenges to 33, 134, 173, 182
debates about 23–4, 25–6, 150, 155, 167, 169, 170, 172–5, 227, 233
history of xix, 20, 26, 86, 171, 173, 175, 205, 231, 233
limitations of 80, 97, 127, 150
reorientation of Australian 23, 96, 110
role of literature to inform xvii, xviii, 12–13, 14–16, 29, 38, 105, 169, 170, 174
stability of 32, 34, 148, 149
strategic policymaking 90, 94, 97, 155–6, 175, 215, 216, 229
shortcomings of Australian 27, 29, 109, 117, 150, 173–4, 176–7, 203
strategic thinking xviii, xix, 84, 85, 94, 96–8, 109, 111, 117–18, 150, 152–3, 159, 162–3, 169, 176, 195, 205, 227, 233, 234
strategy xx, 1, 3, 10, 11, 27, 65, 72, 97, 143, 144, 176, 205, 213–16, 230–6
Australian grand 9, 20, 149, 177
community 13, 94, 97–8, 99–111, 116, 151, 160–1, 228, 235
discourse 10, 12, 13, 23–4, 27, 120, 179
grand 19, 20
Indo-Pacific 159–68, 178
nuclear 96, 175, 196

relevance of literature to xvii, xviii,
12–13, 14–16, 29, 38, 105,
169, 170, 174
shortcomings of xvii, 23, 121–2,
150, 176, 215
underpinnings of 37, 74, 100–1,
105, 106, 108, 172, 209
United States 107, 108
Sweden 124, 171, 183–4, 185, 189,
191, 192, 193, 194, 195–8
air force 183, 189, 196, 197, 198
navy 196, 197, 198
Switzerland 119, 124, 129, 130
Sydney 3, 42, 46, 58

Taiwan 163, 219
Tange, Sir Arthur 176
terrorism 80
Terry, Sue Mi 121
Thompson, Alan 173
Thorpe, Lidia 52, 54
Thucydides xix, 101
Treasury, Department of 83, 177
treaty 44, 45, 53, 63
Trump, Donald 120, 163, 178
truth-telling 45, 50, 53, 56, 59, 60–1,
63
Türkiye 86
Turnbull, Malcolm 42, 45, 46, 54, 82
Turner, Uncle Boydie 46–7

Ukraine 80, 116, 171, 195, 196, 213
Uluru Statement from the Heart 44, 45,
46, 49–50, 58, 61, 62, 63
United Kingdom (UK) 19, 86, 110,
163, 197
and AUKUS 25
as global hegemon 20, 25, 147,
218
Australian ties to 20, 25, 39, 41,
42, 43, 48, 147, 173, 218
military 183, 186, 188, 189, 192,
221
monarchy 42, 43, 44, 47

Parliament 39, 41
Royal Navy 186
see also British Empire
United Nations (UN) 85
Command 124, 129, **140**
United States (US) 15, 96, 103, 167,
214, 222
alliance with Australia 24, 25, 31,
32, 43, 96, 109, 110, 147, 173,
174, 178, 179, 182, 219
and AUKUS 25
and ANZUS 147, 178
and Cold War 104, 108
and Indo-Pacific 163, 165, 166,
167
and Korean Peninsula 120–2, 129,
131, **132**, 133, 134, 140, 141
and NATO 184–90, 194, 198
and Quadrilateral Security
Dialogue 164, 167
and Soviet Union 108
Australian relations with 109, 147,
173, 174, 178, 219
Australian support for 25, 219
decoupling of Australia from 96
defence strategy 32, 107–8, 147
diminishment of power 96
Government 107
hegemony 20, 182
in Korean Demilitarized Zone
(DMZ) 129
intelligence 79, 214
leadership 182, 183
National Intelligence Council 214
Native Americans 221–2
Naval Postgraduate School 185
Navy 185, 186
philosophy 115
policy 32, 86, 167
relations with China 66, 108, 163,
165, 166, 206, 218, 219
Second Fleet 184, 185, 186, 187–8

van Houtryve, Tomas 138
Varghese, Peter 167
Vietnam 140
Vietnam War 23, 172, 176, 177
    post-war 23, 175, 176, 177, 178,
        233
von Clausewitz, Carl 37, 38, 102, 103,
    172

Waddell, Steve 186
Wallis, Joanne 32
Wang, Nils 183
war 21–2, 169, 172, 186, 187
    and strategy 101–3, 172
    Australian mythology about 25,
        26, 152, 172, 210, 223
    Australian War College 221
    frontier wars (Australian) 21–2, 25,
        26, 44, 152
    games 107
    in Ukraine 80, 116, 195, 213
    Korean 23, 120, 124
    nuclear 173, 219
    Peloponnesian 101
    post-Vietnam 23, 175, 176, 177,
        178, 233
    theory 38, 100, 102, 106, 109,
        221, 223
    threat on Korean Peninsula 120,
        124
    United States–China 218–19
    Vietnam 23, 172, 176, 177
    see also Cold War; World War I;
        World War II
Weber, Isabella 74
Weinberger, Caspar 107
Wessels, David 75–6
Western Australia 78–9
West Papua 174
White Australia policy 63, 147
White, Hugh 96, 201, 225
white papers 4
    1987 Defence White Paper 29, 32,
        174, 175n.17

2009 Defence White Paper 166
2013 Defence White Paper xviii, 78,
    79, 159, 166, 168, 178, 227
2017 Foreign Policy White Paper
    148
2020 Defence Strategic Update 29,
    174, 175n.17
'Asian Century' white paper (2012)
    166
defence 28, 81, 82, 83, 230, 232,
    233
White, Patrick 22
Whitlam, Gough 40, 41
Wibben, Annick 133
Williams Foundation 181
Wong, Penny 84
Wordsworth, William 3, 14, 18, 19
World War I 23, 149, 177, 221
World War II 23, 110, 195
    post-war foreign policy 85–6, 147,
        148
    pre-war Australian policy 85

Xi Jinping 84, 165

Yunupingu, Galarrwuy 45